Hiking Waterfalls Wisconsin

Hiking Waterfalls Wisconsin

A Guide to the State's Best Waterfall Hikes

Chad Turner

ESSEX, CONNECTICUT

FALCONGUIDES®

An imprint of Globe Pequot, the trade division of The Rowman & Littlefield Publishing Group, Inc.
4501 Forbes Blvd., Ste. 200
Lanham, MD 20706
www.rowman.com

Falcon and FalconGuides are registered trademarks and Make Adventure Your Story is a trademark of The Rowman & Littlefield Publishing Group, Inc.

Distributed by NATIONAL BOOK NETWORK

Photos by Chad Turner unless otherwise noted
Maps by Melissa Baker and The Rowman & Littlefield Publishing Group, Inc.

British Library Cataloguing in Publication Information available

Library of Congress Cataloging-in-Publication Data available
ISBN 978-1-4930-6682-7 (paper: alk. paper)
ISBN 978-1-4930-6683-4 (electronic)

∞™ The paper used in this publication meets the minimum requirements of American National Standard for Information Sciences—Permanence of Paper for Printed Library Materials, ANSI/NISO Z39.48-1992.

The author and The Rowman & Littlefield Publishing Group, Inc., assume no liability for accidents happening to, or injuries sustained by, readers who engage in the activities described in this book.

This book is dedicated to the
Outdoor Wisconsinite: PROST!
And happy trails!

View from the boardwalk. Tyler Forks River flows over lava rock and empties into the Bad River.

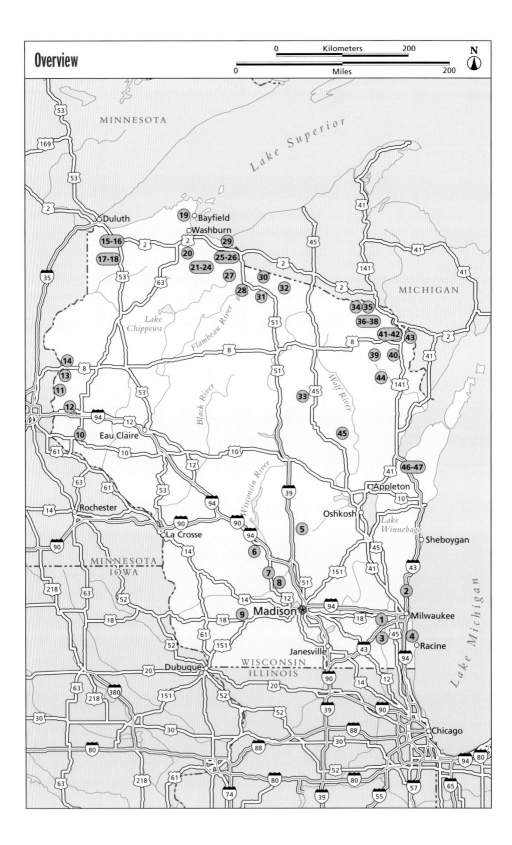

Overview

Contents

The Hikes

Acknowledgments

I am incredibly grateful for the opportunity to write a book like this. I had an unreasonable amount of fun traveling around this beautiful state, hiking, camping, and taking photos of waterfalls. I am fortunate to be working with the talented and hard-working staff at Globe Pequot Press on this book. They are the real pros, and have set the standard for outdoor recreation content as one can see from the impressive number of guidebooks they have published over the years. Thank you for inviting readers to experience the endless adventure and beauty of the great outdoors and allowing me to be a part of it.

A huge thanks goes to my editors Katherine O'Dell, Mason Gadd, Josh Rosenberg, and Meredith Dias. Thank you for being so supportive and pleasant to work with. As one can imagine there are many skilled folks working tirelessly behind the scenes on a book like this. A huge enthusiastic and tearful applause goes to the cartographers, copy editors, and graphic design professionals for making the end product what it is. You're all amazing!

I'd like to extend my appreciation to my good friend, fellow author, and life coach Stacy Tornio. Thank you for your assistance, once again, in helping me obtain this incredible writing opportunity and thank you for your continued friendship and support. I also received guidance and direction from fellow authors Susan Joy Paul, Adam Sawyer, Rebecca Pelky, Kevin Revolinski, and Greg Westrich. So much gratitude goes to you all for replying to my emails and coaching an aspiring young author.

Sincere gratitude is extended to the following individuals for helping bring this project to fruition: Jim McLure, Jesse Voelker, Anthony Willems, Jessica Sartori Wharton, and Jonathon Anderson. Alicia Jee Dimitrova, thank you for the beautiful camera used to take the photographs in this book and thank you for always rooting for me.

This book would have not been possible without my family. My two loving sisters Nicole Holton and Tinameri Turner are the wild women who I shared savage outdoor experiences with growing up. A *big* thanks goes to my parents Richard and Jocelyn Turner for taking us camping and immersing us in the natural world. And thank you for allowing your vagabond son to take up residence in your home while I spent countless hours hiking, researching, mapping, writing, editing, and camping in your backyard. It is your love, kindness, support, and generosity that has allowed me to successfully live my free-spirited and nomadic lifestyle.

A book like this would never come to fruition without the priceless intel, sidebars, fun facts, and anecdotes from fellow hikers, hunters, anglers, bartenders, bar patrons,

The Bad River tumbles over and through many large rocks creating a series of waterfalls.

campsite hosts, and state park workers. Bartenders in rural Wisconsin (and those who occupy the barstools) are some of the most knowledgeable hiking consultants. Many of the best hidden waterfalls and preferred hiking routes located in these pages were shared with me by colorful locals and energetic bartenders at trailside pubs.

And special thanks to everyone reading this. Thank you to the hikers, nature lovers, waterfall hunters, and outdoor enthusiasts for joining me on the trails. Cheers to your health and safety as you enjoy the Wisconsin outdoors.

Meet Your Guide

Chad Turner was born and raised in Wisconsin and is part of a proud family heritage of nature lovers. He is a nomadic scribe, world traveler, adventure sports fanatic, and outdoor recreation junkie. Chad grew up camping, fishing, hiking, swimming, and paddling all over Wisconsin. He is currently a full-time vagabond and spends the majority of his time hiking, cycling, and paddling through each continent and writing about his adventures. No matter where Chad is in the world, he always makes it back to Wisconsin during the warm-weather months to reconnect with nature in his favorite place on earth. Fun Fact: Chad once cut short a trekking adventure in the Himalayas of Nepal to make it back to join friends for a canoe trip down the Wisconsin River.

Chad considers himself a Wisconsinite through and through. He is intimately familiar with the natural landscape of Wisconsin as well as the quirkiness of its inhabitants. He knows the Wisconsinite's affinity for supper clubs, fish fries, cheese curds, the Green Bay Packers, and beer. Chad understands and deeply appreciates that all of these unique facets, along with Wisconsin's love of the outdoors, play a central role in its particular midwestern identity and culture.

One of the thirty-seven boardwalks
supporting you in your nature hike
through the Bayfield County Forest.

Introduction

In a state more commonly known for its farmland, Wisconsin truly is a water-saturated nature-lovers' paradise: a land of many lakes, rivers, and forests, known for free-flowing beer and lots of free-flowing water. Most of the year Wisconsin is a wintery playground, but as the impressive quantity of snow melts, the astounding water within its borders turns into rushing rivers and an impressive cache of bubbling cascades. Wisconsin is home to over one hundred remarkable waterfalls and 2,700 miles of hiking trails, making it a preferred destination for hikers and waterfall enthusiasts.

The water chutes within Wisconsin's borders vary in size and beauty as much as the trails to reach them vary in difficulty and accessibility. Some waterfalls may be described as unassuming gentle tumblers, while others could be described as robust downpours into misty cauldrons. Some are ideal for riverside picnics, while others create exciting environments for kayakers. Wisconsin waterfalls are special in their own way. They are unique to the rushing rivers that propel them and to the natural beauty that frames them.

The liquid landscapes of Wisconsin offer a variety of falls with wildly different attitudes. You'll discover them in tranquil parks, misty gorges, forbidden forests, rocky ravines, and urban centers. Often the disposition of the water feature reflects the natural environment that surrounds it. Some waterfalls are shy, elegant, and unassuming, creating veil-like curtains of water over scenic backdrops. Others are thunderous cascades creating a white torrent of violently falling water. The moods of many Wisconsin waterfalls change with the seasons. After the spring snowmelt they may become significantly ornerier and more voluminous, while drier months bring a more peaceful and serene version.

In the pages to come you will be introduced to forty-seven of the best hikes and most impressive waterfalls that Wisconsin has to offer. Included are a wide variety of hikes showcasing difficulty ratings, easy-to-follow directions to the trailhead, detailed descriptions of the trails, mile-by-mile directional cues, and GPS-compatible maps. This book can be used and enjoyed by both novice hikers and experienced outdoorsmen/outdoorswomen.

This book is for any hiking enthusiast or outdoor adventurer who has a specific affinity for the majesty of waterfalls. The hikes in this book were not strictly chosen by the beauty of the waterfall at the hike's end however; they were chosen by a variety of criteria including length and style of the hike, surrounding natural beauty, trail's-end view, and overall pleasurable experience.

The standout feature that creates the transcendent beauty of Wisconsin is its rushing rivers. These tortuous waterways are the lifeblood of Wisconsin's wilderness and are directly responsible for each of the observable spectacles of falling water. Without the rivers readers would not be able to experience the physical adventure of making it to the rushing waters' edge and breathing in the invigorating air. Waterfall hikes allow us to experience the path less traveled and connect with something greater. This book gives the adventurer the gift of accessibility to Wisconsin's most beautiful and mysterious natural wonders.

Fortunately for waterfall seekers in Wisconsin, no complicated or fancy gear is required. A decent pair of footwear, proper clothing, water, and a photo device is usually all you need. Expect weather common to the area. In the northern part of the state especially near the shores of both Lake Michigan and Lake Superior, you may encounter cold winds or unexpected rainstorms (or sometimes snow!). Many of the shorter hikes on well-groomed trails require little more than a pair of sneakers. On longer hikes your feet may feel better inside a sturdier pair of shoes or hiking boots. In the spring and summer months, it's always a good idea to bring ample amounts of water, sunscreen, and insect repellent. You may want to bring snacks or even a full-on picnic basket on hikes that offer scenic viewpoints or picnic areas.

Safety is important when hiking many of these trails. Some of the hikes meander along bluffs with no guardrails. Some waterfalls may be connected to wetlands or stream- and riverbanks that may be soggy or muddy. A little slip or a wrong step could result in a wet foot or a long fall. Water levels and seasons have a big impact on appearance and approachability. An unassuming trickling waterfall in autumn could be a torrent in spring. Stay safe and happy trails!

Weather

The climate of Wisconsin is a typical continental humid climate: warm humid summers and cold snowy winters. The southern region of the state is slightly warmer than the northern region. The Great Lakes create their own microclimate, which brings substantially more snow during winter months as well as colder temperatures. Winters bring a lot of snow and can feel very long. Between December and February the daytime temperatures rarely make it above 30 degrees F and at night stay well below freezing.

Spring and summer are a very busy time in Wisconsin, especially for hiking, because the long winters make everyone overly excited to get outside while they can. Spring brings snowmelt and rains, which make the rivers full bodied and fast moving and the waterfalls voluminous. Between March and May, the temperatures gradually rise from the upper 30s F to mid 60s F. Temperatures are comfortable, but hiking trails tend to be muddy. Summers are usually very nice, but quite humid. Temperatures will hover in the 80s during the peak of summer between June and August and occasionally push up into the 90s.

Autumn has some of the best weather and best scenery in Wisconsin. Between September and early November, the temperatures gradually drop from the 70s to the low 50s. The leaves changing colors in fall is a major highlight throughout the state and makes hiking during this time especially scenic.

Flora and Fauna

Wisconsin hosts an impressive quantity of animals. Among the waterways, forest floor, and tree canopy, you'll find 668 native vertebrates, including fishes, amphibians, reptiles, birds, and mammals. Many more species of invertebrates also exist including various pollinators, snails, dragonflies, and mussels. Among the state and county forests and their many hiking trails, you'll see a wide variety of birds including bald eagles, sandhill cranes, pileated woodpeckers, and chestnut-sided warblers. Some of the abundant fur-bearing wildlife you may see from the trails are coyote, white-tailed deer, red fox, porcupines, and river otters. Other species that are unique to the northern region of the state and may be harder to spot are timber wolf, black bear, elk, and moose. Be prepared to see some of the braver animals such as northern chipmunk, red squirrel, raccoon, and eastern cottontail rabbit. More elusive species such as mink, fisher, cougar, and badger may be hiding in the bush near the trails and waterways and will quietly observe you as you pass. Many of these animals are more active during the warm-weather months; even if you don't see them, keep your eyes out for nesting sites, tiny footprints, or scat along the trails.

Wisconsin has a diversity of flora and ecozones that support them. The hiking trails in this book will lead you through forests, prairies, wetlands, and savannas. You will have the opportunity to witness a wide and beautiful variety of flora from the tiniest green mosses to towering old-growth oaks.

Forest plants create the understory foliage of the woodlands and include shrubs, vines, ferns, wild grasses, and wildflowers. Prairie plants are a shorter, unique variety of flora that has adapted to spend all day in the sun without drying out. Trees, the megaflora of our state, contribute to colorful landscapes and cool shaded hiking trails. Species you may encounter along the trails include sugar maple, yellow birch, hemlock, spruce-fir, and different varieties of pine. The wetlands introduce fully submerged and partially submerged plants that grow in the wet ground and near the abundant waterways.

One of the elements that makes Wisconsin's outdoors, and specifically the hiking trails, so scenic are wildflowers. Among the forests, wetlands, and prairies, you'll witness some beautiful bloomers including bloodroot, large white trillium, marsh marigold, and prairie coneflower.

Wilderness Restrictions/Regulations

Wisconsin state parks, forests, and trails have special rules to protect the safety of visitors and the environment. Information can be found at the trailheads, park offices, in trail guides, and online. Different trails may have different rules when it comes to such things as camping, alcoholic beverages, pets, picking and gathering, fishing, firewood, admissions stickers, and state trail passes. Information regarding "land status"

View of the Glen Park Falls just below the scenic pedestrian swinging bridge, connecting the east and west banks of the Kinnickinnic River

and "fees/permits" appears in the at-a-glance information that begins each hike. All the hikes are within county, state, or federal land and are open to the public, with the exception of two hikes that are on private land, but are part of a land trust making them available to the public. As you enjoy the hikes and waterfalls in this book, pay close attention to updated information posted on trailhead bulletin boards. Stay on designated trails, obey No Trespassing signs, pack out your trash, keep pets on leashes where necessary, pay entrance and parking fees, and always park in designated areas. Being a good steward of the land will lend itself to a safe and enjoyable experience for you and other hikers.

Accessibility

Some of the hikes in this book are accessible to those in wheelchairs or with limited mobility. Under Accessibility I have categorized each hike as "Yes," "No," or "Limited." "Yes" means that someone with mobility issues or using a wheelchair could easily access the hiking trail. "No" means the trail could not be maneuvered by a wheelchair or by someone with limited mobility. "Limited" means they may include a few stairs or a small stretch of rugged terrain, but could be still be accessed by someone in a wheelchair with a small amount of assistance.

How to Use This Guide

This book is arranged by region in quadrant form: southeast, southwest, northwest, and northeast. I took care in choosing and showcasing some of the most exciting and picturesque waterfalls that punctuate the state. Hopefully this guide contains everything you need to choose, plan, and enjoy a waterfall hike in Wisconsin.

Each chapter starts with a short summary of the hike's highlights. These quick overviews give you an idea of the adventure ahead and the caliber of waterfall to expect at the trail's end. Following the overview, you'll find a series of hike specs—detailed info about the hike and accompanying waterfall that includes:

Start: A solid starting point from which to locate the trailhead.

Elevation gain: Total elevation change from lowest point of the hike to the highest.

Distance: The total distance of the recommended route; out-and-back, loops, and lollipop routes are included in this guide.

Difficulty: Each hike has been categorized by a level of difficulty: easy, moderate, or difficult. The rating system was developed from several sources and personal experiences. The categories are meant to be a guideline only. They may prove easier or harder for different people depending on ability and physical fitness. An easy waterfall hike will generally cover 2 miles or less total trip distance with minimal stairs, minimal elevation gain, and a paved or smooth-surfaced trail. A moderate waterfall hike will cover 3–5 miles total trip distance, with moderate elevation gain and potentially rough terrain. A difficult hike may cover 5 or more miles total trip distance, have rigorous elevation gain, and have rough or rocky terrain.

Hiking time: The average time it will take to cover the route. It is based on the total distance, elevation gain, and condition and difficulty of the trail. Each individual hiker's fitness level will affect their time.

Season/schedule: Best time of the year to hike.

Fees and permits: Information regarding park entrance fees, parking fees, permits, and potential citations.

Trail contacts: This is the location (address in many cases), phone number, and website for the local land manager(s) in charge of all the trails within the selected hike. You are encouraged to get trail access information before you embark on your hike, or contact the land manager after your visit if you see problems with trail erosion, damage, or misuse.

Dog friendly: Trail regulations pertaining to dogs. Dogs are allowed on many Wisconsin trails when leashed (and if you pick up after them).

Trail surface: What to expect you'll be walking on: forested trail, dirt path, boardwalk, paved path, gravel road, etc.

Land status: City park, state park, national park or forest, BLM land, etc.

Nearest town: Nearest substantial town.

Maps: For many hikes there are a wide variety of maps that exist including DNR maps, state park maps, and other auxiliary hiking resources. USGS maps are one of the most accurate sources for topographical information, and local park maps are usually more recent and up-to-date. Hikers are encouraged to use both.

Other trail users: Who you can expect to see on the trail: horseback riders, hunters, mountain bikers, runners, in-line skaters, etc.

Special considerations: Information regarding anything hikers should be prepared for on this trail. Examples: No water, no shade, rugged terrain, no guardrails, steep descent.

Amenities available: Useful features or facilities you may find, such as restrooms, picnic shelters, drinking water, children's play areas, and campsites.

Maximum grade: The steepest part of the hike and how long it lasts. Very few hikes in this book have steep ascents or descents that last more than 0.1 mile.

Cell service: Information regarding the general availability of a signal in the area of the hike. Service may vary by cellphone provider.

Waterway: The river or stream in which the waterfall resides.

Waterfall beauty: This is a 1 to 5 number, 5 being unbelievably beautiful.

Finding the trailhead: Here you'll find dependable driving directions to trailheads including GPS trailhead coordinates for accurate navigation.

Trail conditions: General information regarding the trail surface and what it's made of, including what elements may impact how slippery it gets and whether or not strollers or mobility devices can navigate it.

The Hike: A detailed and carefully researched description of the trail, the waterfall, and interesting things you may see along the way.

Miles and Directions: Here mileage cues identify turns, trail names, and points of interest.

Sidebars: Found throughout the book, these are unique and interesting facts about the area that will enhance your enjoyment of the whole waterfall hiking experience.

Map: A detailed and expertly crafted map is included with each hike. Each map was crafted from GPS tracks and field data collected while on the hikes.

Enjoy your outdoor exploration of Wisconsin waterfalls and remember to leave no trace. Pack out what you pack in.

How to Use the Maps

Overview map: This map shows the location of each hike in the area by hike number.

Route map: This is your primary guide to each hike. It shows the waterfalls, all access roads and trails, points of interest, water, landmarks, and geographical features. It also distinguishes trails from roads, and paved roads from unpaved roads. The selected route is highlighted, and directional arrows point the way.

LAND ACKNOWLEDGMENTS

This book is intended to support your exploration. Readers will come away with a deeper knowledge of the area, and the opportunity to connect more closely and experience more fully the wonders these lands offer. We respectfully acknowledge that this book covers the traditional land of Native Peoples. Wisconsin is home to eleven federally recognized tribes: Bad River Band of Lake Superior Chippewa, Ho-Chunk Nation, Lac Courte Oreilles Band of Lake Superior Chippewa, Lac du Flambeau Band of Lake Superior Chippewa, Menominee Tribe of Wisconsin, Oneida Nation, Forest County Potawatomi, Red Cliff Band of Lake Superior Chippewa, St. Croix Chippewa, Sokaogon Chippewa (Mole Lake), and Stockbridge-Munsee, in addition to other non–federally recognized tribes. Each tribe has its own unique peoples, languages, and spiritual and health practices as well as its own unique connection to the land.

A view of Wequiock Falls from the boardwalk and viewpoint. What lies ahead is the scenic waterfall and the rocky path to get there.

Trail Finder

Hikes to Tall Waterfalls
Morgan Falls
Big Manitou Falls
Superior Falls
Saxon Falls
Willow Falls
Copper Falls
Brownstone Falls
Potato Falls Lower

Hikes to Secluded Waterfalls
Lost Creek Falls
Morgan Falls
Washburn Falls
LaSalle Falls
Meyers Falls
Big Bull Falls
Twelve Foot Falls
Eighteen Foot Falls
Wren Falls
Breakwater Falls
Apple River Falls
Upson Falls

Easy-to-Reach Waterfalls
Greenfield Park Waterfall
Lake Park Waterfall
Montello Street Waterfall
Kimball Falls
Twelve Foot Falls
Big Manitou Falls
Little Manitou Falls
Redstone Falls
Veterans Falls
Cascade Falls
Amnicon Falls

Kid-Friendly Waterfalls
Dells of the Eau Claire Falls
Redstone Falls
Kimball Falls

Greenfield Park Waterfall
Copper Falls
Brownstone Falls
Tyler Forks Cascade
Wequiock Falls
Strong Falls
Glen Park Falls
Keller Lake Falls

Hikes for Nature Lovers
Whitnall Park Waterfall
Pewit's Nest Falls
Parfrey's Glen Falls
Big Bull Falls
LaSalle Falls
Washburn Falls
Interstate Falls
Eighteen Foot Falls
Copper Falls
Brownstone Falls
Tyler Forks Cascade
Dave's Falls
Long Slide Falls
Meyers Falls
Taylors Falls
Potato Falls Upper
Potato Falls Lower
Stephen's Falls

Hikes for Backpackers
Wren Falls

Accessible Hikes
Mill Pond Waterfall
Montello Street Falls
Parfrey's Glen Falls
Pewit's Nest Falls
Kimball Falls
Twelve Foot Falls
Fonferek's Glen Falls
Amnicon Falls

Legend

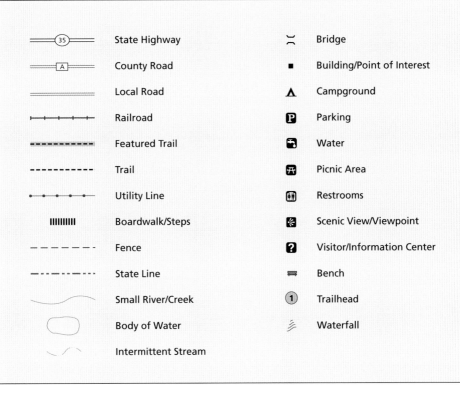

State Highway	Bridge
County Road	Building/Point of Interest
Local Road	Campground
Railroad	Parking
Featured Trail	Water
Trail	Picnic Area
Utility Line	Restrooms
Boardwalk/Steps	Scenic View/Viewpoint
Fence	Visitor/Information Center
State Line	Bench
Small River/Creek	Trailhead
Body of Water	Waterfall
Intermittent Stream	

Southeastern Wisconsin

The southeastern area of the state introduces an intricate landscape with a diversity of unusual waterways and eye-catching rock features. The waterfalls in this quadrant have their own personalities as if naturally crafted to complement the distinctive natural beauty that surrounds them. Steep-sided canyons and sandstone bluffs collide with grid-like farmland and interconnected rivers. Sizeable rivers and marshlands appear unexpectedly and ribbon their way through the countryside, nourishing local crops and creating thriving environments for a rich variety of wildlife. Lumpy forested bluffs dotted with scenic ski and bike trails offer incredible hiking and camping destinations. A magnificent variety of rivers, creeks, and streams pulse and flow through this area like arteries to create beautiful water features and memorable waterfalls.

The Montello Street waterfall in the background plunging into the 150-foot-deep jade-green lake

Many of these waterways meander east like coiled ribbons, eventually emptying into Lake Michigan. These waters, sacred to the Indigenous peoples of southeastern Wisconsin, are woven into the fabric of the urban and suburban landscape resulting in an area that showcases multiple impressive and easy-to-explore waterfalls. The intricate waterways that create them are an integral part of both the health and beauty of the region. The intensity of these various water features and their audible bubbling reflect that of Wisconsin's beer-drenched and motorcycle-loving roots: Miller beer and Harley-Davidson.

This quadrant of the state is home to the bustling metro areas of Milwaukee and Madison as well as quieter towns and villages. Here you will find a variety of farmers' markets, brewery tours, summer festivals, vibrant art and music scenes, and Summerfest: the nation's largest music festival. Many Indigenous groups have called southeastern Wisconsin their home for centuries. Federally recognized tribes including the Ho-Chunk, Menominee, and Potawatomi have active communities throughout the region and still hold significant portions of land. Elaborate museums, artifact shows, and drum and dance festivals occur yearly, offering residents and visitors a look into these tribes' ethnic heritage and their influence on southeastern Wisconsin's history.

1 Greenfield Park Waterfall

This recreation area is an unexpected slice of nature and animal sanctuary nestled into a corner of a suburb southwest of Milwaukee. This paved, wheelchair-accessible path meanders around a central lagoon with shaded picnic areas and public restrooms.

Start: Intersection of 76th Street and Greenfield Avenue in downtown West Allis. This places you 3 miles east of the trailhead.
Elevation gain: Negligible
Distance: 0.51-mile loop
Difficulty: Easy due to minimal elevation change and no stairs or climbing
Hiking time: About 30 minutes
Season/schedule: Greenfield Park is open year-round 6 a.m. to 10 p.m., but it is best used May through Oct.
Fees and permits: None
Trail contacts: Greenfield Park, 2028 South 124th St., West Allis, WI 53227, (414) 257-7275, https://www.ci.greenfield.wi.us/283/Parks-and-Recreation
Dog friendly: Yes, on leashes
Trail surface: Paved and natural
Land status: County park
Nearest town: Greenfield, WI

Maps: USGS Greenfield Park, WI; https://county.milwaukee.gov/files/county/parks-department/Park-Maps/Greenfield.pdf
Other trail users: Dog walkers, anglers, and cyclists
Special considerations: During the cold-weather months, the trail may be covered in snow and ice.
Amenities available: Water and bathrooms are available in the pavilion just south of the trailhead.
Maximum grade: The steepest part of the hike is when you descend from the main trail to the waterfall. The grade is –74 percent, sustained for less than 0.01 mile.
Cell service: Yes
Waterway: Root River Parkway
Waterfall beauty: 3.5
Accessibility: Yes

Finding the trailhead: Greenfield Park is in West Allis, a suburb of Milwaukee. The trailhead is 3 miles west of downtown West Allis. From the intersection of 76th and Greenfield Avenue (downtown West Allis), go 3 miles west on Greenfield Avenue and turn left (south) onto 124th Street. In 0.58 miles turn left onto Park Drive (one of the entrances to the park), directly across the street from a rustic pub and grill called Mary's Caddy Shack. Take your first right (south) into the parking lot. On the southwest end of the parking lot, you will see a waterpark, and on the southeast end, adjacent to the lagoon's fishing platform, you will see a pavilion with water and bathrooms. Walk directly east from the parking lot and you will arrive at the junction of Park Drive (which cuts through the park) and the trailhead. **Trailhead GPS:** N43° 00.451' W88° 03.859'

Trail conditions: The trail is asphalt and requires shoes or sandals; it's a good surface for strollers and wheelchairs. In the cold-weather months, the trail may be icy or covered in snow. There is a small portion of the trail that veers off the asphalt toward the waterfall, which is primarily grass and dirt. This portion of the trail may become muddy and challenging to hike during heavy rains or when snow is thawing in the spring.

The seldom-visited waterfall off the beaten path in Greenfield Park

The Hike

This 0.51-mile hike consists of a well-paved footpath that circles around an emerald green lagoon and finishes exactly where you began. The waterfall is something of a best-kept secret since it is unmarked and many people who visit this beautiful park don't know it exists. It is hidden from the street and located on the north side of the street, across from the eastern end of the lagoon.

To reach the waterfall walk east from the parking lot until you arrive at the trailhead. Follow the footpath and circular trail east around the lagoon in a clockwise loop. You will pass two scenic viewpoints equipped with sitting benches. As you continue on and past the second viewpoint, the path will begin to run directly alongside the road. You will notice a stone wall to your right and matching stone wall on the other side of the street directly to your left: west side and east side. The water that feeds the waterfall from the lagoon is flowing beneath your feet. This is an offshoot trail to the waterfall that you will need to retrace to return to the main trail. Walk across the street to the eastside stone wall and you will see a wooden fence on your right with the word *respect* engraved on it. Follow the wooden fence and the dirt path alongside it to the hidden waterfall. The unpaved path circles clockwise through a pine tree grove and down to a red wood sitting bench and viewpoint that places you directly in front of the waterfall. This is a man-made waterfall with an 8-foot drop and is as visually stunning as it is enjoyable to listen to. This is not a thunderously loud cascade as much as it is a gentle tumbling water feature.

An option for adventurous hikers who don't mind getting their feet wet is to continue east on the soggy grass path opposite the waterfall to discover a hidden lagoon and bird sanctuary. I suggest wearing long pants or high boots because the sharp edges of the tall grass will leave you with some unpleasant scratches from the knees down.

Return to the main trail. You will continue on the trail in a clockwise loop around the lagoon and come across two more remarkable viewpoints on your right side: one view with a sitting bench and slightly farther west, one view without. After you pass a wildflower garden on your right, the walking path begins to turn north and becomes framed by a functional pavilion (on your left) and a fishing platform and canoe launch (on your right). The pavilion is equipped with bathrooms and drinking fountains and is adjacent to a family waterpark due west of the lagoon. Continue hiking north on the path, past the third trail junction, and you will arrive at the trailhead where you started.

As you descend the trail and turn left, you see the lush waterfall in the distance.

On this hike and throughout Greenfield Park, you will find multiple patches of local plants and flowers that were planted to mimic prairies. These are "stopover habitats" that have been carefully created to provide insects, nectar, berries, and nuts for birds to rest and refuel during migration. Here you will find wildflowers such as golden alexander, Michigan lily, and wild indigo, which are equally beautiful and functional. During the summer months if you are observant you just may see a rusty patched bumble bee, hummingbird, clearwing moth, cherry-faced meadowhawk, or yellow warbler.

The small and quiet waterfall nourishing the vegetation around it

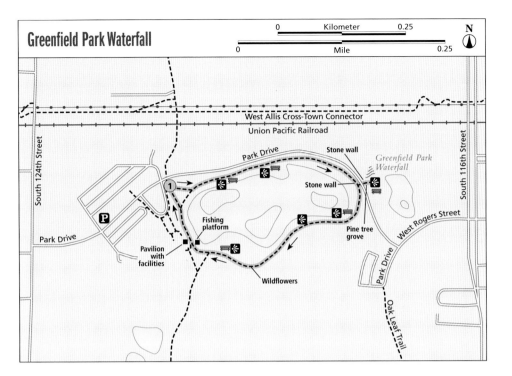

Miles and Directions

0.0 Hike east on the trail toward the first trail junction.

0.14 Pass the second viewpoint with a bench until you reach a stone wall on the west side of the walking path and Park Drive.

0.16 Cross to the other side of Park Drive until you reach the stone wall on the east side of the street.

0.17 Follow the path to your right along the wooden fence, which will lead you through a pine tree grove.

0.18 Pass through the pine trees and arrive at a viewpoint with a red wood sitting bench. The bench is placed to look directly at the waterfall, which is right in front of it.

0.18 Walk directly forward to the waterfall.

0.22 Retrace your steps and return to the walking path. Continue hiking clockwise around the lagoon.

0.45 Arrive at a fishing platform and pavilion. The fishing platform and canoe launch will be on your right and the pavilion will be situated on your left.

0.51 Trail ends.

2 Lake Park Waterfall

Lake Park Waterfall is a 30-foot man-made tumbler nestled in a deep wooded ravine in one of Milwaukee's oldest and most historic parks. This out-and-back hike is wonderful for those looking for a little bit of serenity and escape from the urban jungle.

Start: Start from the centrally located and busy Marquette Interchange in downtown Milwaukee. When you pull into Lake Park, the trailhead is in the southwest corner of the parking lot near the golf course clubhouse.
Elevation gain: Negligible
Distance: 0.1 mile
Difficulty: Easy due to short distance and only one easy-to-navigate staircase
Hiking time: About 10 minutes
Season/schedule: Open year-round from 6 a.m. to 10 p.m.; however, it's best used May through Oct
Fees and permits: None
Trail contacts: 2975 North Lake Park Rd., Milwaukee, WI 53211, (608) 297-2727, https://lakeparkfriends.org/, https://county.milwaukee.gov/EN/Parks/Explore/Find-a-Park
Dog friendly: Yes, on leashes
Trail surface: Paved, woodchips, wooden stairs, gravel

Land status: County park
Nearest town: Milwaukee, WI
Maps: USGS Lake Park, Milwaukee, WI; https://lakeparkfriends.org/visit/lake-park-map/
Other trail users: Runners, bird-watchers, bike riders, and dog walkers
Special considerations: During the winter months the path may be covered in snow or ice.
Amenities available: There is a pavilion on site with water and flush toilets. During the spring and summer, there are porta-potties throughout the park as well.
Maximum grade: -35 percent, during the last 0.01 mile of the hike as you descend the stairs to the base of the falls
Cell service: Yes
Waterway: Spring fed
Waterfall beauty: 1
Accessibility: No

Finding the trailhead: From the Marquette Interchange in downtown Milwaukee take I-794 East for 1.3 miles and take exit #1F for Lincoln Memorial Drive. Head north on Lincoln Memorial Drive for 1.4 miles and turn left (northwest) on Lafayette Hill Road. Go 0.2 mile on Lafayette Hill Road until you reach East Lafayette Place and turn right (east). Go 0.03 mile on Lafayette Place and turn left (northeast) on North Lake Drive. Go 1.1 miles on North Lake Drive and turn right (east) onto North Lake Park Road. Go 0.2 mile and you come to a parking lot. The trailhead is in the southwest corner of the parking lot near the golf course clubhouse. **Trailhead GPS:** N43°04.053' W87°52.220'

Trail conditions: Good. The majority of the hike is a well-maintained paved sidewalk with no uneven surfaces or substantial obstacles. The only rigorous portion of the hike are the stairs leading down to the base of the falls. No special footwear is required.

A view of the Lake Park Waterfall in spring where ▶
the quiet trickle nourishes the surrounding vegetation

The Hike

Situated on a bluff above Lake Michigan and stretching 1 mile long, this 138-acre natural area offers a preserved woodland interspersed with stretches of open meadow-like spaces. Here you'll discover winding footpaths, walking bridges, beautiful views, an abundance of wildlife, and an exceptional native plant community. Over 3 miles of multiuse trails roam the landscape of this park, crisscrossing prairies, community picnic areas, and athletic fields. For those residing in the Milwaukee metro area, Lake Park is a good place to unwind and enjoy the natural beauty of Wisconsin's wilderness while still close to home. Tucked into one of the centrally located wooded ravines is the Lake Park Waterfall, a serene water feature providing an unexpected sanctuary for mental and physical rejuvenation.

In the 1890s forward-thinking Milwaukee leaders decided that a series of parks needed to be designed for the enjoyment and respite of its urban dwellers. Lake Park was one of multiple natural areas in and around the city created as "gardens of the poor." These pockets of preserved wilderness were designed to make nature available to everyone, unlike the well-manicured and private gardens of the wealthy. Lake Park was crafted on a cliff overlooking Lake Michigan and was designed to be enjoyed as a communal place for active sports and nature exploration. "Screens" of trees were planted to allow visitors to feel isolated from the surrounding neighborhoods and urban environment. Today, aside from miles of multiuse hiking and biking trails, this expansive slice of nature hosts an eighteen-hole golf course, children's playground, lawn bowling, upscale French bistro, pavilion with amenities, tennis courts, multipurpose sports fields, multiple deep wooded gullies, and, of course, a majestic 30-foot waterfall.

The trailhead is on the southwest corner of the parking lot near the golf course's clubhouse and just south of the Lake Park Pavilion. To the east and north you will see the dense treeline of the wooded ravine where you'll discover the waterfall. The trailhead is easy to find and is marked with a combination of decorative stones and signage explaining park rules. From the trailhead walk south on the paved footpath until you see a trail junction and seating area with two benches for sitting and two commemorative plaques. Take the path that veers slightly to your left (southeast) and follow it past the first bench until the trail intersects with a woodchip path. Turn left (east) and follow the woodchips along a two-plank wooden fence until you arrive at a descending staircase. At the top of the staircase you are standing at the mouth of the wooded ravine and directly above the waterfall. Descend the first set of thirty-one stairs and you will come to a vista where you can take in the beauty of the upper falls and the picturesque ravine careening to the east. Just beyond this viewpoint there is a second set of eighteen stairs, which brings you down to the base of the falls. Here you have multiple angles to observe or photograph the falls including from a scenic bridge that crosses the ravine. This waterfall is man-made and is a restored version of the original built in the 1930s. It was originally created as a representation of the more robust rivers and streams that flowed through these gulches at an earlier time. To arrive back at the trailhead, return the way you came.

Top: *Standing at the base of the falls: view of the bridge that crosses the ravine*
Bottom: *The path that meanders from the base of the waterfall east through the ravine and toward Lake Michigan*

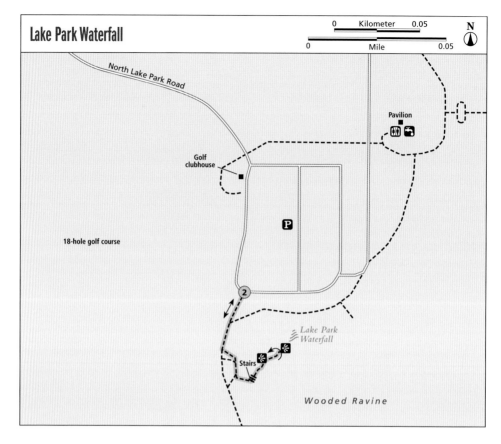

Lake Park Waterfall

Miles and Directions

0.0 From the trailhead head south.

0.03 Arrive at a seating area with a commemorative plaque. Turn left (east) on the woodchip path.

0.04 Arrive at the stairs, which lead down to the waterfall.

0.05 Descend forty-nine stairs to the base of the falls. Return the way you came.

0.1 Arrive back at the trailhead.

Lake Park is known for its meadow-like spaces and for its wild preserved areas. There is a nonprofit called Lake Park Friends dedicated to the preservation, enjoyment, and enhancement of this urban wild space. On their website lakeparkfriends.org, hikers can find two free ebooks: one for identifying native trees of Lake Park and another for identifying wildflowers. Each free publication includes maps that guide you on a walking tour through the park to help you identify the abundant flora (native trees and wildflowers).

View of the upper portion of the falls from the first viewpoint

3 Whitnall Park Waterfall

This waterfall is tucked into a diverse natural area not typically found in parks so close to major cities. Located on Mallard Lake, this easy 1.5-mile loop brings you through prairie-like meadows, accessible wetlands, and lowland forests.

Start: Intersection of 108th Street/Lovers Lane (WI 100) and College Avenue in Franklin. This is a busy intersection of commerce in the heart of Franklin.
Elevation gain: Less than 0.1 mile
Distance: 1.5 miles
Difficulty: Easy
Hiking time: About 1 hour
Season/schedule: Open year-round from sunup to sundown; however, it's most popular May through Oct. During the winter months, the trail may be covered in snow and the lake and waterfall may be frozen.
Fees and permits: Yes (parking only)
Trail contacts: Wehr Nature Center, 6342-6224 Nature Center Dr., Franklin, WI 53132, (414) 425-8550, https://county.milwaukee .gov/EN/Parks/Explore/Wehr-Nature-Center
Dog friendly: No
Trail surface: Gravel, woodchips, and boardwalks
Land status: County park

Nearest town: Franklin, WI
Maps: USGS Wehr Nature Center, Franklin, WI; https://county.milwaukee.gov/files/county /parks-department/Park-Maps/Whitnall11.pdf
Other trail users: None
Special considerations: During the cold-weather months, the trail may be snowy or icy. Be careful and consider wearing winter footwear if you choose to hike it.
Amenities available: Bathrooms and water available at the visitor center, which is open 8 a.m. to 4:30 p.m. daily. Closed on major holidays. A porta-potty is available near the parking lot year-round.
Maximum grade: 40.9 percent for less than 0.1 mile between the eighth and ninth trail junction
Cell service: Yes
Waterway: Mallard Lake/Root River Parkway
Waterfall beauty: 3
Accessibility: No

Finding the trailhead: From the intersection of 108th Street (Lovers Lane) and College Avenue in Franklin, head east on West College Avenue for 0.7 mile. Turn right (south) onto Nature Center Drive and go 0.4 mile. On your right you will see the entrance for Wehr Nature Center Parking. **Trailhead GPS:** N42°47.532' W89°19.566'

Trail conditions: Good. This trail has a combination of surfaces including woodchips, dirt, gravel, grass, and paved. There is minimal elevation change and no substantial obstacles or potential hazards. A good pair of walking shoes is recommended.

Top: Facing the waterfall from downstream in the Root River. Notice the evenly placed fieldstones the CCC put there in the 1930s.
Bottom: View of the falls and Mallard Lake from the fourth trail junction sitting area

The Hike

This visually stunning cascade is nestled in the wild and diverse borders of Whitnall Park, a 220-acre piece of protected land in the southwest suburbs of Milwaukee County. This popular county park offers visitors multiple features for enjoyment and exploration of the natural world year-round. Within the park's borders you'll discover miles of multiuse hiking trails, sledding hills, picnic areas, an archery range, well-maintained and meticulously designed botanical gardens, and a small but picturesque waterfall. Whitnall Park is a rare and beautiful piece of nature worth exploring.

The waterfall and the enjoyable hike are part of the Wehr Nature Center—something of a "nature preserve within a nature preserve"—where Whitnall Park truly offers you a sanctuary of wildness and serenity. Wehr Nature Center was created with a specific vision: to make nature accessible to all people year-round and to inspire current and future generations to explore and value the natural world. It consists of a man-made centrally located lake, 5 miles of interconnected hiking trails, and a photogenic waterfall. The hiking trails within Wehr Nature Center bring you through woodland, wetland, prairie, and oak savanna. On some trails you may find yourself deep in temperate forests thick with sugar maple, red and white oak, and shagbark hickory. Other trails may invite you into small prairie-like communities plentiful with native tall grasses, wildflowers, and herbaceous plants. The hikes vary in both length and difficulty and are perfect for the free-spirited explorer who enjoys a "choose your own adventure"–style experience.

The trailhead is connected to the visitor center, which is on the northwest side of the lake, just southwest of the parking lot. The different hikes in Wehr Nature Center are color coded, and the Lake Loop hike is indicated on the map with the color yellow. To arrive at the waterfall head south from the trailhead and visitor center toward Mallard Lake. Take a left at the first color-coded trail junction and follow it past two more trail junctions until you reach a viewpoint that places you at the top of the waterfall on its northwest corner. Here you have a bench and a picture-perfect view of Mallard Lake. Take a left here and follow the yellow-coded Lake Loop as it brings you on a forested trail. You will pass three more trail junctions, which are all connected to other color-coded hikes. Stay to your right. You'll exit the woods just before arriving at the eighth trail junction, which consists of a paved sidewalk crossing a bridge. Stay to the right and follow the trail back into the woods. The trail returns to woodchips and you will cross two boardwalks that help you pass over potentially swampy terrain before you arrive at the waterfall (lower southeast end).

> Much of what is currently Whitnall Park was built by the Civilian Conservation Corps (CCC) during the 1930s. Mallard Lake was created when approximately 150,000 cubic yards of earth were removed by horse and bucket. The dam that creates the trickling falls was then built by hand using fieldstones found onsite.

Top: Mallard Lake sits quietly behind an old tree stump in the wintertime.
Bottom: A color-coded signpost marker makes it easy for hikers to stay on the Lake Loop Trail.

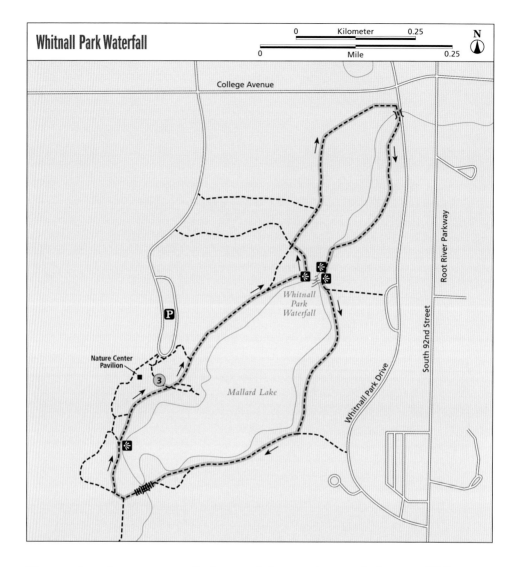

College Avenue

Root River Parkway

South 92nd Street

Whitnall Park Drive

Whitnall Park Waterfall

P

Nature Center Pavilion

3

Mallard Lake

Here you have the option to walk down and view or photograph the waterfall from the base. The path then brings you up a short distance to a second viewpoint at the top of the falls where you have a scenic view of Mallard Lake. Continue walking in a clockwise loop around the lake. You will pass a utility building, and the trail will turn to a series of boardwalks, keeping you elevated over marshland. As you continue onward you will arrive at a trail junction that offers paths to the various color-coded hikes. Stay to your right and follow the yellow signposts for the Lake Loop. You'll pass a pier on the lake with a viewing and sitting area and arrive back at the first trail junction having made a complete 1.5-mile loop. Take a left and you arrive back at the trailhead.

Miles and Directions

0.0 From the trailhead walk southeast toward Mallard Lake.

0.01 Arrive at the first trail junction, which features a sitting bench. Turn left and follow the yellow-marked trail.

0.25 Arrive at a viewpoint with benches on the shores of Mallard Lake. Here you are positioned just northwest of the waterfall with a view from the top. Follow the trail to your left as it veers away from the lake and twists and turns a bit. Continue to follow the yellow trail markers.

0.5 The trail exits the forest and you arrive at a junction that consists of a paved sidewalk and bridge crossing the creek. Follow this path to your right where the sidewalk brings you over the bridge and then veers right back into the forest where the trail returns to woodchips.

0.8 You'll cross two boardwalks that keep you elevated over potentially wet or swampy areas before arriving at the base of the falls, offering you a view of the waterfall from the southeast. Here you have the best options for photos.

0.81 Arrive at a viewpoint with a bench where you have a scenic view of Mallard Lake and a view of the waterfall from above.

1.23 Continue to follow the trail clockwise around the lake until the trail comes to a T-intersection. To your right the trail dead-ends at the shores of the lake with a beautiful view and a bench for sitting. Follow the trail to your left where you will pass a utility building and the trail becomes a boardwalk over the water.

1.28 Arrive at the thirteenth trail junction and keep right as indicated by the yellow signposts. If you take the trail to your left, you will connect with the Woodland Trail (blue line).

1.3 Arrive at a roundabout-style trail junction, which can potentially connect you with multiple other of the color-coded trails. Turn right and continue following the trail marked by the yellow signposts.

1.5 Pass a lakeside pier and sitting area and arrive back at the first trail junction, 0.01 mile southeast of the trailhead where you started.

4 Mill Pond Waterfall—Option #1

This out-and-back hike brings you to a captivating scene that combines the beauty of nature and local history. A scenic 4-acre pond and bird sanctuary spills into a world-class fishing creek that voyages onward to Lake Michigan.

Start: Begin at the intersection of College and Chicago Avenue. At this point you are 1.3 miles northwest of the trailhead.
Elevation gain: 0
Distance: 0.04 mile
Difficulty: Easy
Hiking time: About 2 minutes
Season/schedule: This hike is in Grant Park, which is open year-round from 6 a.m. to 10 p.m. This waterfall is best visited May through Oct. During the cold-weather months, the waterfall may be frozen.
Fees and permits: None
Trail contacts: Grant Park, 100 Hawthorne Ave., South Milwaukee, WI 53172, (414) 762-1550, http://fogp.org
Dog friendly: Yes, on leashes
Trail surface: Paved
Land status: County park

Nearest town: South Milwaukee, WI
Maps: USGS Grant Park, South Milwaukee, WI; https://county.milwaukee.gov/files/county/parks-department/Park-Maps/grant.pdf
Other trail users: Cyclists, dog walkers, foragers, anglers
Special considerations: During the winter months the trail may be icy or covered in snow.
Amenities available: None. There is a coffee shop called Better Together located 0.4 mile northwest of the trailhead at the intersection of Chicago Avenue and Hawthorne Avenue. Here you will find bathrooms as well as an extensive variety of espresso drinks and milkshakes.
Maximum grade: 0
Cell service: Yes
Waterway: Oak Creek Parkway
Waterfall beauty: 3
Accessibility: Yes

Finding the trailhead: From the intersection of College Avenue and Chicago Avenue, head south on Chicago Avenue for 0.9 mile until you come to Oak Creek Parkway at the entrance of Grant Park. Turn left (southeast) and go 0.4 mile until you come to the intersection of Mill Road and Oak Creek Parkway. Park along the street on Oak Creek Parkway just northwest of Mill Road. The trailhead is on the southwest corner of the intersection of Oak Creek Parkway and Mill Road. **Trailhead GPS:** N42° 54.761' W87° 51.197'

Trail conditions: Good. A paved walking path that is mildly cracked and worn from years of use. No substantial obstacles or hazards. No special footwear required.

Top: One of the best views of the falls entails walking up the Oak Creek and through the tunnel. Bottom: From a distance down the creek, you can see the waterfall under the arch of the brick bridge.

The Hike

This medium-sized silvery waterfall can be found in Milwaukee County's second largest public park, which covers 380 acres along the shores of Lake Michigan. This big beautiful green space offers beaches, athletic fields, a golf course, a lakefront beer garden, and miles of wooded trails for all hiking and walking levels. Nearly every trail is oriented so that you regularly come across viewpoints, bluff clearings, and sitting areas that provide remarkable eastern views of Lake Michigan.

When hiking through Grant Park, be prepared for wildlife sightings that may include grey squirrel, eastern cottontail rabbit, raccoon, white-tailed deer, and coyote. Grant Park is known as a birder hotspot. You can witness a wide variety of migratory birds, waterfowl, woodpeckers, and the beautiful but elusive winter finches. There have been 241 different species of birds reported in Grant Park, 118 species spotted on Mill Pond alone.

This waterfall is at a unique juncture of green space between Grant Park and the Oak Creek Parkway where the carefully designed Mill Pond empties into the Oak Creek. Historically this location has been a popular year-round scene for outdoor recreation and enjoyment. During the warm-weather months, anglers of all ages still swarm to the popular fishing hole just below the waterfall in efforts to catch large steelhead trout and king salmon that have traveled upstream from Lake Michigan. During the winter months Mill Pond freezes over and provides locals with a popular ice skating and winter recreation wonderland.

The waterfall and the antique building on its shores are listed on the National Register of Historic Places. The waterfall you are looking at was originally the site of a gristmill constructed in 1841. In fact, the original millstones from the gristmill can still be found there today—one on each side of the spillway. The site was later remodeled and turned into the scenic spillway before you in 1932 by Works Progress Administration (WPA) labor as part of a remodeling project on the Oak Creek Parkway. One of the things that makes the landscape so pretty is the antique building on the north shore of the pond. Also built in 1934 by WPA labor, it was originally designed as a boathouse for the purpose of renting canoes. In most recent years it has been referred to by locals as the "warming house" since it supplied roaring fires and hot cocoa to winter recreation enthusiasts. Local government, volunteers, and historians are revitalizing the pond and boathouse to restore it to its previous nostalgic functionality for the enjoyment of the community.

From the trailhead walk south on the paved trail that runs parallel to Mill Road. The trail crosses over Oak Creek, placing you above and directly in front of the waterfall with the historic boathouse in the background. The view looks like something a landscape artist would paint for a seasonal greeting card or a backdrop intentionally designed for graduation or wedding photos. To return to the trailhead, walk back the way you came.

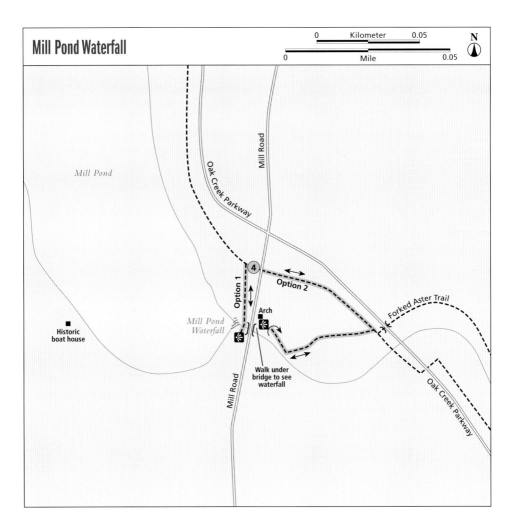

Miles and Directions

0.0 At the trailhead, walk south on the paved footpath, which runs parallel to Mill Road.

0.02 Arrive at the bridge that crosses Oak Creek and puts you directly in front of the waterfall. Return the way you came.

0.04 Arrive back at the trailhead.

4 Mill Pond Waterfall—Option #2

Start: Begin at the intersection of College Avenue and Chicago Avenue. Here you will find a popular coffee and ice cream shop called Better Together. At this starting point you are only 0.9 mile north of the trailhead.
Elevation gain: Negligible
Distance: 0.16 mile
Difficulty: Strenuous due to climbing down a retaining wall and rock hopping up the creek
Hiking time: About 7 minutes
Season/schedule: This hike is in Grant Park, which is open year-round from 6 a.m. to 10 p.m. This waterfall is best visited May through Oct. During the cold-weather months, the creek and waterfall may be frozen.
Fees and permits: None
Trail contacts: Grant Park, 100 Hawthorne Ave., South Milwaukee, WI 53172, (414) 762-1550, http://fogp.org
Dog friendly: Yes, on leashes
Trail surface: Paved, dirt and rocks
Land status: County park

Nearest town: South Milwaukee
Maps: USGS Grant Park, South Milwaukee, WI; https://county.milwaukee.gov/files/county /parks-department/Park-Maps/grant.pdf
Other trail users: Cyclists, dog walkers, foragers, anglers
Special considerations: During the winter months the trail may be icy or covered in snow.
Amenities available: None. There is a coffee shop called Better Together located 0.4 mile northwest of the trailhead at the intersection of Chicago Avenue and Hawthorne Avenue. Here you will find bathrooms as well as an extensive variety of espresso drinks and milkshakes.
Maximum grade: −39.5 at the last part of the hike as you descend the retaining wall and step down to the rock in the creek. Sustained for less than 0.01 mile.
Cell service: Yes
Waterway: Oak Creek Parkway
Waterfall beauty: 3
Accessibility: No

Finding the trailhead: From the intersection of College Avenue and Chicago Avenue, head south on Chicago Avenue for 0.9 mile until you come to Oak Creek Parkway at the entrance of Grant Park. Turn left (southeast) and go 0.4 mile until you come to the intersection of Mill Road and Oak Creek Parkway. Park along the street on Oak Creek Parkway just northwest of Mill Road. The trailhead is on the southeast corner (whereas Option 1 is on the southwest corner) of the intersection of Oak Creek Parkway and Mill Road. **Trailhead GPS:** N42° 54.759' W87° 51.189'

Trail conditions: This hike starts out on a paved sidewalk, which is easy to navigate with no special footwear required. Once you descend toward the river on the dirt path, it gets more challenging. When it is wet this part may be muddy and slippery. It may be covered in snow and ice during the cold-weather months. Part of this hike requires walking along a retaining wall with no guardrails and then stepping down to the water. Sturdy waterproof hiking footwear is strongly recommended.

Top: The Mill Pond Waterfall with the scenic boathouse in the distance
Bottom: A curtain of water falling over evenly placed bricks creates a memorable scene for anglers and park visitors.

The wooded trails along the Oak Creek Parkway are a popular spot for foraging for wild leeks, also called "ramps." With wild leeks, both the leaves and underground bulb smell and taste like onion and are edible. They go great in salads, soups, and other recipes that call for leeks or onion. In other areas of rural Wisconsin, it is reported that dairy farmers don't care for this plant because it produces sour milk in cows who graze on it.

The Hike

This alternate hike option brings you down to the water and allows you to walk upstream to get a view of the falls from the base. From the southeast corner of Mill Road and Oak Creek Parkway, walk along the paved sidewalk as it heads southeast until you reach the bridge where Oak Creek Parkway crosses the creek. Do not cross the bridge, but instead turn right (west) and follow the dirt trail as it veers away from the sidewalk and heads down (southwest) toward the water. When you arrive at the retaining wall you are at the creek's edge, but elevated approximately 6 feet above the water. This is a popular spot for anglers to cast from, and during spawning season you may see them standing on this retaining wall shoulder to shoulder casting for trout and salmon. Take a right (northwest) at the retaining wall and walk until you come to the bridge, which is arching up and over to your left (southwest) crossing the creek. Here you want to carefully descend the retaining wall to the rocks below. Historically anglers and waterfall hikers have stacked up rock against the retaining wall, so that you will not need to jump 6 feet down to arrive at the water. Be careful, since the rocks in the creek may be slippery. From here you can rock hop west through the tunnel and toward the falls. The exposed rocks available to step on stop about halfway under the bridge, bringing you to a stunning up-close view of the falls from below. Wading in the water is also an option, which will bring you right up to the falls. The water is seldom more than approximately 8 to 10 inches deep under the bridge, but the surface you're walking on may be slippery. To return to the trailhead hike back out the way you came.

Miles and Directions

0.0 From the trailhead walk southeast on the paved footpath that runs parallel to Oak Creek Parkway.

0.04 Arrive at the northwest side of the bridge that crosses over Oak Creek. Do not cross the bridge. Turn right (west) and follow the dirt path as it curves and descends southwest toward the creek.

0.06 Arrive at the retaining wall at the water's edge. Turn right (west) and walk along the retaining wall toward the arch.

0.07 Arrive at the arch and turn left (south), which involves stepping down to the rocks in the creek below the arch. Rock hop your way west under the bridge and toward the falls.

0.08 Arrive at the view of the falls from under the Mill Road bridge. Return the way you came.

0.16 Arrive back at the trailhead.

5 Montello Street Waterfall

This out-and-back hike brings you to a picturesque waterfall that punctuates the center of a charming town with a rich history.

Start: The popular intersection of Main Street and Montello Street in downtown Montello
Elevation gain: 0
Distance: 0.04 mile
Difficulty: Easy—a short hike with a flat paved surface
Hiking time: Approximately 3 minutes
Season/schedule: Open year-round; however it's best used May through Oct
Fees and permits: None
Trail contacts: Daggett Memorial Park, 11-31 East Montello St., Montello, WI 53949, (608) 297-2727, www.montellowi.com
Dog friendly: No
Trail surface: Paved
Land status: Daggett Memorial Park

Nearest town: Montello, WI
Maps: USGS Montello, WI
Other trail users: None
Special considerations: During the cold-weather months, the path may be icy or covered in snow.
Amenities available: There are no amenities in the park itself, but there is a Kwik Trip gas station that shares a parking lot with Daggett Memorial Park. The Kwik Trip has bathrooms, water, snacks, and groceries.
Maximum grade: 0
Cell service: Yes
Waterway: Montello Quarry
Waterfall beauty: 4
Accessibility: Yes

Finding the trailhead: From the intersection of Main Street and Montello Street, head east on Montello Street for 0.03 mile. You will see the waterfall and the adjacent park on your left. Turn left (north) into the parking lot and park on the west side of the lot. Daggett Memorial Park shares a parking lot with Kwik Trip. **Trailhead GPS:** N43°47.532' W89°19.566'

Trail conditions: Good. A paved sidewalk that meanders through a well-maintained public park. No special footwear is required. In the cold-weather months, the path may be snow covered and icy.

The Hike

This colorful waterfall appears slightly out of place. While many of the other cascades featured in this book can be found in mist-shrouded forests or rocky gorges, this one sits smack dab on the main highway of a small town. Situated within an old quarry, this man-made tumbler features four cascading falls that elegantly pour over a bluff of multicolored granite and into a 150-foot-deep jade-green lake. To observe this man-made granite wonder, you will find yourself strolling through Daggett Memorial Park, located directly in front of the quarry. The park offers visitors well-groomed footpaths, green lawns, and multiple sitting benches perfect for relaxation and passive

The Montello Street Waterfall with fall colors

reflection. The park is designed so that no matter where you find yourself on its zigzagging foot paths, you always have a perfect view of the falls.

Montello is situated on the confluence of the Montello and Fox Rivers. These two rivers helped put Montello on the map when they became the primary means of transportation between the Great Lakes and the Mississippi River. Now the abundance of lakes, rivers, and waterways surrounding Montello make it a popular destination for lovers of all things outdoors. On Montello's fringe you'll find expansive woodlands and wetlands, perfect for hikers, hunters, and anglers year-round. For individuals looking specifically for hiking and walking trails, you'll discover

This quarry was once Montello's leading industry. Montello Quarry granite gained notoriety as the world's strongest following the death of Ulysses S. Grant. The individuals in charge of building his tomb conducted a worldwide search for the strongest granite and out of nearly 300 samples, Montello's granite was deemed the best.

Granite is considered an igneous rock that was formed as liquid magma solidified deep within the earth. The granite in Montello is believed to be 1.765 million years old. According to geologists, granite consists of mainly quartz, mica, and feldspar. Glacial movement back and forth over many thousands of years scraped away the surrounding land in what is now Montello, exposing the granite.

adventure in John Muir County Park. The boyhood home of the famous naturalist is now a 125-acre park that includes a 30-acre lake with boat access, picnic grounds, restroom, and hiking trails. It also reports being home to the largest measured tree in the state of Wisconsin.

When you drive through downtown Montello, you unexpectedly come upon Daggett Memorial Park and the Montello Quarry. What you are looking at is the site of a once-functioning 10-acre quarry that was the leading industry in this tiny town for generations as well as a national source of high-quality granite. Montello granite is reportedly unique in its density, hardness, and strength and was previously mined to build beautiful monuments and pave roads in many cities. This eye-catching waterfall is man-made and was built in 1992, years after the quarry was closed.

This out-and-back hike brings you through a well-manicured green space featuring excellent views and multiple sitting options. To get the best view of the waterfall, walk northwest from the trailhead through Daggett Memorial Park. You'll pass a trail junction and an inviting sitting area on your left before arriving at a centrally located trail junction with the waterfall directly to your right (north). From here turn right (north) and take a few steps toward the falls where you will find an informational plaque describing the detailed history of the quarry and the waterfall. There are multiple sitting areas in the small park to relax and enjoy the view. To return to the trailhead, walk back the way you came.

The trailhead with the well-groomed Daggett Memorial Park in the background

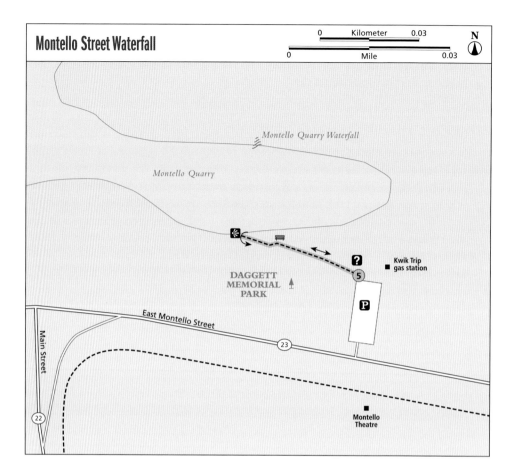

Montello Quarry Waterfall

Montello Quarry

Kwik Trip
gas station

DAGGETT
MEMORIAL
PARK

East Montello Street

23

Main Street

22

Montello
Theatre

Miles and Directions

0.0 From the trailhead walk northwest.

0.01 Pass the trail junction with a sitting bench.

0.02 Arrive at the central view of the waterfall with informative plaque. To return to the trail-head, walk back the way you came.

0.04 Arrive back at the trailhead.

Southwestern Wisconsin

This quadrant of the state is arguably one of the most dynamic. Heading from south-central to southwest, the topography changes from grid-like farmland and rolling hills to colorful bluffs. Prehistoric sandstone composite creates high cliffs decorated with sprouted greenery, resulting in impressive and dramatic views. Vast acres of agricultural land comingle with deep stagnant lakes and feral rivers. Limestone canyons and quartzite bluffs rise and fall among serpentine rivers and their collective tributaries. This picturesque region tells a story unique to Wisconsin's history, particularly interesting for geology buffs. Glaciation as well as the remnants of prehistoric oceans have molded this area into an

A view of Pewit's Nest waterfall after wading upstream and walking through the center of the gorge

unforgettable land for exploration. Southwestern Wisconsin introduces the Baraboo Hills, the "driftless" region, and popular state parks such as Devil's Lake and Governor Dodge. Year-round Wisconsinites gravitate to them for endless possibilities for outdoor recreation. It is a region of abundant natural beauty and historical significance, making it a fascinating region for hikers, waterfall hunters, and geology enthusiasts.

This quadrant of the Dairy State also bumps up against equally beautiful neighboring states Minnesota and Iowa. Before European settlers arrived, this land was Indigenous territory. Dating back approximately 7,000 years, Native Americans lived in this area, used the land for food, and made natural camps and shelters in the bluffs. The high cliffs and bluffs that once protected early inhabitants from the harsh weather are now the reason hikers flock to these regions to enjoy the spectacular views. In this corner of the state, the Mississippi River creates a well-defined border between Wisconsin and its neighbors. Streams, creeks, and tributaries weave in and out of these essential waterways, creating a variety of cascades and waterfalls as well as rocky twisted gorges and steep-sided canyons.

Walk side to side and check out Stephen's Falls from different angles.

6 Redstone Falls

This out-and-back hike that brings you to a stunning thunderous waterfall is hidden away in a far corner of a county park on one of Wisconsin's best recreational lakes. Lake Redstone tumbles into Big Creek, creating a seldom visited swimming hole that is not to be missed.

Start: Intersection of East Main Street (WI 33) and WI 33/Union Street in downtown LaValle

Elevation gain: Less than 0.1 mile

Distance: 0.4 mile

Difficulty: Moderate. A gradual descending path that must be retraced and ascended again upon your return.

Hiking time: About 11 minutes

Season/schedule: Open year-round; however it's best used May through Oct

Fees and permits: Yes

Trail contacts: Lake Redstone Park, S4522 Douglas Rd., LaValle, WI 53941, (608) 355-4800, https://www.co.sauk.wi.us/parksand recreation/lake-redstone-park

Dog friendly: Dogs are allowed on the trails, no leash required. Dogs are *not* allowed on Lake Redstone Beach.

Trail surface: Paved, grass and dirt, wooden bridge

Land status: County park

Nearest town: LaValle, WI

Maps: USGS Lake Redstone, WI

Other trail users: Anglers

Special considerations: The park is surrounded by private land. Keep an eye out for No Trespassing signs and make sure you stay on the park's property.

Amenities available: Pit toilet and hand pump water spigot

Maximum grade: –16 for less than 0.1 mile

Cell service: Yes

Waterway: Big Creek/Lake Redstone

Waterfall beauty: 4

Accessibility: No

Finding the trailhead: From the intersection of East Main Street (WI 33) and WI 33/Union Street, head north on WI 33/Union Street for 0.9 mile until you come to Park Road. Turn right (east) on Park Road, which turns into Douglas Road, and follow it for 1.4 miles until you come to West Redstone Drive. Turn left (north) onto West Redstone Drive, which is also the entrance to Lake Redstone State Park. There is a pay station and drop box to pay entrance fees on your way in. The trailhead is in the northwest corner of the parking lot. **Trailhead GPS:** N43° 35.245' W90° 05.441'

Trail conditions: Good. The trails are indicated either by a paved path, rocks and gravel, or by grass that has been cut intentionally to show where the path in the hike goes. No specific footwear is required.

The first glimpse you get of the scenic falls as you cross the bridge over Big Creek

The Hike

This lesser-known gem is in Lake Redstone County Park on the southeast end of Lake Redstone. This county park is approximately 30 acres and includes a large parking lot, picnic area, children's playground, and sandy beach on the shores of a fun recreational lake. One of the big draws of Lake Redstone is the fishing. Human visitors flock yearly to fish for largemouth bass, musky, northern pike, panfish, and walleye. For those interested in scenic bluffs and cliffs, Lake Redstone has beautiful red rock formations sprinkled throughout the lake, which makes for great scenery for hikers and paddlers.

This region is called the Baraboo Hills and is something of a fascinating place for geology buffs. The distinctly red rock visible on the cliffs and bluffs of Lake Redstone is called quartzite and was deposited 1.7 billion years ago from near-shore ocean sediment. Nowadays these unique formations of quartzite offer visual appeal as well as jump-off points and diving boards for swimmers.

The waterfall, which enhances the scenery of this already beautiful area, is tucked away in a seldom visited corner of the park where the mighty lake empties into Big Creek. The waterfall is man-made, but is so visually stunning that you would never expect it to be an industrial spillway. Quite possibly, the best part of this out-of-the-way attraction is the swimming hole at the base. While some waterfalls throughout the state have wooden guardrails and warning signs keeping hikers at a distance, this one invites you right down to the shores to take a dip. On summer days, it's a clean and cool oasis of misty water that you'll most likely have to yourself.

The trailhead for this hike begins at the north end of the parking lot and circles clockwise down toward the beach. When you come to the first trail junction, stay to your right where the trail descends away from the beach and turns into a combination of dirt, gravel, and rocks. Near the bottom of the short hill, the path turns to a mowed lane of grass where it visibly looks like someone maintains the trail. Continue onward until you arrive at a bridge crossing Big Creek. To your left you see and hear the falls in the distance, and to your right the shallow creek meanders south over multiple rapids. As you cross the bridge, the path becomes a little muddy and you arrive at a second trail junction with a sign prohibiting you from climbing on the waterfall. Take a left at this sign and trail junction and follow the trail until it ends at a photo-worthy view of the falls. If you are so inclined to go for a swim, carefully descend the slippery rocks at the shores of the creek and jump in. To arrive back at the trailhead, return the way you came.

Top: *Admiring the falls head-on from the trail's end*
Bottom: *The sturdy footbridge that crosses picturesque Big Creek as the trail brings you closer to the falls*

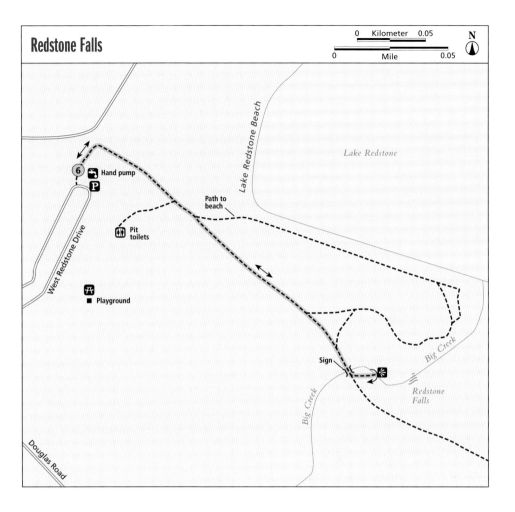

Miles and Directions

0.0 From the trailhead, which is connected to the parking area, head north on the paved trail and follow it as it turns east and down the hill toward the lake.

0.6 Pass the first trail junction and stay to your right as the path descends down a hill and turns to gravel and then mowed grass.

0.15 Follow the mowed grass trail until you arrive at the bridge that crosses Big Creek.

0.16 As you cross the bridge, the trail becomes slightly muddy. Arrive at the second trail junction, which has a sign directing you to the left to see the falls. Turn left.

0.2 Arrive at the view of the waterfall, then retrace the path to the trailhead.

0.4 Arrive back at the trailhead.

7 Pewit's Nest Falls

This out-and-back hike culminates at a hidden waterfall deep within a 40-foot-deep gorge cut into ancient Cambrian sandstone.

Start: Intersection of 8th Street (US 12) and Broadway Street (CR W) in downtown Baraboo
Elevation gain: 0.01 mile
Distance: 0.6 mile
Difficulty: Moderate. The last section of the trail has a short but steep climb.
Hiking time: About 17 minutes
Season/schedule: Open year-round 6 a.m. to 8 p.m., but is best used May through Oct. Getting the best view (and photo) of the waterfall requires wading in shallow water and walking upstream. This may be difficult (or impossible if frozen) during the cold-weather months.
Fees and permits: None
Trail contacts: Pewit's Nest State Natural Area, CR W, Baraboo, WI 53913, (608) 266-0394, dnr.wi.gov
Dog friendly: Yes, on leashes
Trail surface: Gravel and dirt
Land status: DNR state natural area
Nearest town: Baraboo
Maps: USGS Baraboo, WI; https://dnr.wi.gov /topic/lands/naturalareas/documents/topo maps/map200.pdf
Other trail users: None
Special considerations: Historically many visitors to this area have interacted with the landscape by rock climbing and jumping off of the cliffs into the water. At one time this was permitted (or rarely enforced). Now this is strictly prohibited and changed the way most visitors interact with this hike and landscape. There are newly constructed wooden railings built to protect the landscape and keep hikers in designated areas. Visitors must stay behind the split rail fence and out of the protected areas, and anyone who violates this may be subject to a fine of $175–$200. This land is also framed by private property, and you will encounter barbed wire as well as signs indicating where the state natural area ends and private property begins. Parking is very limited, and parking along the road (CR W) is not permitted. The Sauk County sheriff is known to aggressively ticket cars parked on the side of the highway. This location has no toilets or water.
Amenities available: None
Maximum grade: 27 percent the last 0.01 mile of the hike between the first and second trail junction, just before arriving at the trail's end
Cell service: Yes
Waterway: Skillet Creek
Waterfall beauty: 1
Accessibility: Yes. The surface is well-compacted gravel the entire way to the mouth of the gorge and the view of the lower falls. This portion of the route gains very little elevation. Between the first trail junction and the very end of the hike, there is a steep hill to climb, which would be challenging with a wheelchair or stroller.

Finding the trailhead: From the intersection of 8th Avenue/US 12 and Broadway Street (CR W) in southwest Baraboo, go west on US 12/8th Avenue for 1.5 miles until you reach the traffic circle. Take the third exit onto the US 12 East ramp to Madison and head south for 0.8 mile. Take the W ramp (on your right) to US 12/South Boulevard for 0.3 mile. At the traffic circle take the first exit (right) onto CR W. Head west on CR W for 1 mile and then take a left into the parking lot for Pewit's Nest State Natural Area. (Note that CR W does not go in a straight line until you reach the entrance. It begins heading west for 0.5 mile before curving south for another 0.5 mile. Just when it is about to curve west again, you will see the sign for Pewit's Nest.) The sign isn't easy to see from the highway, and if you're going 65 miles per hour you may miss it! **Trailhead GPS:** N43° 27.135' W89°47.361'

Trail conditions: Good. The gravel trail is wide, firmly packed down, and well maintained. Between the first trail junction and the very end of the path there is a steep hill to climb.

The Hike

This hike has geology, history, beauty, and adventure. The hike to Pewit's Nest is an all-around pleasant stroll through nature that ends at a fairytale-like grotto that requires taking your socks and shoes off and getting your feet wet. Pewit's Nest is approximately 2 miles southwest of Baraboo and is quite similar to the more well-known Parfrey's Glen (Hike 8) located in Devil's Lake State Park. This geological feature is a visually stunning narrow canyon with multiple rippling rapids and a popular swimming area right at the mouth of the gorge. The gorge was formed by Skillet Creek cutting a narrow canyon through ancient Cambrian sandstone, the result being unique rock formations in the way of potholes and waterfalls.

Cambrian sandstone is a beautiful layered stone formed over a billion years ago from the ancient oceans' (Cambrian Seas) near-shore sediment. Aside from its color-ful beauty, Cambrian stone has biological significance since it is some of the earliest stone to contain diverse fossils of animals. In Pewit's Nest, layers of this prehistoric stone composite create high cliffs decorated with sprouted greenery resulting in a truly otherworldly environment.

The hike to the canyon brings you through a shaded landscape of understory foli-age common in Wisconsin woodlands. Ostrich ferns, wild raspberries, and vibrantly colored flowering perennials are dispersed alongside the trail. The forest, both on the hike and above the gorge, is dominated by red cedar, white pine, hemlock, and yellow birch. Keep an ear and eye out for vivacious wildlife such as turkeys, white-tailed deer, and grey and red fox.

According to Sauk County historical records, at one time an eccentric mechanic lived in this canyon in a hard-to-get-to abode built into the solid sandstone about 10 feet above a deep pool of water. According to legend the resident of this gorge repaired watches, clocks, guns, and farming utensils. His machinery was powered by an old-fashioned centrifugal water-wheel powered by water moving through the gorge. Pewit is another name for a phoebe bird and, similar to the eccentric mechanic, they build their nests in protected nooks such as the sides of cliffs. As a result, early settlers named this gorge "Pewit's Nest."

Top: As you stroll down Skillet Creek away from the falls, take a look over your shoulder and catch a glimpse of this geological wonder in all its glory.
Bottom: Looking at Skillet Creek as it continues its quiet voyage east and away from the gorge

The trail starts out wide and is firmly packed gravel. This trail is not paved, but the first 0.13 mile could be navigated by strollers, wheelchairs, or mobility devices. It isn't until the first trail junction when the path turns to dirt and presents more uneven surfaces. At the first trail junction, there is a fork in the trail, providing two paths that bring you to different viewpoints. Take the path to the right (continuing south) first and it will bring you down to the mouth of the gorge, which is a popular spot for people to wade in the cool water. At this viewpoint you have an absolutely beautiful view of the canyon, which looks like a giant sandstone cave with the creek pouring out of its mouth. To get the best view of the most accessible waterfall, walk in the shallow water toward the mouth of the gorge.

To arrive at the second viewpoint, return the way you came. At the first trail junction turn right (east) and walk up the steep hill. The path will be framed by two plank wooden fences on your right. Just follow the contour of the fences until you can't go any farther and you have arrived at the viewpoint overlooking the gorge. Behold, one of Mother Nature's geological masterpieces! Being able to see the other water features deeper into the gorge may depend on the time of the year. It is easier to see the creek and other waterfalls in early spring or late fall when there is slightly less foliage growing in and around the gorge.

From the trail's end, and within the fenced-in confines, you peer down into the ravine.

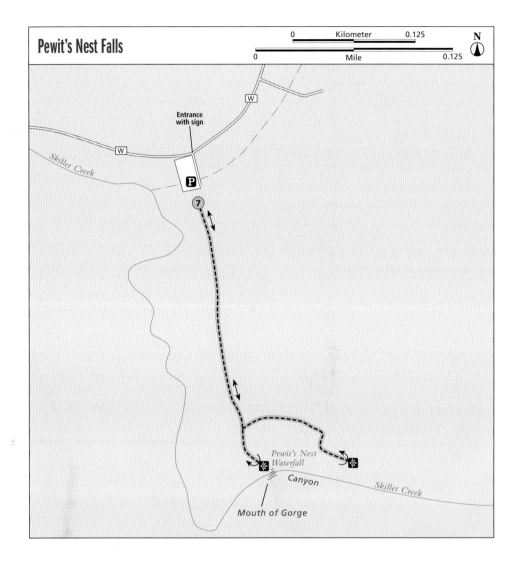

Miles and Directions

0.0 The trailhead is in the southeast corner of the parking lot. From the trailhead walk south on the footpath.

0.13 Arrive at the first trail junction and follow the path along the split rail fence to the right.

0.16 Arrive at the mouth of the gorge, the swimming hole, and the view of the lower falls. Retrace your steps and return to the first trail junction. Take a right (east) and walk up the steep hill that is framed on your right side by a split rail fence.

0.3 Follow the contour of the split rail fence and arrive at the trail's end. Here you have a view of the gorge from above, including the middle and upper falls. Retrace the path to the trailhead.

0.6 Arrive back at the trailhead.

8 Parfrey's Glen Falls

This simple and quiet waterfall is hidden deep in the far reaches of a fairytale-like sandstone canyon. A leisurely stroll along a beautiful mountain-like stream will bring you there.

Start: Intersection of Broadway Street (US 12) and Water Street/WI 113 in downtown Baraboo. Statz Park is at this intersection.

Elevation gain: Less than 0.1 mile from beginning to end

Distance: 1.74 miles

Difficulty: Moderate with a difficult ending. The initial 0.7 mile of this hike takes place on a spacious well-groomed path with very few obstacles and plenty of benches for resting. The last 1.7 miles of the hike is an adventurous gauntlet of moss-covered boulders that you must climb over to get a view of the falls.

Hiking time: About 40 minutes

Season/schedule: Open year-round 6 a.m. to 8 p.m., but is best used May through Oct

Fees and permits: Yes. State Park sticker is required. A payment drop box is onsite for one-time day visitors.

Trail contacts: 1377 CR DL, Merrimac, WI 53561, (608) 266-2621, http://dnr.wi

Dog friendly: No

Trail surface: Paved, gravel, dirt, and rocks

Land status: State park and designated DNR State Natural Area

Nearest town: Baraboo, WI

Maps: USGS Baraboo, WI

Other trail users: None

Special considerations: Parfrey's Glen is open daily 6 a.m. to 8 p.m. and a Wisconsin State Park sticker is required to park in the parking lot. The park rules, which are posted within the natural area, as well as online, report that it is permissible to hike all the way up to the waterfall, but absolutely *not* beyond it.

Amenities available: Pit toilets and hand pump water fountain

Maximum grade: From the beginning of the hike to the end, the trail fluctuates between 5 percent and 10 percent. It is a slow and steady climb for 0.7 mile.

Cell service: Yes

Waterway: Parfrey's Glen Creek

Waterfall beauty: 2

Accessibility: Limited. The first 0.14 mile of the hike is paved. After the pavement ends the hike continues as a wide, well-compacted gravel trail until you come to the stream crossing 0.55 mile into the hike.

Finding the trailhead: From the intersection of Broadway Street (Business 12) and WI 113 in downtown Baraboo, take WI 113 south for 6.4 miles and turn left (east) on to CR DL. Take CR DL for 2 miles and turn left (north) onto Glen Lane. Drive 0.06 mile and turn right into the parking lot. You will see the signage for Parfrey's Glen from CR DL. **Trailhead GPS:** N43°24.601' / W89° 38.210'

Trail conditions: This is a well-maintained trail that is open year-round for hikers and snowshoeing. The first portion is paved, but then it turns to gravel and eventually dirt. Some areas have scattered rocks and exposed tree roots that make for a lot of uneven surfaces and may be slightly precarious for less athletic hikers. There is one part that requires a stream crossing on large rocks that are surprisingly stable. The last portion of the hike brings you through a boulder-strewn ravine and requires some athletic rock hopping. A sturdy pair of waterproof boots or footwear for hiking is strongly encouraged.

*For those willing to
venture past the end
of the designated trail*

The Hike

This well-trafficked out-and-back hike is within Devil's Lake State Park, one of Wisconsin's most visited natural areas. Devil's Lake offers incredible hiking, fishing, canoeing, camping, and rock climbing. Parfrey's Glen is one of the many hiking trails that exist within the state park's 9,127 acres. *Glen* is a Scottish word for a narrow rocky ravine, and this hike culminates at a waterfall secluded deep in a moss-covered glen cut through the sandstone of the Baraboo Hills. Due to its geological beauty and ecological diversity, it was designated by the Wisconsin Department of Natural Resources as the first ever designated State Natural Area in 1952.

The ecosystem within Devil's Lake State Park supports wonderfully diverse wildlife, much of which may be spotted from the Parfrey's Glen trail. Wild turkeys, fishers, white-tailed deer, coyotes, wolves, and even black bears have been spotted on the hiking trails within the park. The glen's walls are sandstone and are embedded with pebbles and larger boulders of a substance called quartzite. Quartzite is a hard, non-foliated metamorphic rock also referred to as "plum pudding stone." Sandstone, abundant in the Baraboo Hills, was transformed into quartzite millions of years ago through heating and pressure usually related to tectonic compression.

Nearly the entire path, all the way to the end, closely hugs a mountain-type stream, which, due to beautifully dispersed rocks and logs, features a nonstop array of bubbling cascades and mini rapids. The dynamics of this stream make the entire hike visually pleasant as well as auditorily enjoyable. This is a hike of moderate difficulty due to the last 0.1 mile of the hike, which requires some athletic rock hopping and boulder climbing. There are many benches strategically placed throughout the hike, which allow frequent opportunities to rest if needed. Due to the visual beauty and sound of the creek, nearly every bench is a noteworthy viewpoint. This hike is also unique because it intersects with Wisconsin's famous Ice Age Trail, a 1,200-mile footpath that passes through some of the state's most beautiful and unique glacial landscapes.

The trail begins on a paved path for 0.13 mile and then widens as it turns to gravel. The firmly packed gravel continues on for 0.26 mile and then turns to dirt as

Due to the glen's cool moist wooded environment, rare species of plants and animals have been found there. Uncommon species of diving beetle (*Agabus confusus*) and caddisfly (*Limnephilus rossi*) as well as two unique birds, the Acadian flycatcher and the cerulean warbler, have been found there.

Devil's Lake State Park, where Parfrey's Glen is located, has a "critter cam," a motion-activated trail camera to photograph and document wildlife sightings. Deer, coyotes, fox, turkeys, fisher, raccoons, and black bear have all been spotted, and the photos are on the Devil's Lake website for viewing.

The Cambrian sandstone cliff of Parfrey's Glen

One of the many serene sitting areas along the creek

it enters a forest of mountain maple and yellow birch. The path continues to alternate between gravel, dirt, and loose rock until the trail's end. There is a stream crossing 0.6 mile into the hike, which requires stepping across large stones to get to the other side. The end of the designated trail confronts you with a breathtaking view of the glen with a series of mini cascades skipping over moss-covered rocks and logs. At the trail's end, the DNR have a clearly posted sign that states that visitors may proceed into Parfrey's Glen at their own risk and that there is no designated trail beyond this point. Hike past the sign and through the gorge and in 0.17 mile you'll arrive at the trail's end. This last portion of the hike involves crisscrossing the creek and climbing up and over some large moss-covered boulders, and will lead you directly to the falls. To return to the trailhead, walk back the way you came.

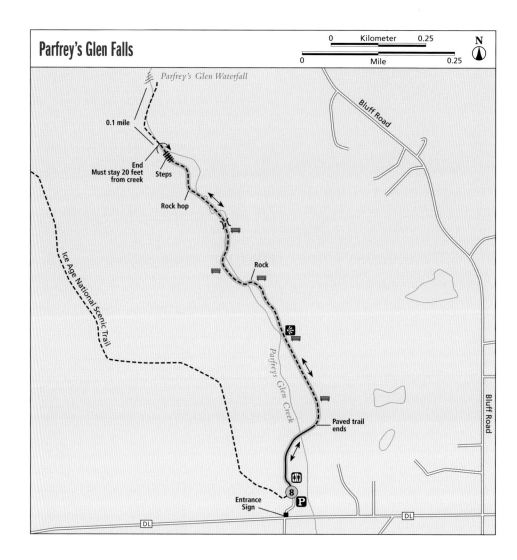

Parfrey's Glen Falls

Parfrey's Glen Waterfall

0.1 mile

End
Must stay 20 feet
from creek

Steps

Rock hop

Rock

Ice Age National Scenic Trail

Parfrey's Glen Creek

Paved trail
ends

Entrance
Sign

8

P

Bluff Road

Bluff Road

DL

DL

Miles and Directions

0.0 Hike north at the trailhead and parking lot.

0.55 Arrive at a stream crossing where you will need to rock hop across.

0.6 Arrive at the stone stairs. Ascend the 16 steps.

0.7 Arrive at the end of the designated trail. Continue hiking through the glen.

0.87 Arrive at the trail's end and waterfall. Return the way you came.

1.74 Arrive back at the trailhead.

9 Stephen's Falls

This out-and-back hike brings you face to face with the fascinating geology of Wisconsin's "driftless area." A slender waterfall pours like transparent vines over layers of ancient sandstone and into a shallow pool.

Start: The busy intersection of WI 18 and WI 23 in Dodgeville

Elevation gain: A total descent of less than 0.1 mile

Distance: 0.4 mile

Difficulty: Difficult. The first portion of the trail, just over 0.1 mile, is paved and is accessible for wheelchairs, strollers, or mobility devices. Later, the trail turns to dirt and gravel before a steep set of stone stairs to the base of the falls.

Hiking time: About 16 minutes

Season/schedule: Open year-round from 6 a.m. to 11 p.m.; however, it's best used May through Oct

Fees and permits: Yes

Trail contacts: Governor Dodge State Park, 4175 WI 23, Dodgeville, WI 53533, (608) 935-2315, https://dnr.wisconsin.gov/topic /parks/govdodge

Dog friendly: Yes, on leashes

Trail surface: Paved, gravel, dirt, and stone steps. Athletic shoes or hiking boots are recommended.

Land status: State park

Nearest town: Dodgeville, WI

Maps: USGS Governor Dodge State Park, WI; https://dnr.wisconsin.gov/topic/parks/gov dodge/recreation/camping

Other trail users: This trail is typically just hikers looking to see the waterfall; however,

the trails in Governor Dodge State Park are also open to bikers and horseback riders and, in the winter, cross-country skiers.

Special considerations: During the cold-weather months, the stairs leading to the falls may be icy and slippery.

Amenities available: Water, showers, restrooms, pit toilets, dumping station, concessions (available Memorial Day through Labor Day). Water systems are seasonal so flush toilets, showers, drinking fountains, and dump stations are not available fall through spring (approximately Oct 1 through May 15). Pit toilets are available year-round.

Maximum grade: Approximately -25 percent for less than 0.1 mile of the hike from the top of the stairs to the end of the hike at the base of the falls

Cell service: Yes

Waterway: An unnamed tributary to Cox Hollow Lake

Waterfall beauty: 3

Accessibility: Limited. The first 0.16 mile of the trail is paved. This brings you to a view of the upper falls as well as a seating area equipped with a sitting bench overlooking the bluff. Strollers, wheelchairs, or mobility devices should not continue past this point.

Finding the trailhead: From the intersection of WI 18 and WI 23, head north on WI 23 (North Bequette Street) for 3.1 miles until you reach the entrance of Governor Dodge State Park. Turn right (east) into the park and go 0.2 mile until you reach the park office where you will need to pay an entrance fee. Continue past the park office for 0.9 mile until you reach the parking area for Stephen's Falls. You will see a sign on the right (east) side of the road. Designated parking is along the east side of the street. **Trailhead GPS:** N43°01.629' W90°07.872'

Trail conditions: Good. Well maintained, but quite possibly muddy and slippery when it rains. The trail may also be covered in snow or ice during the cold-weather months.

Top: From the end of the hike, a scenic view of the creek pouring over ancient sandstone
Bottom: View of the upper falls from the first viewpoint with the guardrails

The Hike

Governor Dodge State Park is one of Wisconsin's oldest and largest state parks. Covering 5,270 acres it offers modern-day explorers many opportunities to engage and interact with the natural world. Since the 1940s this has been a popular destination for a wide variety of activities including camping, canoeing, off-road biking, cross-country skiing, horseback riding, and nature hikes. The geography of Governor Dodge State Park comprises rolling hills, bluffs, lakes, streams, deep valleys, and a tucked away thinly veiled waterfall. The quantity, variety, mileage, and landscape of the hiking trails in Governor Dodge State Park are what make it so remarkable.

Like most beautiful and fertile areas of Wisconsin, Governor Dodge State Park was originally Indigenous territory dating back approximately 7,000 years. Native Americans lived in the area, used the land for food, and made natural camps and shelters in the bluffs. The hills and valley that visitors find so eye-catching once provided protection from the harsh weather for early inhabitants. Many of the original white settlers to the area were miners and farmers. In 1948 a farmstead was handed over to the local conservation commission and slowly all the areas around it were obtained to create the state park.

To arrive at the waterfall, walk east from the trailhead. The path starts out paved and makes an S shape while it passes a prairie of wild tall grasses on your right and a forest on your left. Continue on the trail past the first junction, which has a sign directing you toward the falls straight ahead. Continue forward (east) and you'll come to a second trail junction where you will find multiple large informative signs explaining the history of Governor Dodge State Park as well as the history of Stephen's Falls. Here the trail comes to a fork giving you the option to stay on the paved path (right) or take a short detour and veer to your left. The path to your left leads you to a dirt trail, which brings you to a view of the upper falls. Follow this detour along the wooden guardrail and then continue southeast on the path. It will reconnect with the paved trail and you'll arrive at a second viewpoint with a bench. Here you have a view looking out over the bluff and down to where the waterfall drops. This viewpoint is also where the paved trail ends, so strollers, wheelchairs, or mobility

It is also believed that the famous Jesuit missionaries and fur traders Marquette and Joliet passed through here on their expedition exploring the unsettled territory of the Great Lakes region.

If you travel north on WI 23 from the entrance of the state park, you will find the Museum of Minerals and Crystals. Allegedly the owner has a wealth of knowledge and is a great storyteller. The museum hosts many fascinating specimens including interesting fossils, and it's a fun place to check out for any geology buffs who want to learn more about the different types of rocks that make this driftless region such a huge draw.

View of the stream below the upper falls just before tumbling over the sandstone bluff

devices should not continue past this point. Walk southeast and you'll arrive at a set of stairs. The stairs are forty-six steps made of a combination of intentionally placed concrete and naturally occurring stones with a railing. At the base of the stairs, walk northeast until you are standing in front of the waterfall. It's not one of Wisconsin's 100-foot-tall gushers, but still a visually imposing work of nature. Streams of water appear to paint the side of a tall moss-covered bluff, which increases in beauty when you look at it from different vantage points. The sandstone cliff you are looking at is over 400 million years old.

If you're feeling adventurous continue your hike along the creek, which will bring you on the Lost Canyon Trail, where you can do a moderate 1.2-mile loop or connect to other nearby trails such as the Meadow Valley Trail. Many of these wooded trails are known for their wildlife. Deer, turkeys, foxes, and smaller animals such as woodchucks, muskrats, and various species of birds are common.

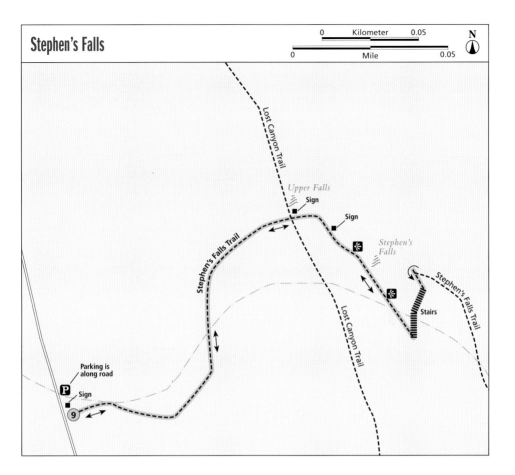

Miles and Directions

0.0 From the trailhead head east on the paved trail.

0.13 Arrive at a trail junction with a sign explaining the history of the falls.

0.16 Follow the trail to the left, which veers off the paved path and turns to dirt and gravel. Here you arrive at a view of the upper falls. The path then reconnects with the paved trail.

0.17 Pass a viewpoint with a bench, where the paved trail ends, and arrive at the top of a set of stairs.

0.19 Descend forty-six steps and arrive at the bottom of the stairs.

0.2 Arrive at the end of the trail with a view of the falls. Return the way you came.

0.4 Arrive back at the trailhead.

Northwestern Wisconsin

Northwestern Wisconsin makes it easy to fall in love with the Midwest. In this quadrant Wisconsin bumps up against the Land of 10,000 Lakes. Lake Superior gives Minnesota and Wisconsin equal bragging rights for scenic shorelines and coastal wilderness. The St. Croix River cuts its way south between the two neighboring states attempting to equally divvy up scenic bluffs and waterfalls for both sides to celebrate and enjoy. Here exists a land of scenic gorges and robust watersheds. Breathtaking scenery and undomesticated wildlife set the backdrop along thousands of miles of shoreline where Wisconsin residents can enjoy hiking, camping, fishing, boating, and swimming.

A view of the majestic water feature, Cascade Falls, from farther down the Cascade Falls Trail

From southwest to northwest, Wisconsin's topography changes as it slowly fades from farmland and rolling hills to dense forest thanks to a glacial boundary. This hilly rock-strewn landscape introduces the Blue Hills rising 600 feet above deep "kettles" of poorly drained bowl-shaped depressions. Here you'll discover some of the state's tallest waterfalls being birthed by some of Wisconsin's most noteworthy rivers. Reddish-brown waterways voyage toward Lake Superior plunging over exposed rock and allowing you to observe billions of years of volcanic geological activity. On all sides of these waterways are an impressive acreage of county forests that seem to go on forever. Here you'll discover all the necessary ingredients for magical waterfall hiking. Powerful and scenic rivers wind their way through impenetrable forests and plunge over jagged rock formations.

Twenty-three of the waterfalls in this book are located in this quadrant, making it one of the most concentrated regions of waterfalls in the state. It offers the perfect combination of wild rivers, unique geology, descending gradients, and lush green forests. Northwestern Wisconsin packs in a lot, creating the perfect place for nature lovers and waterfall seekers.

10 Glen Park Falls

This out-and-back hike is something of a waterfall "two for one." A pleasant stroll through a park brings you past a powerful industrial spillway and ends in a shaded glen before a distant but pretty waterfall.

Start: 0.09 mile northwest of the swinging bridge where the trail veers off from the paved footpath and becomes gravel and dirt
Elevation gain: Less than 0.1 mile
Distance: 0.4 mile
Difficulty: Difficult. Involves steep hills and wading through water and/or rock hopping.
Hiking time: Approximately 27 minutes
Season/schedule: Open year-round from 6 a.m. to 11 p.m.; however, it's best used May through Oct
Fees and permits: None
Trail contacts: 361 West Park St., River Falls, WI 54022, (715) 425-0924, rfcity.org
Dog friendly: Yes, on leash
Trail surface: Blacktop, dirt, rocks, gravel

Land status: City park
Nearest town: River Falls, WI
Maps: USGS River Falls, WI; https://www.rfcity .org/DocumentCenter/View/61/Glen-Park-Trail -Map?bidId=
Other trail users: Anglers
Special considerations: Rapidly rising water
Amenities available: Water and restrooms (closed during the fall and winter)
Maximum grade: –511 percent. Less then 0.1 mile between the trailhead and the first trail junction at the bottom of the hill.
Cell service: Yes
Waterway: Kinnickinic River
Waterfall beauty: 2
Accessibility: No

Finding the trailhead: From the intersection of East Locust Street and South Main Street in downtown River Hills, head southwest on South Main Street for 0.4 mile until you come to West Park Street. Turn right (west) on West Park Street and travel west for 0.2 mile until you come to the entrance of Glen Park on your right (north). Turn right into the park and drive less than 0.1 mile to a parking lot adjacent to the pavilion and Glen Park swimming pool. From the parking lot walk northwest on the S-shaped footpath for 0.09 mile until you reach the swinging bridge that crosses the Kinnickinnic River. Here you will also see a Glen Park sign and information regarding the falls and the park's history. From here walk 0.02 mile northwest until a gravel path diverges from the paved footpath and veers off to your right (north). You have arrived at the trailhead. **Trailhead GPS:** N44°51.235' W92°38.030'

Trail conditions: The first 0.09 mile of the trail is a combination of gravel and blacktop, which descend from the park on a cliff down to the water's edge. This first portion of the hike could be maneuvered by a wheelchair or stroller, as long as you can make it back up the hill. The grade fluctuates between –6 percent and –511 percent. Due to the incline, this may be slippery in cold weather. From the first trail junction until the trail's end, you are walking along the banks of the river, then crossing a stream and continuing on an island. Sturdy footwear such as a quality pair of hiking boots is recommended. Your feet may get wet at the stream crossing. Rapidly rising water is a potential hazard.

Top: View of the falls from the southeast end of the island at the trail's end
Bottom: Once you reach the junction between the Kinnickinnic River and Lake Louise, you get a surprise view of the Lake George Spillway, making this hike a waterfall two for one.

The Hike

This small but impressive waterfall is in a wooded glen just below a swinging foot-bridge in the quaint town of River Falls. The casual stroll to arrive at this water feature is in Glen Park, a 40-acre community park located southwest of downtown. The waterfall hike featured here brings you to the convergence of the Kinnickinnic River and the Lake George Spillway in the quaint town of River Falls. What makes this hike so charming is that a casual walk in a park brings you face to face with a massive industrial spillway, just before you enter a peaceful wooded ravine with a serene multitiered waterfall.

Glen Park is River Falls's oldest park and was built during the Great Depression as a Civil Works Administration project. It allegedly had a zoo at one point, but its current highlights are a public swimming pool, picnic shelters, and hiking trails. The scenic swinging bridge was designed and built by the Minneapolis Bridge Company in 1925 to connect pedestrian traffic to Glen Park. It now hovers just over the water-fall, creating a backdrop for the waterfall when looking at the whole scene from the mouth of the river.

All the trails on this hike are well maintained and easy to follow. To arrive at the waterfall, start out at the swinging footbridge, which is centrally located. The trail-head is on the west bank of the river just northeast of the bridge. Head northeast on the paved path and follow the gravel trail, which diverges to your right. The path descends down a hill and curves left (west) and then right (north) again, creating an S shape. The last portion of the descent is a steep blacktop hill, which brings you to a trail junction where you will turn right (north). Walk straight (north) and you come to the water's edge, the banks of Lake Louise. Here you have a view of the massive Lake George Spillway to your right (northeast). Walk along the banks of Lake Louise toward the spillway and you'll arrive at the mouth of the Kinnickinnic River. You'll need to cross the stream to get to the island, which sits directly in the middle of the river. When the water is low, there are many exposed rocks to rock hop across. Be careful, because the rocks are not all stable and when they are wet they become quite slippery. Carefully make your way to the island and join the island trail, which heads southeast. Take this path up the center of the island until you've arrived at the farthest

The location of the Glen Park Falls used to be a fully functioning mill that was powered by the moving water from the river. Dating back to 1957, it was originally used to make flour and grist, but later was used as a sawmill to cut wood for the production of beehives. As years passed the Kinnickinnic River had less and less water, and eventually the mill had no power to operate effectively. It stood vacant and useless for many years until one year the spring floods washed out the dam and mill. Now all you'll find is the serenity of a modest waterfall shaded by beautiful limestone outcroppings.

View of the Glen Park Falls as it quietly pours over moss-covered stones in the distance

end and you can't go any farther. It's a well-worn and easy-to-follow gravel and sand path. Directly in front of you is the Glen Park waterfall with limestone bluffs rising up on both sides of you.

This hike is part of the Glen Park habitat restoration and nature preserve on the banks of the South Kinnickinnic River and Lake Louise. Keep an eye out for white-tailed deer, turkey, pheasant, rabbits, ducks, and other wildlife.

Note: As you descend the path from the footbridge, you'll notice multiple off-shoot trails from the main path that would take you down significantly more aggressive and adventurous trails. These offshoot trails may help you arrive to the water's edge faster, but could be hard on your joints.

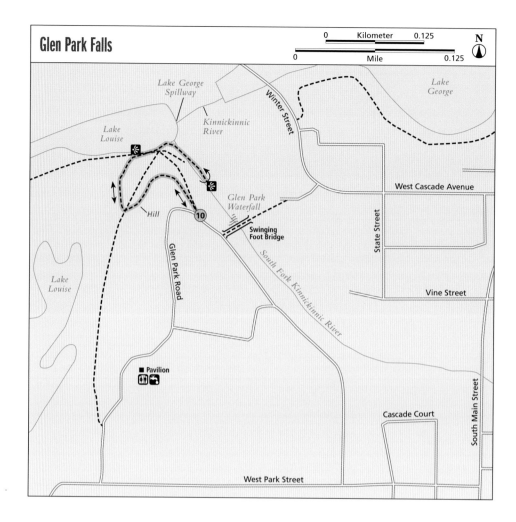

Glen Park Falls

Lake George Spillway

Kinnickinnic River

Lake George

Winter Street

Lake Louise

Lake George

West Cascade Avenue

Glen Park Waterfall

Hill

10

Swinging Foot Bridge

State Street

Glen Park Road

South Fork Kinnickinnic River

Vine Street

Lake Louise

Pavilion

Cascade Court

South Main Street

West Park Street

0   Kilometer   0.125
0   Mile   0.125

N

Miles and Directions

0.0 From the trailhead follow the path northwest as it curves slightly counterclockwise and descends down toward the riverbank.

0.09 At the bottom of the hill, arrive at a trail junction and go right (north) toward the water's edge. This trail changes briefly from gravel to blacktop but then turns back to gravel at the water's edge.

0.1 Arrive at a scenic view of the Lake George Spillway.

0.16 Arrive at the intersecting shores where the Kinnickinnic River spills into Lake Louise.

0.16 Rock hop across the river (east) from the shore to the island. Here you'll find a trail that heads southeast across the island in the direction of the waterfall.

0.2 Walk southeast until you arrive at the end of the island and have a clear view of the falls, which are situated just below the swinging bridge above you. Return the way you came.

0.4 Arrive back at the trailhead.

11 Apple River Falls

This out-and-back hike spells mystery and adventure. A hard-to-find trail brings you to a shaded and secluded ravine decorated with moss-covered boulders and a profoundly beautiful waterfall.

Start: Start out at the intersection of Main Street and CR I in downtown Somerset. Once you park in the designated parking areas on the shoulder of CR I, walk along the west side of the highway for 0.07 mile until you reach the trailhead.
Elevation gain: 0.02 mile
Distance: 0.3 mile
Difficulty: Moderate. This hike contains some uneven surfaces as well as a steep hill near the end that brings you down to the river's edge. To get the best view of the falls, you'll be required to descend some moss-covered rocks to get directly in front of the falls.
Hiking time: About 25 minutes
Season/schedule: Best visited May through Oct
Fees and permits: None
Trail contacts: Apple River Falls, Somerset, WI 54025, https://dnr.wi.gov/topic/Lands/natu ralareas/index.asp?SNA=145
Dog friendly: Yes, no restrictions
Trail surface: A combination of gravel, dirt, and, at the very end, large mossy rocks that require a bit of athletic rock hopping to reach the best view of the waterfall
Land status: Public canoe portage
Nearest town: Somerset, WI

Maps: USGS Somerset, WI; https://dnr.wi.gov /topic/lands/naturalareas/documents/topo maps/map145.pdf
Other trail users: Paddlers (kayaks and canoers) and anglers
Special considerations: This trail is on public land, but if you veer off the designated trail you will be trespassing. Also, this waterfall is adjacent to an Xcel Energy power plant and the river may be subject to a rapid change in water levels. There are signs notifying anyone near the water to get to high ground immediately if you hear alarms or see flashing lights.
Amenities available: None. The Kwik Trip gas station near the intersection of Main Street and CR I in downtown Somerset is the closest place to get water or use the bathroom.
Maximum grade: The entire hike slowly descends toward the water's edge at an average grade of approximately –5.7 percent. The steepest part of the hike is the last hill which has a grade of –14 percent for 0.01 mile before arriving at the end of the hike.
Cell service: Limited.
Waterway: Apple River
Waterfall beauty: 4
Accessibility: No

Finding the trailhead: From the intersection of Main Street (WI 64) and North CR I/Spring Street, head northwest on CR I for 3.5 miles. The designated parking areas for this hike are located on the shoulders of CR I just before the highway crosses the Apple River. As CR I is approaching the Apple River bridge, you'll see a horse pasture on the north side of the highway and a farmhouse (address: 2021 County Hwy I, Somerset, WI 54025—put this address in Google Maps and it will bring you right to the trailhead parking) on the south side. There are signs indicating where you can and cannot park. This designated parking is just alongside of the highway and is most commonly used by anglers and paddlers. From the parking area, head to

the west side of CR I and walk 0.07 mile until you come to the guardrail on the west side of CR I.
Trailhead GPS: N45° 09.379' W92°42.830'

Trail conditions: The majority of this hike is dirt and grass and slowly descends toward the river. When it rains this hike could be quite slippery. This hike is not recommended for wheelchairs, strollers, or mobility devices. A pair of hiking boots or sturdy athletic footwear is recommended.

The Hike

On this hike you will begin by thinking *is this legal?* and end by wondering *where did this amazing waterfall come from?* One minute you're on the shoulder of a highway, and then a short hike later you are in a secluded ravine that looks like something out of a hobbit fairy tale. This unassuming and seldom used canoe portage guides you along the fence of a power plant and thrusts you into the woods. The trail emerges on the banks of the Apple River as it begins morphing into a wildly scenic canyon.

The Apple River has a vastly different landscape after the falls than it does before it. Just upstream in the town of Somerset, the Apple River is a wide slow-moving river popular with anglers, canoers, and tubers. Below the Apple River Falls, it's a completely different story. The falls skip off multiple levels of rock and empty into a sudsy pool. Jagged stone outcroppings begin to appear as if caving in on all sides of the river, making it more mysterious and secluded. These dazzling falls are the gateway to one of the most interesting stretches of this 77-mile river: the Apple River Canyon.

To arrive at the trailhead for the Apple River Falls, take CR I north and pull over before the highway crosses the Apple River. The trailhead begins just behind the guardrail on the west side of the highway. Walk north until you see a stone path leading you

The Apple River Falls mark the beginning of the Apple River Canyon, which is approximately 0.5 mile downriver. It is a shallow steep-sided canyon known for revealing fascinating layers of geology. For those who can identify their rocks, the cliffs of the Apple River Canyon display Oneota dolomite, Jordan sandstone, Lodi shale, and Franconia sandstone. As the canyon twists and turns and rises and falls between the waterfall and the St. Croix River, the surrounding vegetation becomes quite interesting as well. The walls of the canyon can be anywhere from 100 to 140 feet high and they run primarily east and west. This creates north and south walls with contrasting sunlight, moisture, and temperature. Southern-facing slopes of the canyon grow the vibrant green lichens and mosses and prairie grasses, while northern-facing slopes are more hospitable to northern dry mesic forests. For anyone interested in exploring this canyon east of the falls, there is an area protected by the DNR called the Apple River Canyon State Natural Area. This protected piece of nature offers great hiking, fishing, and beautiful views.

down a small hill and away from the highway (northwest). At the bottom of the hill you'll see a fence with a No Trespassing sign. This is actually a public canoe portage, and it is completely legal to follow the trail behind the fence. For a first-time hiker on this trail, it may seem alarming. There is a place on the left side of the fence to go around it. Once on the other side of the fence, take a hard right (north) and follow the trail over a huge slab of concrete. Just after the concrete slab, the trail veers left (west), away from the fence and down a small hill. At the bottom of the hill, you arrive at a fork in the trail: stay to your right (north). If you go straight you end up on Xcel Energy property. Continue north on the path over a gravel road until you see a yellow sign with the word *portage* on it at the next trail junction. Follow that sign and you'll cross a paved road before the trail enters the woods. Stay on the trail and walk into the woods and down a small decline. You'll pass a diverging trail that veers off to your left (north), but you want to stay right (east). You will begin to hear the sounds of the falls. Continue heading east until you come to a trail junction with an Xcel Energy sign warning you that there is potential for rapidly rising water. Turn left (north) and follow the trail through the woods until you arrive at a steep hill. Carefully descend the hill and you'll arrive at the trail's end with an incredible view of the falls. You'll be standing on a short cliff at this point with many large boulders below you. There is potential to descend the cliff and get closer to the falls; however, the rocks can be very slippery. The depth of the pool that the falls empty into is unknown, so swimming is possible but be careful. To arrive back at the trailhead, walk back the way you came.

After you maneuver the trails of this concealed hike, you come upon this gorgeous torrential waterfall.

Above: A view of the falls from downstream as the Apple River voyages onward
Below: The secluded waterfall pouring over stone ledges in the rocky ravine

The unassuming trailhead for this concealed and adventurous hike

Miles and Directions

0.0 From the trailhead on the west side of CR I walk north behind the highway guardrail until you reach a descending stone path.

0.01 Follow the descending stone path as it curves left (northwest) and turns toward a fence.

0.02 Arrive at a fence with a No Trespassing sign. There is an opening on the left side of the fence where you can go around it. Turn right (north) behind the fence and walk along the backside of the fence. Stay to the right and you can follow this trail almost all the way to the water's edge.

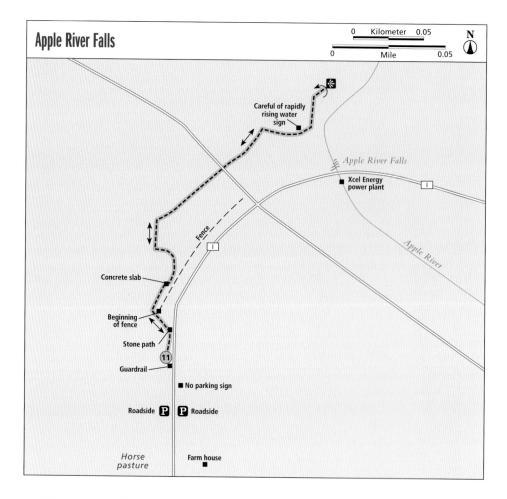

Apple River Falls

0 Kilometer 0.05

0 Mile 0.05

N

Careful of rapidly rising water sign

Apple River Falls

Xcel Energy power plant

Fence

Concrete slab

Beginning of fence

Stone path

(11)

Guardrail

No parking sign

Roadside **P** **P** Roadside

Horse pasture

Farm house

Apple River

0.11 Arrive at a trail junction with the canoe portage sign. Continue straight (northeast) and follow the trail into the woods. (If you go left or right you will end up on private Xcel Energy property.)

0.13 Arrive at the fourth trail junction, which presents a fork in the trail where two diverging grass paths split left and right. Stay to your right (east) and follow the sound of the falls.

0.15 Stay to your right and follow the path until you come to a trail junction marked with an Xcel Energy sign warning you about the potential of rapidly rising water. Take the path to your left (north) and continue following the trail through the woods.

0.16 Arrive at the top of a steep hill. Carefully walk down the hill until the path ends at the edge of the ravine.

0.17 Arrive at the trail's end with the best view of the falls. Walk back the way you came.

0.34 Arrive back at the trailhead.

12 Willow Falls

An invigorating hike that winds through a state park with an abundance of inter-connected trails to explore. The main attraction: a stunning and thunderous waterfall with geological and historical significance.

Start: The parking lot for this hike is on the southeast end of the state park. The trailhead is in the northwest corner of the parking lot.

Elevation gain: Less than 0.03 mile

Distance: 1.0 mile

Difficulty: Moderate. This is a wide and well-groomed path with a gradual descent of 0.03 mile between 0.1 and 0.3 mile into the hike. This requires climbing back up this hill when returning to the trailhead.

Hiking time: About 1 hour

Season/schedule: Willow River Park is open year-round from 6 a.m. to 11 p.m.; however, it is best used May through Oct.

Fees and permits: Yes

Trail contacts: Willow River State Park, 1034 CR A, Hudson, WI 54016, (715) 386-5931, www.wiparks.net

Dog friendly: Yes, on leashes

Trail surface: The trail surface varies between gravel, pavement, dirt, and sand. A wooden bridge at the end brings you over the river and directly in front of the waterfall.

Land status: State park

Nearest town: Hudson, WI

Maps: USGS Willow River State Park, WI; https://dnr.wisconsin.gov/topic/parks/willowriver/maps

Other trail users: Hunters, anglers, and rock climbers

Special considerations: Hunting season

Amenities available: The park has flush toilets, showers, water, and vault toilets. During the cold-weather months, there is no running water and only the vault toilets are operational. This particular hike has no amenities nearby.

Maximum grade: After the second trail junction until the end of the hike, there is a maximum grade of –28.6 percent that only occurs briefly (less than 0.1 mile of the hike).

Cell service: Yes

Waterway: Willow River

Waterfall beauty: 5

Accessibility: Limited. The trail could be navigated by wheelchairs, strollers, or mobility devices. Even the areas that are dirt, gravel, or sand are wide, flat, and compacted. The challenge is in the descending nature of the trail, from the first sharp turn 0.08 mile into the hike until the third trail junction 0.3 mile in. Descending the hill would be manageable, but returning back up it may be difficult.

Finding the trailhead: From the intersection of I-94 and US 12, head north on US 12 E for 1.7 miles until it turns into CR A (WI A). Continue north on CR A for 1.5 miles until you reach the entrance of Willow River State Park. Turn left (west) into Willow River State Park and go straight for 0.2 mile, which will bring you to the park office where you will need to pay an entrance fee for the day or show your Wisconsin State Park sticker. From the park office turn right (east) on an unnamed road and follow it for 0.5 mile until it ends at the Willow Falls parking lot. The trailhead is on the northeast side of the parking lot and is marked by signs saying "access restricted to foot travel only." **Trailhead GPS:** N45° 01.050' W92° 42.361'

Trail conditions: This is a wide well-maintained trail that varies between gravel, pavement, dirt, and sand. From the second trail junction to the end, the trail steadily descends. The trail could be potentially slippery when wet, covered in fall leaves, or when snowy and icy. No potential hazards or obstacles. A good pair of walking shoes is encouraged.

The mighty Willow Falls as it tumbles down each step of the river

The Hike

Willow Falls State Park is a great destination for an abundance of well-maintained trails and a magnificent waterfall with a rich and interesting history. This hike brings you down a sloping nature trail that winds through a shaded forest and ends with a startling view of the massive falls. A viewing platform equipped with multiple benches for your enjoyment allows you to relax and take in the view of the river as it tumbles in layers between high dolomite stone cliffs before lumbering eastward and emptying into Little Falls Lake.

Human activity over time has changed the landscape of the Willow River Waterfall. Before 1910 this was a pristine hidden gem untouched and unaffected by humans. In 1914 German immigrant Christian Burkhardt saw potential in the forceful fast-moving water and built a mill, which later turned into a hydroelectric dam. In 1992 the dam was no longer functioning and was removed, restoring this natural area back to its majestic state. The trout population returned to normal levels, and the powerful and scenic waterfall became the primary feature of the park.

> **Bonus Hike:** Cross the bridge and you'll see an ascending staircase on your right that will bring you up (177 stairs) to a viewpoint above the falls that overlooks the river, surrounding cliffs, and lake in the distance. An additional sixty-six steps will take you even higher as you connect with the Burkhardt Trail north of the falls.

Top: *From the high cliffs on the north side of the falls, you can see Little Falls Lake in the background. Wisconsin is so beautiful in the autumn.*
Bottom: *With your back to the falls, you watch and admire the Willow River journeying westward.*

Willow River State Park offers many opportunities for year-round recreation aside from just waterfall viewing. Visitors to the park can enjoy camping, fishing, rock climbing, wildlife viewing, and a visit to the onsite nature center. While the forested trails are the ideal place to spot wildlife, many of the most unusual ones can be hard to spot. Painted turtles, corn snakes, five-lined skinks, and yellow-spotted salamanders may be spotted throughout the park, but they can be seen up close and personal in the nature center.

One of the fun things about the trails in this park are the unique names like Knapweed Trail, Nature's Playground Trail, and Hidden Ponds Nature Trail. Each trail name gives you an idea of what you're in for, and each trail seems to bring you to a memorable view of the surrounding river landscape. An added charm of this hike is the diverse forest you walk through to get to the end. Basswood, ash, maple, pin cherry, elm, and oak surround you as you take the slow-descending trail to the river's edge. Interspersed among the understory brush are wildflowers like bloodroot, spring beauty, wood violet, and St. John's wort.

To arrive at the waterfall, begin at the trailhead and walk northwest on the gravel and dirt trail. You'll come to a junction with a sign indicating the path to the falls is to your left. Follow the trail left (west) until you arrive at a second trail junction where the path intersects with the Pioneer Trail. This intersecting trail connects the park office with a viewpoint above the falls. Continue straight (northwest) past this junction and the trail takes a hard left (south) before descending down a hill. This begins the paved portion of the trail, which is navigable by wheelchairs, strollers, and mobility devices. The trail curves in a clockwise turn until you arrive at the third trail junction. Here you will see a park map to help re-orient yourself. At this junction the hike connects with the Willow Falls Trail, which if you followed it left (west) would bring you to the park's 300 Campground. Take the path to your right (east) and follow it as the trail returns to a combination of sand and dirt. This path will bring you to the trail's end where you'll arrive at a bridge crossing the Willow River. Here you stand directly in front of the falls. To arrive back at the trailhead, walk back the way you came.

The beautiful dolomite formations you see on the cliffs surrounding the falls contain the compressed remains of chemical and biological sediment that was deposited when much of Wisconsin and Minnesota was covered by a shallow sea.

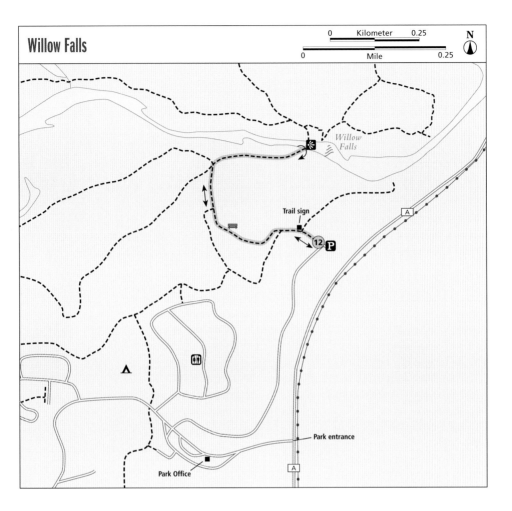

Willow Falls

Willow Falls

Trail sign

Park entrance

Park Office

Miles and Directions

0.0 From the trailhead walk northwest.

0.03 Arrive at the first trail junction. Here you'll see a sign directing you toward the falls to your left (west).

0.06 Arrive at the second trail junction. Here is where the hike intersects with another park hike called the Pioneer Trail. Continue straight (west).

0.08 Arrive at a bend in the trail where it takes a sharp left. The trail turns to pavement and begins the hike's downhill descent.

0.3 Arrive at the third trail junction. Here you will see a park map to help re-orient yourself. At this junction the hike connects with the Willow Falls Trail, which if you followed it left would bring you to the park's 300 Campground. Stay to your right.

0.5 Arrive at the view of the falls. Walk back the way you came.

1.0 Arrive back at the trailhead.

13 Cascade Falls

This unassuming hike leads you down 135 steps to a stunning waterfall that quietly empties into a shallow stream. If you're feeling extra curious and adventurous, follow the hike all the way to the St. Croix River.

Start: Begin at the intersection of North Cascade Street (WI 35) and Osceola Road (WI 243) in downtown Osceola. You are within walking distance of the trailhead.
Elevation gain: Less than 0.1 mile
Distance: 0.08 mile
Difficulty: Vigorous due to 135 steps
Hiking time: About 8 minutes
Season/schedule: Open year-round; however, best used May through Oct. In the cold-weather months, the waterfall may be frozen and the stairs slippery.
Fees and permits: None
Trail contacts: 101 North Cascade St., Osceola, WI 54020, (715) 755-3300, https://www.myosceolachamber.org/hiking.html
Dog friendly: Yes, on leashes
Trail surface: Stairs and a wooden bridge
Land status: City owned, property managed by the Osceola Area Chamber, Volunteers of Osceola Rivertown Trails Coalition

Nearest town: Osceola, WI
Maps: USGS Osceola, WI; https://www.myosceolachamber.org/hiking.html
Other trail users: Cross-country skiers
Special considerations: Nearly the entirety of this hike consists of descending stairs, and you will need to ascend them on the way back. In the cold-weather months, the stairs may be icy and slippery.
Amenities available: None
Maximum grade: From the top of the stairs to the bottom, you are descending at a consistent grade of approximately –60 percent, over a distance of 0.02 mile.
Cell service: Yes
Waterway: Osceola Creek
Waterfall beauty: 5
Accessibility: No

Finding the trailhead: From the intersection of North Cascade Street (WI 35) and Osceola Road (WI 243) in downtown Osceola, head north on Cascade Street (WI 35) for 0.08 mile. The trailhead is on your left (west side of the street) between PY's Bar and Grill and The Watershed Cafe. You can park on either side of the street. The trailhead is indicated by a wooden platform and a large statue of Chief Osceola. Here you will also find a large, easy-to-read map of all the local hikes. **Trailhead GPS:** N45° 19.183' W92° 42.361'

Trail conditions: This hike consists of sturdy wooden stairs with a wood bridge at the end bringing you in front of the falls. There are no uneven surfaces and no substantial obstacles. No specific footwear is required. This hike is not navigable by strollers, wheelchairs, or other mobility devices.

Osceola Creek and the Cascade Falls Trail meander northwest toward the St. Croix River.

The Hike

What makes this hike so interesting is that one minute you find yourself standing on a busy sidewalk in Osceola's historic main street, but after descending a rigorous 135 steps, you arrive in a misty glen directly in front of a breathtaking waterfall. You'll also discover a picnic area and the opportunity to wade in cool water on a hot summer's day. It is reported that due to the orientation of the ravine, at dusk the waterfall becomes illuminated with changing colored lighting. When this is combined with the naturally occurring fireflies in the summer, the glen transforms into a truly magical place. In the winter, the falls freeze to create a glistening ice sculpture. Wilke Glen and Cascade Falls offer a peaceful getaway for those looking to step away from the noisy streets above.

Cascade Falls is in the heart of downtown Osceola. Legend has it that in 1884 William Kent and his companions halted their journey from St. Croix Falls to explore a stream that was gurgling its way through the glen and emptying into the St. Croix River. When he and his companions saw the magical 25-foot waterfall and the surrounding land, they instantly saw its potential. Kent and his comrades staked claim to the waterfall and glen, and it eventually became the Village of Osceola. From the Osceola Creek to the St. Croix River, the geography drops a total of 108 feet. According to historical records the falls were a popular stop for excursion steamboats in the late 1800s.

The trailhead is on the west side of South Cascade Street and is indicated by a large wooden platform with a statue of Chief Osceola. On this platform you'll find trail maps and information about the history of the area and the falls. The trail that leads you down to the base of the falls is part of three scenic interconnected trails called the Falls Bluff Trail Loop. This hiking loop boasts being a preservation of historic trails that combine the terrain of bluff, river, stream, and waterfall. The trail that brings you into the glen and to the falls is called the Cascade Falls Trail and gives you the option of hiking all the way to the St. Croix River.

To find the waterfall start out at the trailhead and locate the stairs on the south side of the platform. Carefully walk down the 135 stairs until you arrive at the bot-

> **Bonus Waterfall:** Just above Cascade Falls is another waterfall called Geiger Falls where a small creek pours into Osceola Creek. To arrive at Geiger Falls from the Cascade Falls trailhead, walk south on Cascade Street (WI 35) and take the first sidewalk off to your right, which goes behind The Watershed Cafe. The sidewalk will lead you to a footbridge that Geiger Falls flows under. These falls were named after Veit Geiger, who operated a brewery at this location between 1867 and 1878. The different springs and creeks provided an abundance of pure water, and the nearby caves provided a constant 50-degree storage cellar—one of the many pieces of Osceola history connected to the waterfalls.

After you descend 135 stairs into a wooded ravine, you arrive at this captivating waterfall.

tom. Although the stairs are on the south side of the platform, they descend west, placing you on the east side of Osceola Creek. The trail continues west on a wooden bridge that crosses the creek and places you directly in front of the waterfall. If you continue to the other side, there is a path that allows you to go behind approximately one-quarter of the falls, allowing the water to pour on your head. To return to the trailhead, walk back the way you came.

Osceola has a more comprehensive hike called the Falls Bluff Loop, which combines three of their most scenic and challenging hikes. This hike comprises the Cascade Falls Trail, Eagle Bluff Trail, and Simenstad Trail, offering a lot of scenic diversity. On this 45-minute hike, you will discover a waterfall, a river, a creek, a natural spring, and a bluff overlooking a valley. Maps can be found online and posted at the trailhead as well as supplied in pamphlet form.

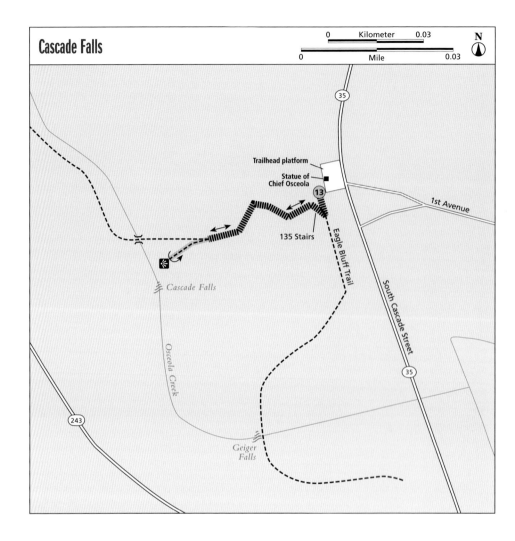

Miles and Directions

0.0 From the trailhead descend the 135 steps that are on the south side of the platform, but descend west toward Osceola Creek.

0.02 Arrive at the base of the stairs. Walk straight (west) toward Osceola Creek.

0.04 Arrive at the bridge that crosses the creek with a view of the waterfall. Return the way you came.

0.08 Arrive back at the trailhead.

14 Taylors Falls

A rigorous, but visually rewarding hike in Wisconsin's oldest state park showcasing ancient glacial geology. This closed-loop trail brings you to a modest water feature surrounded by jaw-dropping scenery in a deep-walled gorge.

Start: The intersection of East State Street and South Washington Street (WI 87). This is a popular intersection of commerce in downtown St. Croix Falls, WI. Here you will find a popular Indian restaurant called The Vegetarian, a coffee shop called Dalles Café and Coffee House, and one block east, St. Croix Regional Medical Center.
Elevation gain: 0.01 mile
Distance: 0.4 mile
Difficulty: Strenuous due to elevation change, multiple sets of stairs, and technical terrain
Hiking time: About 34 minutes
Season/schedule: Open year-round 6 a.m. to 11 p.m., but it's best used May through Oct
Fees and permits: Yes
Trail contacts: Interstate Park, 1275 WI 35, St. Croix Falls, WI 54024, (715) 483-3747, https://dnr.wisconsin.gov/topic/parks/interstate
Dog friendly: Yes, on leashes
Trail surface: Dirt and large rocks
Land status: State park
Nearest town: St. Croix Falls, WI
Maps: USGS Interstate Park, MN (there is both a Wisconsin and Minnesota side); https://

files.dnr.state.mn.us/maps/state_parks/spk00178.pdf
Other trail users: None
Special considerations: This trail is considered one of Interstate Park's "Summer Trails," meaning it is open and well maintained during summer months. It's still open during winter months, but is not maintained and as a result may be covered in snow and ice. Since this is a bluff trail with no guardrails, please use caution.
Amenities available: The park has water, flush toilets, vault toilets, picnic areas, a nature center, and a boat launch. Water and flush toilets are only available during the warm-weather months, approximately mid-May through October.
Maximum grade: This trail ascends and then descends before arriving back at the trailhead. During the descent it has a maximum grade of –575 percent, which lasts for less than 0.01 mile. During the ascent it has a maximum grade of 84 percent, which lasts less than 0.01 mile.
Cell service: Yes
Waterway: St. Croix River
Waterfall beauty: 1
Accessibility: No

Finding the trailhead: From the intersection of East State Street and South Washington Street (WI 87), head east on East State Street for 0.3 mile. East State Street turns into South Vincent Street for 0.4 mile and then becomes WI 35 South. Continue on WI 35 South until you reach the entrance for Interstate Park. Turn right (west) on to Park Road, which brings you into Interstate Park. Go 0.4 mile and you'll arrive at the park office where you will need to pay a fee or show your Wisconsin State Park sticker. Continue on Park Road for 0.6 mile until you arrive at the parking area for Pothole Trail, also named the Western Terminus of the Ice Age Trail (you can put "Western Terminus of the Ice Age Trail" in Google Maps and it will bring you directly to the trailhead parking area). From the parking area walk southwest 0.01 mile to the trailhead.
Trailhead GPS: N45° 24.011' W92° 38.865'

Trail conditions: This is a rigorous bluff trail with many descending and ascending rocks and stone steps. There are no railings at the bluff, so take precautions when getting close to the edge for a view of the waterfall and surrounding scenery. Hiking boots or a sturdy pair of athletic footwear is advised. This hike is not maneuverable by strollers, wheelchairs, or other mobility devices. Potential hazards would be when the trail is icy or snow covered during the cold-weather months, especially near the bluffs.

The Hike

Some hikes in this book are known for their scenic waterfall at the end. Other hikes are more popular because of the entertaining hike that brings you to them. The waterfall at the end of this trail is modest at best, but the hike to arrive at it is so much fun, and so interesting, that I felt obliged to include it in the book. A geologically fascinating walk brings you to the edge of a famous deep-walled gorge called Dalles of the St. Croix River. The views at the edge of the gorge are breathtaking and seem to go on in all directions to the extent that you'll be forced to twist and turn your head, potentially straining your neck. What also makes this hike relevant is that the trailhead for it is the western terminus of the famous 1,200-mile Ice Age Trail. Looking for a bonus hike? When you're done with the Pothole Trail, start walking east and you'll be busy for the next few months.

The hike to arrive at the falls is called the Pothole Trail, which gets its name from the strange stone features observable throughout this hike. The uneven terrain

Over one billion years ago, balsatic lava flowed out of the earth to form thick layers of the black rock found along the St. Croix River near Taylors Falls. Now it is the location of 295-acre Interstate Park, which was created in 1895 making it one of the oldest parks in Wisconsin and Minnesota. It was the first state park to be located in two states. The parks are operated separately by the states' Departments of Natural Resources.

There was a period in the last ice age called the "Wisconsin Glaciation," which ended about 10,000 years ago. When the glaciers melted they deposited debris across the state creating an amazing variety of features called "glacial landscapes." Two of the main features of this hike are the "potholes" and the basalt gorge. Both were created as a result of torrential meltwater from the glaciers. When meltwater from the glaciers surged through this valley, sand, gravel, and small boulders became trapped in whirlpools by the swirling water. Over time the abrasive action of the grinding rocks drilled holes into the bedrock creating the potholes. The potholes you'll see on this trail range in size from small soup bowl–shaped cavities to craters 10 feet wide and 15 feet deep. According to park reports, the Minnesota side of the gorge has even larger ones.

Top: *A view of Taylors Falls from the rocks below the cliff*
Bottom: *View of The Dalles of the St. Croix River with Taylors Falls behind you*

The reason they call it Pothole Trail

is riddled with different-sized bowling ball–shaped holes that appear to be drilled into the larger rocks. The holes look very industrial in nature, but the truth is that glaciers are to blame.

To get to the falls, walk east from the trailhead. Immediately you'll see a fork in the trail giving you the option to go left or right. This is a closed-loop trail, so either direction will bring you to the falls and the view of the gorge. For the sake of creating the most enjoyable hike, I suggest going right (northwest). The trail has regular markings and does not intersect with any other trails in the park, so it's difficult to get lost. As you begin hiking northwest, you'll encounter multiple small staircases of stone steps helping you descend and ascend the rocky landscape and uneven terrain. After you descend the first set of stone steps, you'll come to a trail junction with a sign depicting a hiker and an arrow pointing to the left (west). Follow the trail west and you pass between two enormous rock formations. At 0.15 mile around the loop, you'll arrive at a viewpoint with a bench and an informative sign about the trail. You'll see Taylors Falls below to your right, which are truthfully more of a series of small rapids than a proper waterfall.

To arrive at the next viewpoint, walk south on the trail and cross a wooden bridge. You'll come to a short path to your right (southwest) directing you to a second viewpoint. This is an out-and-back path that brings you to a lookout where you can see the Dalles of the St. Croix River and the entire gorge in both directions. Return to the main trail and walk up ten stairs, which brings you to a third viewpoint and overlook. This one is the highest lookout on the hike and allows you to see the farthest in all directions. It also has a selfie station where you can set the timer on your camera and take photos of yourself with the gorge in the background. After the last viewpoint there is 0.1 mile left of the hike, which involves ascending one more stone staircase before arriving back at the trailhead.

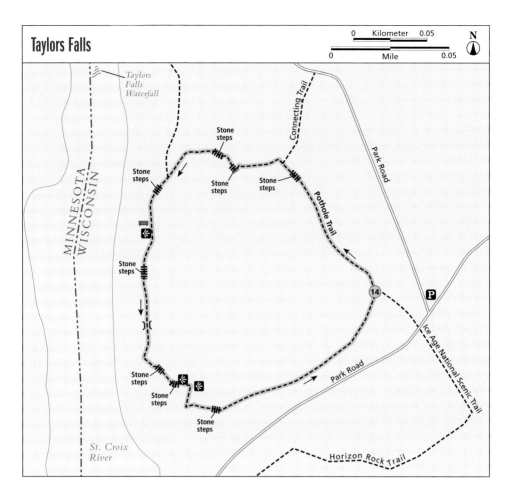

Miles and Directions

0.0 From the trailhead follow the path to your right heading northwest.

0.07 Arrive at the first trail junction. You will see a sign with a picture of a hiker and an arrow pointing left: turn left (west).

0.15 Arrive at the first viewpoint. You have a view of the falls to your right and the St. Croix River to your left.

0.24 Arrive at the second viewpoint with an informational sign. Turn right (east).

0.25 Arrive at a third viewpoint of the St. Croix River and bluffs in the distance. Follow the path south and it will curve to the left (east).

0.4 Arrive back at the trailhead.

15 Amnicon Falls (Upper, Lower, and Now and Then Falls)

This out-and-back hike features three incredible waterfalls and multiple stretches of roaring rapids along the Amnicon River. At the trail's end you get up close with the beauty and sheer power of the thunderous waterfall.

Start: Intersection of Tower Avenue (WI 35) and Belknap Street (US 12) in downtown Superior. This is a busy intersection of commerce, but also the location of Superior's Center City Park.
Elevation gain: 0.01 mile
Distance: 0.6 mile
Difficulty: Moderate. The hike has some uneven surfaces, but minimal stairs and climbing.
Hiking time: About 53 minutes
Season/schedule: Open year-round 6 p.m. to 11 p.m., but it's best used May through Oct
Fees and permits: Yes
Trail contacts: Amnicon Falls State Park, 4279 CR U, South Range, WI 54874, (715) 398-3000, https://dnr.wisconsin.gov/topic/parks /amnicon
Dog friendly: Yes, on leashes
Trail surface: Dirt and rocks
Land status: State park
Nearest town: Superior, WI

Maps: USGS Amnicon Falls State Park, WI; https://dnr.wisconsin.gov/topic/parks /amnicon/maps
Other trail users: None
Special considerations: When it rains the trail may be muddy.
Amenities available: Water and toilets at the trailhead. Additional toilets can be found near the end of the hike.
Maximum grade: –372 percent sustained for less than 0.01 mile
Cell service: Spotty in the entire area including on the way in
Waterway: Amnicon River
Waterfall beauty: 5
Accessibility: Yes. When you enter the park, just after the pay station and just before the bridge, turn right and a road will lead you right to a parking lot situated right between the Upper, Lower, and Now and Then Falls. From here the viewpoints for all three falls are approachable by wheelchairs, strollers, and mobility devices.

Finding the trailhead: From the intersection of Tower Avenue (WI 35) and Belknap Street (US 12) in downtown Superior, head east on Belknap (US 12) for 2 miles until you reach East 2nd Street (US 2/US 53). Turn right (southeast) on East 2nd Street (US 2/US 53) and follow it south for 11.3 miles. Take exit 222 on your left (east) for US 2 East for Ashland and go 0.1 mile until you come to CR U. Turn left on CR U and go 0.3 mile until you come to Park Road and the entrance of Amnicon Falls State Park. Turn left into the park and follow Park Road for 0.3 mile, crossing a bridge over the Amnicon River, and arriving at a parking lot and picnic area adjacent to the trailhead. Many Wisconsin state parks have park offices as gatekeepers to the entrance of the park, keeping any cars from entering without speaking to a park ranger and paying a fee. Amnicon State Park does not have a park office near the entrance, but they do have a pay station where you can register your vehicle and put money in an envelope. ***Note:*** If you need to speak with a ranger or park staff, there is a contact station farther inside the park near the campground. **Note:** To hike Amnicon Falls or any of its adjacent waterfalls, you need to pay an entrance fee or have a current Wisconsin State Park sticker displayed in your window. Failure to do so may result in receiving a citation (which usually costs more than the entrance fee for most state parks). **Trailhead GPS:** N46° 36.484' W91° 53.400'

Trail conditions: This trail is mainly dirt and rocks, with the occasional uneven surface, random rocks, and exposed tree roots. A pair of hiking boots or sturdy athletic footwear is encouraged. The hike is primarily shaded with minimal sun exposure. The trail slowly descends at a mild grade from the trailhead to the Horton Covered Bridge just before the end. There are no potential hazards or substantial obstacles. This hike is not accessible for strollers, wheelchairs, or other mobility devices. There is a parking lot and toilets located northwest of the falls that can be reached by vehicle, making the viewpoint for the falls accessible.

The Hike

These waterfalls are three of the featured attractions in Amnicon State Park, where the Amnicon River winds through the northwest landscape providing a wealth of scenic beauty. Each waterfall tells a different story involving billions of years of geological activity. It is rare that a state park has a river that is this uniquely beautiful and harbors this quantity of scenic water features.

The Upper Falls is arguably one of the most powerful in the state park whereas the lower falls is one of the more visually appealing. Now and Then Falls gets its clever name because witnessing its beauty depends on the rainfall and whether or not the creek that feeds it is flowing. What you are observing at the Upper Falls is the river pouring over a dark rock called basalt, or trap rock. This rock is remnants of ancient lava flows which are now solidified and have created interesting structures. According to park geology reports, the lava flows that created the Upper Falls are widespread and can be seen more than 100 miles away. When observing basalt, you'll notice that it is massive and lacks layering. When you compare it to other sedimentary rock such as sandstone, you'll notice the lack of visible lines.

There are many ways to arrive at these three famous park attractions, including driving right up to the parking lot adjacent to them. For the sake of creating an enjoyable, scenic, and adventurous hike, I suggest starting out at the trailhead 0.3 mile away where you follow a trail that brings you on a nature hike to see multiple other

Interested in geology? This park has a self-guided geology walk that brings you through the park and explains the events responsible for the development of this area and how it is recorded in the rocks and landscape. An informative booklet, "Amnicon Falls State Park Geology Walk," can be obtained at the park office. This instructional walk explains how tremendous forces of nature have combined to produce the state park's outstanding scenery.

Top: A head-on view of the falls from the covered bridge
Bottom: A view of the lower falls northwest of the covered bridge

A beautiful side angle of the falls

features of the Amnicon River. There are two trails that start out at the trailhead, east and west, but they both connect and merge into one trail in less than 0.1 mile. Take the trail on your left (west) and walk north. Pass the first trail junction and follow the path as it veers left (west). You'll pass two viewpoints on your right and a picnic area before you arrive at a campsite and a trail sign indicating the trail goes

Now and Then Falls hidden in the forest

right (northeast). Pass a bench and sitting area and you'll arrive at a bridge. Cross the bridge and you have stepped foot onto the island that is a central feature in the park (and the home to Snake Pit Falls, which you'll read about in Hike 16). Once on the island stay to your right as the trail follows the contour of the Amnicon River along the northeast banks of the island. You'll descend a set of stairs and come to the park's famous covered bridge, which will give you your first glimpse of Upper Falls. This is one of the best vantage points and photography angles of the Upper Falls. After you cross the bridge, take a hard right and you'll follow the trail along a guardrail until you arrive at a sign for the falls and a descending staircase. Retrace your steps (heading northeast) to the other side of the covered bridge where you will arrive at the viewpoint for the Lower Falls. Return to the trail and head northeast, which will bring you across the parking lot, where you will see a sign for Now and Then Falls. Head southeast on the short trail, and you will see the falls tucked away slightly in the forest. To return to the trailhead, walk back the way you came. An alternate route back to the trailhead would be to walk to the parking lot just north of the falls and walk back along the road. This is all paved and will bring you back to where you started. There are also bathrooms adjacent to the parking lot.

Miles and Directions

0.0 From the trailhead head north into the woods.

0.13 Arrive at a trail sign near a picnic table: follow the path as it veers to your right (northeast).

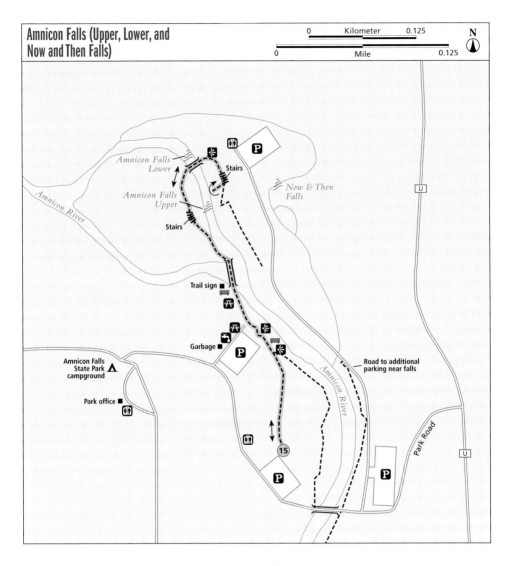

0   Kilometer   0.125

0   Mile   0.125

N

0.14 Arrive at a bridge. Cross the bridge and follow the path left (northwest).

0.21 Ascend a set of stairs and continue straight (northwest). Follow the path as it turns clockwise and begins heading northeast until you arrive at a covered bridge.

0.25 Cross the covered bridge: turn right.

0.26 Arrive at the first view of the Upper Amnicon Falls. Turn around and walk to the other side of the covered bridge.

0.29 Arrive at the view of the Lower Falls. Return to the view of the Upper Falls, walk less than 0.1 mile, and turn left. Walk across the parking lot and you'll see a sign that says "Now and Then Falls."

0.3 Arrive at Now and Then Falls. Walk back the way you came.

0.6 Arrive back at the trailhead.

16 Snake Pit Falls

This hike brings you to a wooded island formed by the Amnicon River splitting in two and blazing a second trail. The resulting attraction is the highest waterfall in the park as fast-flowing water pours over bedrock and into a narrow rocky gorge.

Start: Intersection of Tower Avenue (WI 35) and Belknap Street (US 12) in downtown Superior. This is a busy intersection of commerce, but also the location of Superior's Center City Park.
Elevation gain: 0.01 mile
Distance: 0.6 mile
Difficulty: Moderate. The hike has some uneven surfaces, and involves some stairs and climbing, but minimal elevation change.
Hiking time: About 20 minutes
Season/schedule: Amnicon State Park is open year-round from 6 a.m. to 11 p.m.; however, it's best used May through Oct.
Fees and permits: Yes
Trail contacts: Amnicon Falls State Park, 4279 CR U, South Range, WI 54874, (715) 398-3000, https://dnr.wisconsin.gov/topic/parks /amnicon
Dog friendly: Yes, on leashes

Trail surface: Dirt and rocks
Land status: State park
Nearest town: Superior, WI
Maps: USGS Amnicon Falls State Park, WI; https://dnr.wisconsin.gov/topic/parks /amnicon/maps
Other trail users: None
Special considerations: When it rains the trail may be muddy.
Amenities available: Water and toilets at the trailhead
Maximum grade: –15.8 percent on the descent and 27.2 percent on the ascent. Both are less than 0.01 mile.
Cell service: Spotty in the entire area including on the way in
Waterway: Amnicon River
Waterfall beauty: 2
Accessibility: No

Finding the trailhead: From the intersection of Tower Avenue (WI 35) and Belknap Street (US 12) in downtown Superior, head east on Belknap (US 12) for 2 miles until you reach East 2nd Street (US 2/US 53). Turn right (southeast) on East 2nd Street (US 2/US 53) and follow it south for 11.3 miles. Take exit 222 on your left (east) for US 2 East for Ashland and go 0.1 mile until you come to CR U. Turn left on CR U and go 0.3 mile until you come to Park Road and the entrance of Amnicon Falls State Park. Turn left into the park and follow Park Road for 0.3 mile, crossing a bridge over the Amnicon River, and arriving at a parking lot and picnic area adjacent to the trailhead. Many Wisconsin state parks have park offices as gatekeepers to the entrance of the park, keeping any cars from entering without speaking to a park ranger and paying a fee. Amnicon State Park does not have a park office near the entrance, but they do have a pay station where you can register your vehicle and put money in an envelope. **Note:** To hike Amnicon Falls or any of its adjacent waterfalls, you need to pay an entrance fee or have a current Wisconsin State Park sticker displayed in your window. Failure to do so may result in receiving a citation (which usually costs more than the entrance fee for most state parks). If you need to speak with a ranger or park staff, there is a contact station farther in near the campground. **Trailhead GPS:** N46° 36.490' W91° 53.402'

Trail conditions: This trail is mainly dirt and rocks, with the occasional uneven surface, random rocks, and exposed tree roots. A pair of hiking boots or sturdy athletic footwear is recommended. The hike is primarily shaded with minimal sun exposure. There are no potential hazards or substantial obstacles. This hike is not accessible for strollers, wheelchairs, or other mobility devices.

The Hike

Snake Pit Falls is one more piece of evidence of the Amnicon River providing scenic beauty as it moves through different channels in the park. This gem of a multitiered cascade occurs when a small branch of the river forks off and flows over two narrow ledges before dumping into a narrow rocky gorge. The gorge flows a little less than 50 yards before opening back up to the main channel of the Amnicon River again. This hike brings you to an island where, standing before the falls, you witness the erosive ability of flowing water.

The flow of the river changes throughout the year. During spring snowmelt, the Amnicon River is a raging torrent pulsing through the various channels of the river including Snake Pit Falls and Now and Then Falls. During drought periods many of the channels dry up to barely a narrow creek. Just below Snake Pit Falls is the Douglas Fault line separating sandstone bedrock and basal bedrock. The constant flow of moving water with variable intensities is slowly eroding the different types of rock and changing the shape of the river.

One thing you'll notice is that the river seems to be one continuous series of mini waterfalls and rapids. Aside from the four primary falls in the park designated with proper signage, as you hike the trails you pass countless smaller falls that are equally noteworthy. Some of the smaller no-name falls are so picturesque that they could rival many of the more well-known falls in other areas of Wisconsin. It's as if Amnicon State Park has an over-abundance of interesting water features and just can't name them all.

This hike is a lollipop loop. To get to Snake Pit Falls, start out at the same trailhead you did for the Upper, Lower, and Now and Then Falls. Head north on the trail. Pass the first trail junction and follow the path as it veers left (west). You'll pass two viewpoints on your right that offer opportunities to pause and enjoy a view of the Amnicon River. The trail passes a parking lot with an adjacent picnic area before entering a cedar forest. As you continue on the path, you'll arrive at a campsite with a trail sign indicating that the trail goes right (northeast). Pass a bench and sitting area and arrive at a bridge. Cross the bridge and you step foot onto the island, which is a central feature in the various hiking trails that you would have crossed if you went to see the Upper Falls, Lower Falls, and Now and Then Falls from Hike 15. To arrive at Snake Pit Falls, you will make an entire loop around this island, before re-crossing the bridge and returning to the trailhead. Once on the island stay to your right as the trail follows the contour of the Amnicon River and the northeast banks of the island. Pass the entrance to the covered bridge and continue left (northwest). Make

Snake Pit Falls

a counterclockwise loop and you'll arrive on the west side of the island where you have a view of Snake Pit Falls. Continue walking south and then east until you return to the bridge which brought you over to the island. Cross the bridge and walk back the way you came to return to the trailhead.

Top: The root beer–colored water of the Amnicon River
Bottom: The Amnicon River pouring into a steamy sudsy cauldron

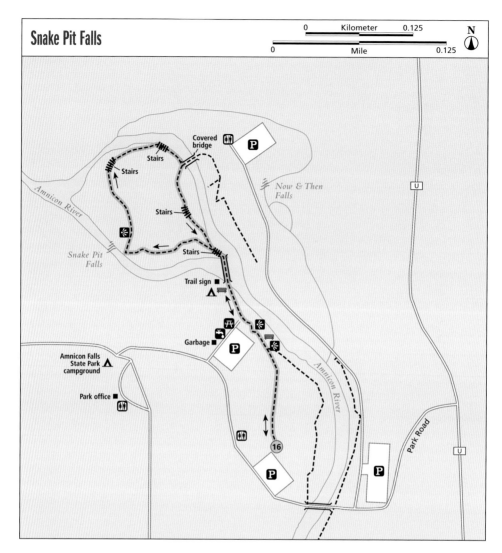

Snake Pit Falls

Covered bridge

Stairs

Stairs

Stairs

Stairs

Amnicon River

Now & Then Falls

Snake Pit Falls

Trail sign

Garbage

Amnicon Falls State Park campground

Park office

16

Amnicon River

Park Road

Miles and Directions

0.0 From the trailhead head north into the woods.

0.13 Arrive at a trail sign near a picnic table: follow the path as it veers to your right (northeast).

0.14 Arrive at a bridge. Cross the bridge and follow the path left (northwest).

0.21 Ascend a set of stairs and continue straight (northwest). Follow the path as it turns clockwise and begins heading northeast until you arrive at a covered bridge.

0.25 Arrive at the covered bridge, but do not cross. Follow the path to your left as it circles clockwise around the island. You will see a sign directing you to Snake Pit Falls.

0.37 Arrive at the viewpoint for Snake Pit Falls. Follow the loop (south and then east) back to the bridge that brought you over to the island. Return the way you came.

0.6 Arrive back at the trailhead.

17 Big Manitou Falls

This hike brings you to the cliffs of a unique river gorge carved out of sandstone and basalt. Behold, the tallest waterfall in Wisconsin thunderously cascades into the slithery canyon–walled Black River.

Start: Intersection of Tower Avenue (WI 35) and Belknap Street (US 12) in down-town Superior. This is a busy intersection of commerce, but also the location of Superior's Center City Park.
Elevation gain: Negligible
Distance: 0.2 mile
Difficulty: Easy due to short distance and minimal climbing
Hiking time: Approximately 12 minutes
Season/schedule: Pattison State Park is open year-round from 6 a.m. to 11 p.m. Each sea-son offers a different caliber of visual appeal, including winter when the frozen waterfall is covered in a fresh blanket of snow.
Fees and permits: Yes
Trail contacts: Pattison State Park, 6294 WI 35, Superior, WI 54880, (715) 399-3111, https://dnr.wisconsin.gov/topic/parks /pattison
Dog friendly: Yes, on leashes
Trail surface: A combination of pavement, blacktop, and gravel

Land status: State park
Nearest town: Superior, WI
Maps: USGS Pattison State Park, Superior, WI; https://dnr.wisconsin.gov/topic/parks/patti son/maps
Other trail users: Anglers
Special considerations: None
Amenities available: Pattison State Park has flush toilets, showers, water, and vault toilets. Near the trailhead for Big Manitou Falls are only vault toilets.
Maximum grade: –28.9 percent near the very end of the hike, sustained for less than 0.01 mile
Cell service: Yes
Waterway: Black River
Waterfall beauty: 3
Accessibility: Yes. It could be maneuvered by a wheelchair, stroller, or mobility device, but due to the inconsistent trail surface, proceed with caution.

Finding the trailhead: From the intersection of Tower Avenue (WI 35) and Belknap Street (US 12) in downtown Superior, head south on Tower Avenue (WI 35) for 13.1 miles until you come to CR B. Turn right on to CR B and go 0.05 mile and you'll see a parking lot for Big Manitou Falls on your left. Turn left into the parking lot. From the parking lot walk north 0.02 mile to the trailhead, which is on the north side of CR B. **Trailhead GPS:** N46° 32.131' W92° 07.386'

Trail conditions: The trail is a combination of pavement, blacktop, and gravel, and doesn't appear to be consistently maintained. It may be slippery when it rains or during cold-weather months. There are no potential hazards or substantial obstacles. No specific footwear is required.

The tallest waterfall in Wisconsin falling elegantly to the Black River ▶

The Hike

This giant geological spectacle is the main attraction of Pattison State Park. It's an impressive 165-foot vertical drop making it the tallest waterfall in Wisconsin (Niagara Falls is only 2 feet higher) and the fourth highest waterfall east of the Rockies. This hike brings you to multiple different viewpoints where you can see this impressive waterfall. It is a portion of a longer 0.5-mile trail called the Big Manitou Falls River Trail that brings you all the way down to the Black River gorge.

Pattison State Park is a 1,400-acre state park with a lake, beach area, camping, nature center, and some of the most scenic hiking trails in the state. Pulsing through the state park is the Black River. This serpentine river enters Pattison State Park in its southeastern corner, plunges over Little Manitou Falls, and then winds through a series of rapids and mini waterfalls before forming Interfalls Lake. The river exits the lake on its northwest side and thunders over the mighty Big Manitou Falls as it enters the steep-sided gorge. Pattison State Park has over 7 miles of hiking trails, many of which stick very closely to this scenic river with lookouts near all of its popular water features.

The waterfall and the steep-sided rocky walls in the Black River gorge are the product of multiple ancient geological events. Lava flow covered the surrounding region over a billion years ago creating basalt bedrock. Later, a massive fracturing caused a crack in the bedrock, which is called the Douglas Fault. This fault line starts on the floor of Lake Superior just north of Ashland and extends as far west as the Twin Cities in Minnesota. This fault line can also be observed in Amnicon State Park as discussed in Hike 16.

This hike brings you to two designated viewpoints of the falls. From the trailhead walk northwest on the paved trail. The path leads you past a picnic area on your right and vault toilets on your left. The trail curves in a clockwise loop until you arrive at the first viewpoint with a bench. Here you are looking at the falls from the southwest. From this viewpoint take a left (northwest) on the paved trail. You'll walk along a fence as the trail slowly descends in elevation. When the fence ends, the trail begins to curve clockwise until you're walking north, then northeast and you arrive at the last scenic viewpoint. To return to the trailhead walk back the way you came. If you're feeling curious and adventurous, follow the rest of the 0.4-mile trail down to the Black River gorge. It is a beautiful sight to see, but the descent is steep and you will have to walk back up.

Option: From the trailhead there is a path you can take to your right (north) that will bring you to the top of the falls looking down over it. Of course, it's not as impressive as being able to view the falls from the front, but it offers a different vantage point. Also, there is a bonus waterfall. This hike brings you over a bridge that crosses the Black River between Interfalls Lake and Big Manitou Falls. A modest spillway under WI 35 is visible from the small bridge.

A view of Big Manitou Falls, the fourth highest waterfall east of the Rocky Mountains, through the trees

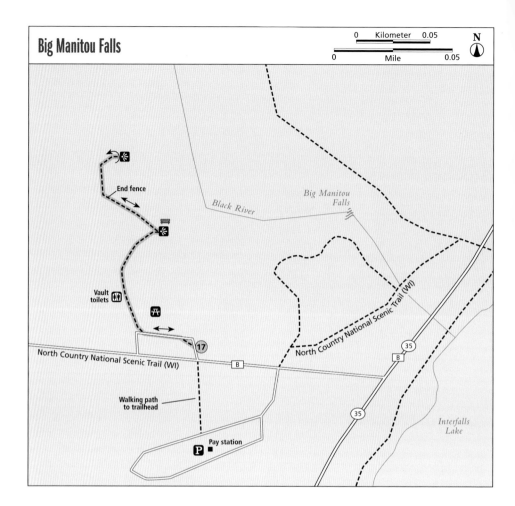

Big Manitou Falls

0   Kilometer   0.05

0   Mile   0.05

N

End fence

Black River

Big Manitou Falls

Vault toilets

North Country National Scenic Trail (WI)

North Country National Scenic Trail (WI)

17

35

B

B

35

Walking path to trailhead

Interfalls Lake

Pay station

P

Miles and Directions

0.0 From the trailhead head west on the paved footpath.

0.01 Pass the bathrooms and picnic area.

0.07 Arrive at the first viewpoint with a bench: take a left (northwest). Follow the path along a fence.

0.1 Arrive at the end of the trail with a view of the falls. Walk back the way you came.

0.2 Arrive back at the trailhead.

Top: Big Manitou Falls cascading over ancient lava rock
Bottom: View of the top of the falls through the trees

18 Little Manitou Falls

Despite its name, this is a decent-sized waterfall and arguably better looking than its older brother down the street. Surrounded by a forest of cedar and red pine, the Black River impresses us by splitting over remnants of ancient lava flows.

Start: Intersection of Tower Avenue (WI 35) and Belknap Street (US 12) in downtown Superior. This is a busy intersection of commerce, but also the location of Superior's Center City Park.
Elevation gain: Negligible
Distance: 0.08 mile
Difficulty: Easy due to short distance and minimal climbing
Hiking time: Approximately 10 minutes
Season/schedule: Pattison State Park is open year-round from 6 a.m. to 11 p.m. Each season offers a different caliber of visual appeal. The autumn colors create a scenic backdrop in the fall, whereas in winter the frozen waterfall looks like a shiny ice sculpture.
Fees and permits: Yes
Trail contacts: Pattison State Park, 6294 WI 35, Superior, WI 54880, (715) 399-3111, https://dnr.wisconsin.gov/topic/parks/pattison
Dog friendly: Yes, on leashes

Trail surface: Dirt and rocks
Land status: State park
Nearest town: Superior, WI
Maps: USGS Pattison State Park, Superior, WI; https://dnr.wisconsin.gov/topic/parks/pattison/maps
Other trail users: Anglers
Special considerations: There are many great views of this waterfall from different vantage points, but if you want to get to the base of the falls, it requires descending some sharp and jagged rocks. Hiking boots are strongly encouraged. Proceed with caution.
Amenities available: Water and toilets are available near the trailhead.
Maximum grade: -64 percent sustained for less than 0.01 mile at the end of the hike to arrive at the base of the falls
Cell service: Yes
Waterway: Black River
Waterfall beauty: 4
Accessibility: No

Finding the trailhead: From the intersection of Tower Avenue (WI 35) and Belknap Street (US 12) in downtown Superior, head south on Tower Avenue (WI 35) for 14 miles until you arrive at a sign for Little Manitou Falls on your left (west side). The entrance is just past CR B, and the parking lot for Big Manitou Falls, by 1 mile. Turn left (south) into the entrance for Little Manitou Falls and drive 0.1 mile. You will arrive at a parking lot on your right (south). From the parking walk east and cross the park road to arrive at the trailhead. **Trailhead GPS:** N46° 31.321' W92° 07.386'

Trail conditions: This trail has the potential to get muddy and slippery when it rains. The rocks you descend at trail's end are wet and slippery from the spray from the falls. Sturdy footwear is encouraged.

The falls framed by autumn colors

LITTLE MANITOU FALLS

The Hike

Despite its title, this 30-foot gusher can hold its own. Little Manitou Falls is an impressive water feature in Pattison State Park. This short out-and-back hike brings you to the shores of the Black River where a vibrant forest decorates the fringe of a river that plunges over remnants of ancient geological events. This waterfall and its associated hiking trails have no guardrails, so unlike the bigger Manitou, you can get right up close to this one.

When confronted with natural beauty like these falls, it's easy to suspect that a waterway such as this and the surrounding land was once sacred to its Indigenous inhabitants. Pattison State Park is known for having a rich Native American heritage. According to Department of Natural Resources records, nomadic hunters have been passing through this area since approximately 9,000 years ago. There is evidence that over a long period of time different cultures of Native Americans hunted the forests, fished the rivers, and searched the rocky outcrops for copper. The Ojibwe were here when the first European settlers arrived. In the 1800s, it was reported that there was a trading post at the base of the Big Falls just down the road (see Hike 17). It was a well-known landmark and gathering place for the Ojibwe, and they believed that they could hear the voice of the Great Spirit, Gitchi Monido, in the rushing falling waters of the falls.

This hike is designed to get you down to the base of the falls. On the Pattison State Park map, there is a trail called Little Manitou Falls Trail that starts out at the northwest corner of the parking lot. This wonderful little park trail brings you to a view of the falls, but then continues on for 0.5 mile along the Black River. That trail and the one described here are different. They start at different trailheads.

To arrive at the trailhead, from the parking lot head northeast and walk across the main park road. From here descend a small set of six stairs. At the bottom of the stairs, take a hard left (east) and you'll arrive at a viewpoint with a sign. This an excellent location for photography. Turn right (south) and descend a small set of seven stairs. Arrive at a second view of the falls from a western vantage point. From here head northeast down a rocky incline to arrive at the water's edge. Be careful—the rocks are sharp and quite slippery. This will bring you down to a place where you are on the banks of the river directly in front of the falls. You will feel the spray of the cascading water on your face and be reinvigorated by its power. To arrive back at the trailhead, carefully walk back the way you came. *Note:* The last portion of this climb is an option, but is not necessary. There are multiple different viewpoints to enjoy the beauty of the falls without the last rigorous climb.

Top: *The Black River leaping over lava rock formations*
Bottom: *Multiple viewpoints of Little Manitou Falls*

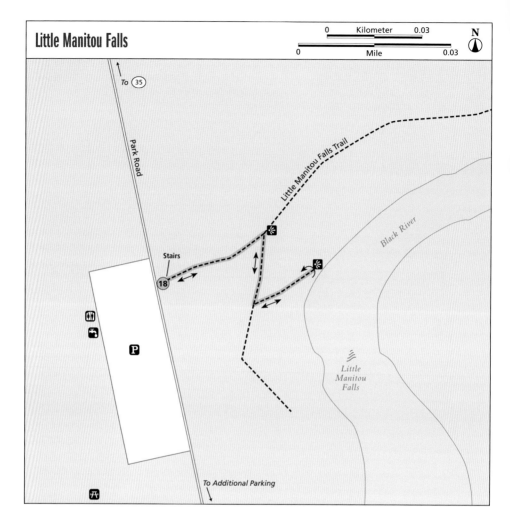

Little Manitou Falls

0   Kilometer   0.03

0   Mile   0.03

N

To (35)

Park Road

Little Manitou Falls Trail

Black River

Stairs

18

Little Manitou Falls

P

To Additional Parking

Miles and Directions

0.0 From the trailhead head east and walk down a set of six stairs.

0.01 Arrive at the first view of the falls with a sign indicating that you are looking at Little Manitou Falls: turn right (south) and walk down seven steps.

0.03 Arrive at a second (closer) view of the falls. Turn left and descend a rocky path. Be careful!

0.04 Arrive at the trail end. Walk back the way you came.

0.08 Arrive back at the trailhead.

19 Lost Creek Falls

A nicely developed trail winds gently through a forest of maple, black oak, basswood, and aspen. At the hike's end you arrive at an enchanting 8-foot waterfall that looks like something out of a postcard.

Start: Intersection of CR C and WI 13 at the west end of downtown Cornucopia. There is a restaurant at this intersection called The Fat Radish and a Star North gas station 1 block east.

Elevation gain: 0.04 mile

Distance: 2.6 miles

Difficulty: Moderate due to length and one stretch of descending switchbacks near the end

Hiking time: About 80 minutes

Season/schedule: Open year-round; however, it's best used May through Oct

Fees and permits: None

Trail contacts: Bayfield County Forestry and Parks, Lost Creek Falls Walking Trail, Trail Drive, Cornucopia, WI 54827, (715) 373-6114, bayfieldcounty.org

Dog friendly: Yes

Trail surface: Dirt and wooden boardwalks

Land status: Bayfield County Forest

Nearest town: Cornucopia, WI

Maps: USGS Cornucopia, WI; https://www.bayfieldcounty.wi.gov/DocumentCenter/View/9020/Lost-Creek-Falls-Trail-PDF?bidId=

Other trail users: None

Special considerations: During the cold-weather months, the trail may be covered in ice and snow. The trail is still easy to find when covered in snow due to frequent trail signs as well as blue guide marks on trees approximately every 28 feet.

Amenities available: None

Maximum grade: –132 percent for less than 0.01 mile at the very end of the hike

Cell service: No

Waterway: Lost Creek

Waterfall beauty: 5

Accessibility: No

Finding the trailhead: From the intersection of CR C and WI 13, head east on CR C for 2.1 miles. Turn right (west) onto Trail Drive when you see a sign for "Lost Creek Falls Trailhead." On Trail Drive the road turns from paved to dirt and gravel. Drive 0.4 mile on Trail Drive and you will arrive at the trailhead on your left. Pull into the parking lot and you will see the trailhead in the southwest corner of the parking lot indicated by a sign and posted trail map. **Trailhead GPS:** N46° 49.957' W91° 06.215'

Trail conditions: This hike is a slow descent on a well-groomed path with very few potential hazards. From the beginning of the hike to the waterfall there are 37 boardwalks keeping you off of muddy or uneven surfaces. The last 0.05 mile are descending switchbacks down a dirt trail, which could be potentially slippery when it is rainy or covered in fall leaves.

Transparent vines of water falling quietly in the woods

The Hike

This 2.6-mile out-and-back hike is hidden on the Bayfield Peninsula in a lush forest southwest of Cornucopia. It is a very well-maintained and easy-to-follow trail protected by the canopy above and surrounded by eye-catching greenery. To keep your feet dry and mud-free, boardwalks have been built and strategically placed throughout the hike to keep you elevated over lowland areas.

The waterfall at the end is an 8-foot cascade that you can walk behind. There are some smaller bonus falls above and below the main falls to enjoy for the adventurous hiker who enjoys exploring. During the spring snowmelt is the best time to see these falls. If you do this hike at the right time of year, the trail is lined with raspberries, thimbleberries, and blackberries, providing ornamental foliage to gaze at and trail snacks to enjoy.

The hike brings you through a northern mesic hardwood forest. Red and white pine, sugar maple, yellow birch, and basswood are dispersed along the hike. In the understory herbage, you'll find tree saplings, American fly honeysuckle, beaked hazelnut, and leatherwood. In the surrounding forest keep an eye out for white-tailed deer, red and grey fox, black bear, and even the occasional moose.

Top: View of Lost Creek Falls from the trail's end
Bottom: The falls from a distance

To arrive at the waterfall, head south on the trail. The path will transition between gravel, dirt, and boardwalks nearly the entire way with a few bridges placed here and there. You will continue for 0.5 mile before you arrive at your first trail junction. Keep to your right and descend a small hill. Continue on the trail as it heads northwest for another 0.5 mile until you arrive at a sharp hairpin turn where the trail heads south briefly and then makes a sharp turn northwest. Continue following the trail until you arrive at a series of switchback trails that lead you down to the creek. Descend the switchback trails until you reach the bottom where you'll find a sign directing you to the falls to your left (south). You have arrived at the view of the falls. There are no railings or Do Not Enter signs. The area is free to explore, which includes many great opportunities for photographs. To arrive back at the trailhead, return the way you came.

Miles and Directions

0.0   From the trailhead walk south.

0.5   Arrive at the first trail junction. Follow the path as it veers to your right and descends a small hill.

0.6   Cross a wooden bridge and continue straight (west).

1.0   Arrive at a sharp hairpin turn in the trail. Follow the trail as it turns south and then northwest.

1.2   Arrive at the hill above the trailhead. Descend the switchback trail.

1.2   Arrive at trail sign indicating the falls are to your left (south).

1.3   Arrive at the trail's end with view of the falls. Walk back the way you came.

2.6   Arrive back at the trailhead.

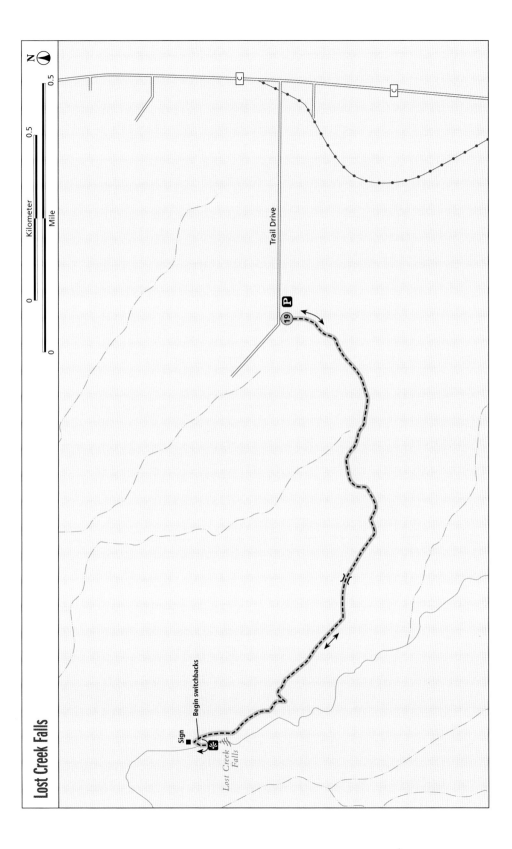

Lost Creek Falls

20 Morgan Falls

Here you'll discover one of the highest waterfalls in Wisconsin. This out-and-back hike brings you to an elegant cascade that diagonally traverses a 70-foot granite face and settles into a cool and shallow pool.

Start: Intersection of Lakeshore Drive (US 2) and Ellis Avenue South (WI 13) in downtown Ashland

Elevation gain: Less than 0.1 mile

Distance: 1.8 miles

Difficulty: Moderate due to length

Hiking time: About 1.5 hours

Season/schedule: Open year-round. This is a popular winter hike, but snowshoes are recommended due to deep snow and icy conditions.

Fees and permits: Yes

Trail contacts: Morgan Falls, Marengo, WI 54855, (715) 362-1300, https://www.fs.usda.gov/recarea/cnnf/recarea/?recid=27749

Dog friendly: Yes, on leashes

Trail surface: A combination of dirt, gravel, bridges, and boardwalks

Land status: Chequamegon-Nicolet National Forest

Nearest town: Ashland, WI

Maps: USGS Marengo, WI

Other trail users: None

Special considerations: The trailhead has no source of drinking water.

Amenities available: Vault toilets and picnic area

Maximum grade: Less than 0.1 mile

Cell service: Limited.

Waterway: Morgan Creek

Waterfall beauty: 3

Accessibility: Yes. This hike traverses a flat, well-developed trail that crosses a variety of bridges and boardwalks.

Finding the trailhead: From the intersection of Lake Shore Drive E (US 2) and Ellis Avenue South (WI 13), head southwest for 1.3 miles. Turn left onto Sanborn Avenue (WI 112) and head south for 9.7 miles. When you pass Petrin Road, the highway changes to CR E (WI E); continue straight for 2.6 miles. Turn left onto Ashland Bayfield Road/County Line Road and in 4.5 miles you will arrive at the parking lot and trailhead for Morgan Falls. Turn left into the parking lot. The trailhead is in the southeast corner of the parking lot. **Trailhead GPS:** 46°21.141' W90°55.337'

Trail conditions: Natural and boardwalks. This trail presents few uneven surfaces, obstacles, or potential hazards. No specific footwear is needed.

The Hike

This hike and its unforgettable waterfall are nestled into a well-preserved portion of the Chequamegon-Nicolet National Forest near Ashland, Wisconsin. This large slice of unfragmented forest contains exposed cliffs, rippling streams, breathtaking overlooks, and, of course, an unforgettable 70-foot waterfall. This moderate hike brings you through a wildflower prairie and into a forested terrain of birch, aspen, and tam-

The base of Morgan Falls as the final cascade skips off of granite into a shallow pool

arack. One of the things that makes this hike so approachable is the number of sturdy and well-constructed boardwalks and bridges that cross over streams and marshy terrain, making it accessible for people with disabilities. Another feature of this trail is that it's open year-round and reportedly popular with snowshoeing and winter hikers. According to many waterfall hunters, Morgan Falls is uniquely picture-worthy during the cold-weather months when it's frozen and covered in a blanket of snow. For anyone looking for a longer scenic hike, there is an option to hike beyond the second trail junction to discover a scenic overlook called St. Peter's Dome.

From the trailhead walk southeast on the wide gravel trail. The path is surrounded on both sides by a diversity of local ferns and patches of wildflowers, making you wish you had the plant identification skills of a botanist. Large-flowered trilliums, wild violets, Dutchman's breeches, varieties of hemlock, and Canada yew surround you as the trail curves south and then southwest in a clockwise fashion. The path crosses a large beautiful bridge and then continues on an elevated boardwalk keeping you above the sedge meadow and hardwood swamp. At 0.25 mile into the hike, you'll arrive at a trail junction with a sign telling you to turn left for Morgan Falls: turn left (east) here and follow the trail into the forest. The trail is primarily gravel and dirt and the slopes are fairly flat. As you continue hiking east, the wet-and-dry-mesic conifer forest and northern hardwoods begin to surround you and shade the trail. All sides of the walking path are ruggedly decorated with exposed rocks, small cliffs, and vegetation. The path crisscrosses Morgan Creek as you see signs of past human settlement and enterprises in the way of brick and stone formations where buildings used to be. What you're seeing are the remnants of old CCC (Civilian Conservation Corps) camps and an abandoned stone quarry. Hike past the first trail junction and you'll arrive at a second trail junction with a sign directing you right (south) for Morgan Falls or straight (east) for St. Peter's Dome. Turn right (south) and you'll begin to hear the falls; they begin to make themselves evident with their pleasant sound. In 0.1

Bonus Hike: The hike to Morgan Falls is part of a longer hike that culminates at a breathtaking overlook called St. Peter's Dome (known by local hikers as "Old Baldy"). From the top of St. Peter's Dome, you'll see an outstanding view of Chequamegon Bay of Lake Superior and the colorful Apostle Islands. The St. Peter's Dome hike is a 3.6-mile there-and-back hike that begins at the same trailhead as Morgan Falls.

This hike in particular will make you wish you could recognize the incredible diversity of wildflowers and animals all around you while hiking. Fortunately, we live in an age of mind-blowing technological advances. There is a smartphone application called Seek by iNaturalist that uses the power of image recognition technology to identify plants and animals all around you. With Seek you can take photos of wildflowers, plants, fungus, and animals and the app will help you identify them and learn about the organisms all around you.

A view from the trail as this boardwalk brings you from wildflower prairie into a forest of birch, aspen, and tamarack

The shallow pool and scenic granite rock at the base of Morgan Falls

mile you'll arrive at Morgan Falls. You'll see stone steps that will bring you down to a sandy beach at the base of the falls. There is also an accessible well-groomed gravel path that circumvents the stairs and leads to the base of the fall as well.

Morgan Falls is a mystical and serene oasis tucked away in an uninterrupted forest rich in geological and botanical diversity. Here Morgan Creek diagonally traverses a mossy granite face and then settles into a shallow pool perfect for wading in. The turbulent creek water appears to burst through cracks as well as tumble down the rocky façade. This waterfall invites you to observe it from all angles to enjoy its various vantage points and intricacies, which can be hard to capture with a camera. To arrive back at the trailhead, hike back the way you came.

Morgan Falls as it diagonally traverses a 70-foot granite face ▶

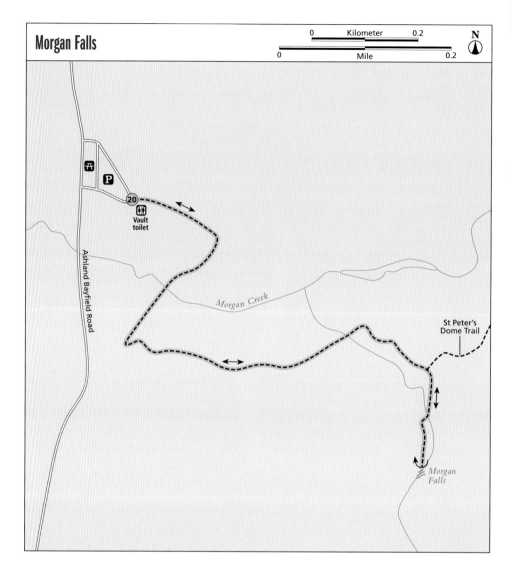

Miles and Directions

0.0 From the trailhead walk southeast on the trail.

0.25 Arrive at a trail junction with a sign: turn left (east).

0.6 Arrive at a second trail junction with a sign: turn right (south).

0.9 Arrive at the end. Walk back the way you came.

1.8 Arrive back at the trailhead.

21 Copper Falls

Part of the North Country National Scenic Trail, this hike brings you to a spectacular waterfall that pours over ancient lava rock and into a colorful deep gorge.

Start: Intersection of Lakeshore Drive (US 2) and Ellis Avenue South (WI 13) in downtown Ashland
Elevation gain: Negligible
Distance: 0.2 mile
Difficulty: Moderate due to multiple sets of stairs
Hiking time: About 6 minutes
Season/schedule: Open year-round from 6 a.m. to 11 p.m.; however, it's best used May through Oct
Fees and permits: Yes
Trail contacts: Copper Falls State Park, 36764 Copper Falls Rd., Mellon, WI 54546, (715) 274-5123, https://dnr.wisconsin.gov/topic /parks/copperfalls
Dog friendly: No
Trail surface: Stone steps, dirt, gravel, occasional pavement, forested, and wooden footbridge

Land status: State park
Nearest town: Ashland, WI
Maps: USGS Copper Falls State Park; https:// dnr.wisconsin.gov/topic/parks/copperfalls /maps
Other trail users: None
Special considerations: During the cold-weather months, the trail may be icy or covered in snow. Flush toilets in state parks are generally closed mid-Oct through mid-May.
Amenities available: Flush toilets, water, picnic area, designated pet area
Maximum grade: 410 percent for less than 0.01 mile
Cell service: Spotty in the entire area, including road in
Waterway: Bad River
Waterfall beauty: 4
Accessibility: No

Finding the trailhead: From the intersection of Lakeshore Drive (US 12) and Ellis Avenue (WI 13), head southeast on Ellis Avenue (WI 13) for 23.6 miles. Turn left (northeast) on WI 169 and go 1.7 miles. Turn left (north) on Copper Falls Road and in 0.1 mile you will come to the park office. Copper Falls Road is the main road that runs through the state park. Continue straight (north) for 1.6 miles through the park, past the south and north camping areas, until you arrive at the parking lot for the North Country Scenic and Doughboy Loop trailhead. Turn right (east) into the parking lot. From the parking lot walk 0.2 mile east to the trailhead. **Trailhead GPS:** N46° 22.317' W90° 38.477'

Trail conditions: The most athletic portion of the trail is at the beginning. The path begins with a series of stairs followed by a wooden bridge and then more stairs. After the second set of stairs, the trail brings you to a forested path that is a combination of dirt, gravel, and random stretches of pavement. This trail presents few uneven surfaces, obstacles, or potential hazards. Strollers, wheelchairs, or mobility devices cannot navigate this trail. A pair of hiking boots or athletic footwear is recommended.

The beautiful and elusive Copper Falls

The Hike

Copper Falls State Park is a geological wonder with unique rock formations formed by ancient lava, deep colorful gorges, and multiple incredible waterfalls. It is considered by many to be one of Wisconsin's most scenic parks. In addition to the waterfall selection, the state park offers great camping, bicycling, picnicking, fishing, and swimming.

Copper Falls State Park sits on the convergence of the Bad River and the Tyler Forks River. It is a wealth of scenic beauty and a place of fascinating historical significance. Human activity over time has changed the landscape of this area. Throughout the park you'll notice construction that looks like it may have come from a different era. Lookout towers, footbridges, cabins, and buildings were constructed in the park by two Depression-era government agencies, the Civilian Conservation Corps (CCC) and Works Progress Administration (WPA). Buildings, bridges, and trails were built by relief workers to provide visitors with opportunities to swim, hike, snowshoe, fish, hunt, and picnic at Copper Falls State Park. Since then the park has continued to be a gathering place for people to enjoy the unique geology and natural beauty.

What you are seeing when you look at Copper Falls is a large igneous bedrock formation of black basalt that splits the Bad River in two as it drops into the canyon to form Copper Falls. Essentially, hot lava poured out of the earth millions of years ago and then cooled in these interesting and fun to look at formations. In 1902, miners rerouted the Bad River by blasting through a bedrock formation upstream. This redirection caused more river volume to flow over the east side of the falls, accelerating rock erosion. Since its redirection, the falls have dropped from their original height of 30 feet to the 8 feet of today.

To arrive at Copper Falls, we hike the Doughboy Trail. On park maps, the Doughboy Trail starts at the parking lot. For this hike and its description, the trail will begin at the base of a set of stairs: east of the parking lot and just northwest of the pavilion.

From the trailhead at the base of the stairs walk northeast, ascend the steps, and cross the bridge over the Bad River. Ascend another set of stairs and you'll arrive on the dirt trail that brings you into the woods. Continue northeast on the trail as its

The North Country National Scenic Trail (NCNST) is the longest of the US National Trails, stretching 4,800 miles across eight states. From Vermont to North Dakota, hikers traverse forests, rugged mountains, rural landscapes, wild terrain, farmland, and rural communities. The NCNST crosses Wisconsin between Michigan's Upper Peninsula and Minnesota, where it passes through Copper Falls State Park from north to south. The NCNST runs parallel with the Doughboy Trail, allowing you to hike a portion of this historic scenic route while visiting Brownstone Falls and Copper Falls. For more information, visit www.northcountrytrail.org.

The rock-strewn Bad River just
upstream from Copper Falls

The Bad River snaking through composite rock, which it has been cutting through for millions of years

surface changes between dirt, red gravel, and randomly poured concrete. You'll pass two trail junctions, and arrive at the view of the falls equipped with an informative sign about its unique geology and history. It's a beautiful view, but due to the way the waterfall twists and turns, it's difficult to get a good photo. There are also wooden railings and tree branches in the way at the viewpoint, making it even more challenging to get a good photo. To arrive back at the trailhead, return the way you came.

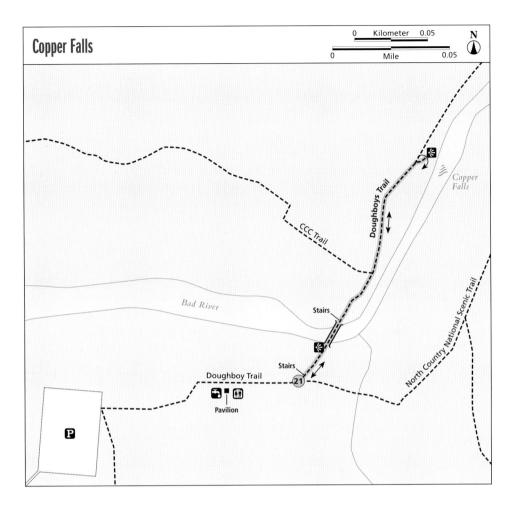

Copper Falls

Copper Falls

Doughboys Trail

CCC Trail

Bad River

Stairs

Stairs

Doughboy Trail

Pavilion

North Country National Scenic Trail

21

Miles and Directions

0.0 Walk up the stone stairs from the trailhead and head northeast.

0.01 Cross the bridge over the Bad River.

0.03 Ascend a second set of stairs.

0.04 Pass the first trail junction: keep straight (northeast).

0.05 Pass a second trail junction: keep straight (northeast).

0.1 Arrive at the view of the falls. Walk back the way you came.

0.2 Arrive back at the trailhead.

The dry-mesic forest decorating the banks of the Bad River and hovering just over the falls

22 Brownstone Falls

This hike offers an enjoyable forested trek along a colorful canyon. This waterfall features the Tyler Forks River plunging 30 feet over red and brown rock into the Bad River Gorge.

Start: Intersection of Lakeshore Drive (US 2) and Ellis Avenue South (WI 13) in downtown Ashland
Elevation gain: Negligible
Distance: 0.8 mile
Difficulty: Moderate due to multiple sets of stairs
Hiking time: About 50 minutes
Season/schedule: Open year-round from 6 a.m. to 11 p.m.; however, it's best used May through Oct
Fees and permits: Yes
Trail contacts: Copper Falls State Park, 36764 Copper Falls Rd., Mellon, WI 54546, (715) 274-5123, https://dnr.wisconsin.gov/topic/parks/copperfalls
Dog friendly: No
Trail surface: Stone steps, forested, wooden footbridge, and wooden stairs
Land status: State park
Nearest town: Ashland, WI
Maps: USGS Copper Falls State Park; https://dnr.wisconsin.gov/topic/parks/copperfalls/maps
Other trail users: None
Special considerations: During the cold-weather months, the trail may be icy or covered in snow. Flush toilets in state parks are generally closed mid-Oct through mid-May.
Amenities available: Flush toilets, water, picnic area, designated pet area
Maximum grade: 410 percent for less than 0.01 mile
Cell service: Spotty in the entire area, including road in
Waterway: Bad River
Waterfall beauty: 3
Accessibility: No

Finding the trailhead: From the intersection of US 12 and WI 13 (aka Ellis and Lakeshore Drive), head southeast on WI 13 South for 23.6 miles. Turn left (northeast) on WI 169 and go 1.7 miles. Turn left (north) on Copper Falls Road and in 0.1 mile you will come to the park office. Copper Falls Road is the main road that runs through the state park. Continue straight (north) for 1.6 miles through the park, past the south and north camping areas, until you arrive at the parking lot for the North Country Scenic and Doughboy Loop trailhead. Turn right (east) into the parking lot. From the parking lot walk 0.2 mile east to the trailhead. **Trailhead GPS:** N46° 22.398' W90° 38.407'

Trail conditions: The most athletic portion of the trail is at the beginning. The path begins with a series of stairs followed by a wooden bridge and then more stairs. After the second set of stairs, the trail brings you to a forested path that is a combination of dirt, gravel, and random stretches of pavement. This trail presents few uneven surfaces, obstacles, or potential hazards. Strollers, wheelchairs, or mobility devices cannot navigate this trail. A pair of hiking boots or athletic footwear is recommended.

*Brownstone Falls
plummeting into
the Bad River*

The Tyler Forks River emptying into the Bad River

The Hike

This waterfall is in Copper Falls State Park on the Doughboy Trail, 0.16 mile northeast of Copper Falls. This cascade is created by the Tyler Forks River plunging 40 feet into the Bad River and is arguably one of the most impressive in the park. This display of falling water is surrounded by reddish-brown rocks, hence the name. On either side of the turbulent fast-moving water, the walls of the gorge rise up 60–100 feet high making it all the more scenic. The uniquely colored rock you're looking at was formed from red lava flowing through a 100- to 200-foot canyon of colorful conglomerates, shells, and sandstones. The end result is a stunning waterfall and an enjoyable nature hike to arrive at it.

The Bad River is known for these picturesque waterfalls, geological wonders, and scenic gorges. In fact, these features have been attracting visitors for centuries. Some report that the Bad River got its name for its lasting legacy of damaging floods. According to park records, the Bad River has flooded multiple times in the past, which has washed out and destroyed swimming areas, footbridges, and stairs. Others report that "Bad River" was a mistranslation by French traders of the Ojibwe word *Mashkiziibi*. Either way, the Bad River is definitely a force to be reckoned with.

To get to Brownstone Falls, walk northeast from the trailhead, ascend the steps, and cross the bridge over the Bad River. Ascend another set of stairs and you'll arrive on the dirt trail that brings you into the woods. Continue northwest on the trail as its surface alternates between dirt, red gravel, and randomly poured concrete. You'll pass two trail junctions, where you'll continue straight (northeast) until you arrive at Copper Falls. From Copper Falls continue northeast. Pass a third trail

Reddish-brown lava rock making the falls stand out

View of the Bad River looking not-so-bad

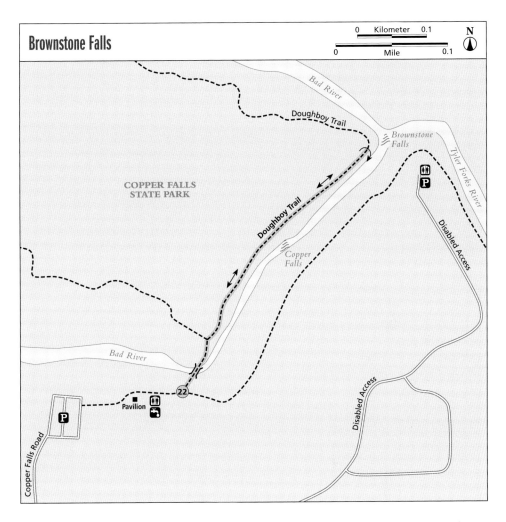

junction and you'll arrive at a view of Brownstone Falls, which is marked by an informative sign explaining its history and unique geology. To arrive back at the trailhead, walk back the way you came.

Miles and Directions

0.0   Walk up the stone stairs from the trailhead and head northeast.

0.01 Cross the bridge over the Bad River.

0.03 Ascend a second set of stairs.

0.04 Pass the first trail junction: keep straight (northeast).

0.1   Pass Copper Falls.

0.3   Pass a third trail junction.

0.4   Arrive at the view of Brownstone Falls. Walk back the way you came.

0.8   Arrive back at the trailhead.

23 Tyler Forks Cascade

This loop trail includes a shaded forested hike with multiple adventurous staircases. This 1.83-mile loop brings you to three waterfalls and the best view in the gorge.

Start: Intersection of Lakeshore Drive (US 2) and Ellis Avenue South (WI 13) in downtown Ashland

Elevation gain: 0.02 mile

Distance: 1.83 miles

Difficulty: Strenuous due to multiple stairs

Hiking time: About 1 hour 15 minutes

Season/schedule: Open year-round from 6 a.m. to 11 p.m.; however, it's best used May through Oct

Fees and permits: Yes

Trail contacts: 36764 Copper Falls Rd., Mellen, WI 54546, (715) 274-5123, https://dnr .wisconsin.gov/topic/parks/copperfalls

Dog friendly: No (not allowed)

Trail surface: Paved and dirt with wooden bridges, stairs, and boardwalks

Land status: State park

Nearest town: Ashland, WI

Maps: USGS Copper Falls State Park; https:// dnr.wisconsin.gov/topic/parks/copperfalls /maps

Other trail users: None

Special considerations: During the cold-weather months, the trail may be icy or covered in snow. Flush toilets in state parks are generally closed mid-Oct through mid-May.

Amenities available: Flush toilets, water, picnic area, designated pet area

Maximum grade: –64 percent for less than 0.01 mile

Cell service: Spotty in the entire area, including road in

Waterway: Tyler Forks River and Bad River

Waterfall beauty: 4

Accessibility: Yes. A 0.5-mile paved access road connects the trailhead to the falls viewpoint.

Finding the trailhead: From the intersection of US 12 and WI 13 (aka Ellis and Lakeshore Drive), head southeast on WI 13 for 23.6 miles. Turn left (northeast) on WI 169 and go 1.7 miles. Turn left (north) on Copper Falls Road and in 0.1 mile you will come to the park office. Copper Falls Road is the main road that runs through the state park. Continue straight (north) for 1.6 miles through the park, past the south and north camping areas, until you arrive at the parking lot for the North Country Scenic and Doughboy Loop trailhead. Turn right (east) into the parking lot. From the parking lot walk 0.1 mile east to the trailhead. **Trailhead GPS:** N46°22.323' W90° 38.475'

Trail conditions: This is a forested path that is a combination of dirt, gravel, wooden stairs, and random stretches of pavement. This trail presents few uneven surfaces, obstacles, or potential hazards. Strollers, wheelchairs, or mobility devices cannot navigate this trail. A pair of hiking boots or athletic footwear is recommended.

Framed by pine trees and emptying into shallow pools ▶

The Hike

This 1.83-mile loop incorporates all the best parts of the Bad River Gorge and Tyler Forks River. The full circle hike immerses you in a woodland trail and includes many of the best views in Copper Falls State Park. This rigorous hike involves a lot of stairs and winding paths, but the payoff is visiting three incredible waterfalls, some of which you get to view from multiple vantage points.

As you stroll along the shores of the meandering Bad River, you'll find yourself in a northern dry-mesic forest. The path is surrounded on all sides by hemlock, sugar maple, white pine, and yellow birch. The forest floor and slopes of the gorge have a thick understory blanket made up of ferns, clubmosses, and saplings. This hike brings you deep into the enchanted woods as you follow an easy-to-follow path along the river. This area of the forest is known for fishers, black bears, grey wolves, porcupines, and even elk. For bird enthusiasts, many migratory birds have been sighted and documented on the Doughboy Trail. Keep an ear and eye out for big northern raven, great pileated woodpecker, sassy chickadees, riffed grouse, and eagles.

The main attraction of this hike is the Tyler Forks Cascade, which appears as a gentle collision of the Tyler Forks River and the Bad River. The Tyler Forks River is more of a wide-open valley, whereas the Bad River is a fast-moving canyon. To arrive at this waterfall and the union of these two very different waterways, start out at the same trailhead as you did for Copper Falls and Brownstone Falls. Walk northeast from the trailhead, ascend the steps, and cross the bridge over the Bad River. Continue on the trail past Copper Falls and Brownstone Falls until you arrive at a viewpoint called Devil's Gate. Here you have a view of unique rock formations with an interesting history and significance to the geology of the gorge. Devil's Gate is an outcropping of conglomerate rock that was formed after the lava flow stopped and streams full of rocks and sediment poured over layers of basalt. The conglomerate was then deposited in a layer-cake fashion and tilted by tremendous pressure from within the earth. The Bad River cut through this cement-like rock to form the rocky gate known as "Devil's Gate." From Devil's Gate go left (west) and follow the path past a rest area with a shelter. From here the trail circles clockwise as it descends multiple sets of stairs until you arrive at a bridge crossing the Bad River. After you cross the river, the path then ascends a staircase: at the top go right (southeast). You'll follow the trail for 0.3 mile, which includes ascending another set of stairs and passing a rest area before you arrive at the boardwalk for Tyler Forks Cascade. From the main trail it's an out-and-back path that brings you to two stunning views of the cascade as well as the gorge in the distance. After visiting the view of the cascade, return to the main trail. Head southeast for 0.14 mile until you cross a bridge and come to a trail junction. Take a hard right (southwest) and walk across the bridge until you arrive at another trail junction with a sign: turn right (northwest). Follow this path for 0.12 mile northwest past a rest area and toilets until you come to a trail junction: turn hard left (southwest). After this turn you will arrive at an alternate viewpoint

The boardwalk comingling with nature to bring you to the view of the falls

The Tyler Forks River elegantly pouring over shelves of rock

of Brownstone Falls. Continue southwest for 0.2 mile on the trail until you arrive at an alternate viewpoint for Copper Falls. This brings you less than 0.1 mile from the trailhead. Continue southwest on the trail and follow it as it turns clockwise, then faces east and the trail returns to pavement. Arrive back at the trailhead.

Miles and Directions

0.0 Walk up the stone stairs from the trailhead and head northeast.

0.01 Cross the bridge over the Bad River, ascend a set of stairs, and continue on the trail past Copper Falls and Brownstone Falls.

0.7 Arrive at Devil's Gate: turn left (east). Follow the trail as it circles clockwise.

0.82 Descend a set of stairs and walk straight (north).

0.84 Cross a bridge with a beautiful view over the Bad River.

0.85 Ascend a set of stairs and at the top, turn right (southeast). Continue straight (southeast), ascend a set of stairs, and continue past the rest area.

1.17 Arrive at the boardwalk to see Tyler Forks Cascade. This is an out-and-back path that requires descending 116 steps to arrive at two scenic viewpoints. Retrace your steps.

1.23 Arrive back at the main trail: head southeast. Continue past the vault toilets and over a bridge.

1.37 Arrive at a trail junction. Turn right (southwest) and cross a bridge.

1.39 Arrive at another trail junction with a trail sign: turn right (northwest). Continue straight past a rest area and toilets.

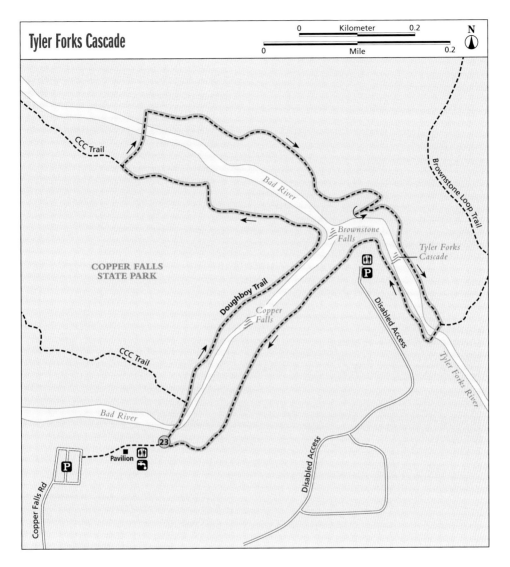

1.52 Arrive at a trail junction. Turn left (southwest).

1.53 Arrive at alternate view of Brownstone Falls. Follow the path southeast, which zigzags briefly before arriving at a trail junction.

1.74 Cross a bridge that has an alternate view of Copper Falls. Continue straight (southwest).

1.81 Paved path begins.

1.83 Arrive back at the trailhead.

24 Red Granite Falls

This hike is a lollipop loop that brings you from glassy/scenic Loon Lake through a high-canopy forest, along moss-covered marshes and down to the banks of the Bad River. While some falls in the state park keep you at a distance with aggressive signage and protective guardrails, this series of rapids lets you get up close and personal.

Start: Intersection of Lakeshore Drive (US 2) and Ellis Avenue South (WI 13) in downtown Ashland
Elevation gain: Negligible
Distance: 2.5 miles
Difficulty: Strenuous due to length and hills
Hiking time: About 2 hours, 5 minutes
Season/schedule: Open year-round from 6 a.m. to 11 p.m.; however, it's best used May through Oct
Fees and permits: Yes
Trail contacts: Copper Falls State Park, 36764 Copper Falls Rd., Mellen, WI 54546, (715) 274-5123, https://dnr.wisconsin.gov/topic/parks/copperfalls
Dog friendly: Yes, on leashes
Trail surface: Forested
Land status: State park

Nearest town: Ashland, WI
Maps: USGS Copper Falls State Park; https://dnr.wisconsin.gov/topic/parks/copperfalls/maps
Other trail users: None
Special considerations: During the cold-weather months, the trail may be icy or covered in snow. Flush toilets in state parks are generally closed mid-Oct through mid-May.
Amenities available: Water, flush toilets, and picnic area
Maximum grade: –29.7 percent for less than 0.01 mile
Cell service: Spotty in the entire area, including road in
Waterway: Bad River
Waterfall beauty: 4
Accessibility: No

Finding the trailhead: From the intersection of WI 2 and WI 13 in downtown Ashland, head south on WI 13 for 23.6 miles and turn left onto WI 169/Copper Falls Drive. Go 1.7 miles and turn left on Copper Falls Road. Here is where you enter the state park and will have to pay a daily fee or show your Wisconsin State Park sticker. Go 0.3 mile and you'll come to Power House Road where you will see signs directing you left (southwest) to a parking lot. Turn left on Power House Road and go 0.1 mile and park in the parking lot. From the parking lot walk toward Loon Lake on a paved path for less than 0.1 mile. You will see a sign for "Red Granite Falls Trail 2.5 Miles" directing you off of the paved path and to your right (west). Follow this dirt and grass path for less than 0.1 mile until you reach the trailhead. Here you will find a clearly marked trailhead and information about invasive species and the importance of cleaning off your shoes before you hike. **Trailhead GPS:** N46° 21.187' W90° 38.880'

Trail conditions: This is a well-groomed trail that switches between gravel and dirt. The path twists and turns and includes a few hills, but there are not many uneven surfaces or large rocks to maneuver. There is a dirt path from the main trail that diverges down to the falls. This may be slippery when it rains or when it is covered in fall leaves.

The Hike

This 2.5-mile lollipop loop starts out near the shores of Loon Lake in the southeast corner of the Copper Falls State Park and ends on the banks of the Bad River. The main attraction here is a seldom visited hike and an eye-level view of multiple tumbling water features. Here you have the opportunity to swim below the falls or rock hop the boulder-strewn shores. What makes this hike unique is that, unlike other waterfalls in the park, there are no climbing or swimming restrictions. You will find yourself right at the water's edge, on one of Wisconsin's most beautiful natural playgrounds.

To arrive at the trailhead, walk southeast toward Loon Lake. Before you arrive at Moon Beach or the pavilion, you'll see a sign stating "Red Granite Trail 2.5 Miles" directing you off the paved path and toward the woods (southwest). Follow the path to the trailhead. The trail begins as you walk into the woods and you find yourself surrounded by a forest of birch, maple, ash, and varieties of pines. The trail is well groomed and easy to follow. The trail surface transitions from dirt to gravel and back to dirt. You walk 0.5 mile, pass three trail junctions, and arrive at a fork in the road at the fourth trail junction. This is where the loop begins. Follow the path to your right (west). The path continues to turn in a counterclockwise loop. At 0.7 mile into the hike you come to a clearing where you pass under power lines before re-entering the woods again. You arrive at a fifth trail junction, which is a there-and-back path to the falls. Up ahead there is a sixth trail junction, which is a different path leading off the main trail to the river's edge above the main falls. Return to the trail and continue

One of the few falls in Copper Falls State Park that allows you to get this close

The easy-to-access falls offer opportunities for rock climbing.

following the clockwise loop as it veers away from the river and back into the woods heading southwest. The trail brings you under the power lines again, before directing you back to the fork in the path that originally brought you to the falls. Stay to the right (northeast) and follow the path back to the trailhead.

Miles and Directions

0.0 From the trailhead walk southwest.

0.5 You'll pass three trail junctions before arriving at a fork in the trail: follow the path to your right (west).

0.7 Pass a clearing in the woods, which brings you under power lines. Continue straight.

0.8 Arrive at a trail junction with an out-and-back path to the falls. Take a right (north) and walk down to the river's edge for a view of the falls. Return to the trail.

0.9 Arrive at another trail junction with another out-and-back path to the falls. Return to the trail. Follow the trail as it veers away from the Black River in a clockwise loop and back into the woods (southwest).

1.4 Pass a clearing in the woods and walk under power lines (same ones you previously crossed under). Continue straight (northeast).

2.0 Arrive back at the first trail junction where you began the loop. Stay to your right (northeast).

2.5 Arrive back at the trailhead.

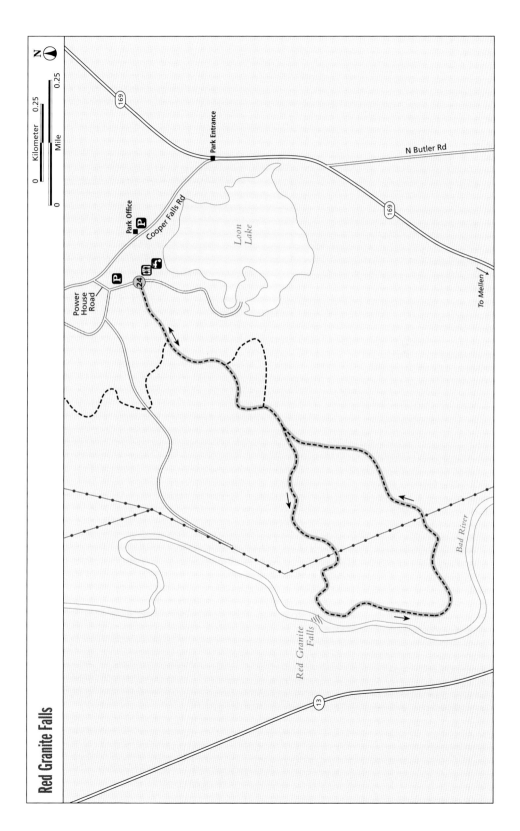

Red Granite Falls

N

0   Kilometer   0.25
0   Mile   0.25

169

Park Entrance

N Butler Rd

Park Office

Cooper Falls Rd

Loon Lake

169

To Mellen

Power House Road

24

Red Granite Falls

Bad River

13

25 Potato Falls Upper

This waterfall is considered one of the most beautiful in Wisconsin, and, to some, the entire Midwest. This forested hike descends a timber staircase and delivers you to a viewing platform with a perfect view of the Upper Falls.

Start: Frontier Bar and Campground at the intersection of US 2 and WI 169 in Saxon, WI

Elevation gain: Less than 0.1 mile

Distance: 0.2 mile

Difficulty: This is not a long hike, and it would be considered easy—however, the many stairs (130) put it in the category of difficult for some ability levels.

Hiking time: Approximately 27 minutes

Season/schedule: Open year-round from 6 a.m. to 10 p.m.; however, it's best used Apr through Oct

Fees and permits: None

Trail contacts: Potato River Falls Rd., Gurney, WI 54528, (715) 561-2922, https://www .ironcountyforest.org/

Dog friendly: Yes, on leashes

Trail surface: Dirt and wooden stairs

Land status: County park

Nearest town: Gurney, WI

Maps: USGS Potato Falls Campground

Other trail users: None

Special considerations: Many steps. Best time to hike is Apr through Oct.

Amenities available: 5 rustic campsites, a picnic shelter, vault toilets, and ATV access

Maximum grade: –83 percent for less than 0.1 mile

Cell service: Limited

Waterway: Potato River

Waterfall beauty: 5

Accessibility: No

Finding the trailhead: To find the trailhead, start from Frontier Bar and Campground at the intersection of US 2 and WI 169 and head south on WI 169 for 2.8 miles. Turn right (west) on Falls Road for 1.5 miles, which will bring you to the Potato Falls County Park. As you enter the park, you'll see a parking lot on your right side (west). Here you'll see signs for the trailhead for both the Upper Falls and Lower Falls. **Trailhead GPS:** N46° 27.772' W90° 31.777'

Trail conditions: This is a well-maintained trail of dirt and wooden stairs. The county park is open year-round, and these waterfalls in winter are particularly beautiful. During the rainy or winter months, the trail may be slippery.

The Hike

What makes the Iron County region so interesting for hikers, and specifically water-fall seekers, is that it borders Lake Superior and Michigan's Upper Peninsula. Year-round this water-saturated region of the state offers plenty of recreational opportuni-ties, from hunting and fishing to ATV-ing, hiking, and camping. In the cold-weather months, this region gets *a lot* of snowfall, turning it into a winter playground for anyone who enjoys activities like snowmobiling, cross-country skiing, snowshoeing, and ice fishing. When the snow melts in the spring, the numerous rivers and streams

The Potato River as it traverses the unique topography of Iron County, WI

When the snow melts in spring, Potato Falls and many nearby waterfalls start gushing, making this specific region excellent for waterfall exploration. Within a 20-minute drive of Potato Falls County Park, you can visit Copper Falls State Park (Hikes 20 to 23), Wren Falls (Hike 27), Foster Falls (Hike 27), Upson Falls (Hike 28), Superior Falls (Hike 29), Saxon Falls (Hike 30), Kimball Falls (Hike 31), and Interstate Falls (Hike 32). These waterfalls could easily all be visited in a weekend, or for the more aggressive hiker, all in one day!

come alive with fabulous caches of waterfalls, two of the most exciting being Potato Falls Upper and Lower.

The star attraction of this waterfall adventure is the Potato River, which is not just one waterway, but actually encompasses multiple different streams and creeks. The rust-colored water of the Potato River twists its way across the county and then plunges over a series of stunning rock features—most notably here in Gurney and in Upson Town Park (see Hike 28)—before joining the Bad River east of Marengo. In Potato Falls County Park, you'll witness this eastern tributary of the Bad River watershed dropping a total of 90 feet with a dramatic show of whitewater and ancient rock. Iron County boasts being home to the state's ten highest waterfalls and the Potato Falls is on that list. The Upper and adjacent Lower Falls are in a rustic county park with wooden boardwalks and staircases leading the way to the best viewing locations.

From the designated parking area, you'll see a sign to your left (northwest) for the Upper Falls indicating where the trail begins. From the trailhead walk southeast. The trail is primarily dirt and brings you into a forest where you'll follow a path that extends along the upper ridge of the gorge. Stay on the dirt trail for 0.08 mile until you come to the top of a wooden staircase. Descend the 130 wooden steps and walk less than 0.1 mile south to arrive at the lookout platform for the Upper Falls. To arrive back at the trailhead, return the way you came. Both the Upper and Lower Falls require climbing down and then back up an impressive quantity of stairs, making the physical adventure of getting to the falls equally as magical as witnessing their breathtaking views and sounds.

Above: The Potato River as it skips off 400-year-old volcanic rock unique to the Lake Superior region
Below: The Upper Falls cloaked in the seasonal yellow-greens of local Scots pines

A waterfall with no guardrails allows you to get up close and view the falls from different vantage points.

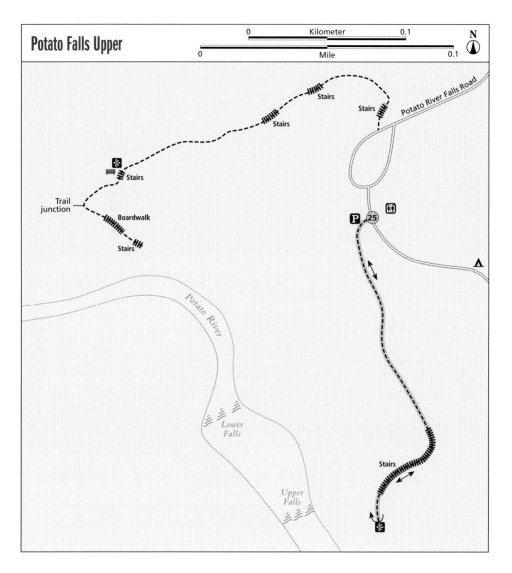

Miles and Directions

0.0 From the trailhead walk southeast.

0.08 Descend 130 stairs.

0.1 Arrive at the viewing platform. Walk back the way you came.

0.2 Arrive back at the trailhead.

26 Potato Falls Lower

When the rust-colored Potato River roars, foams, and crashes over the Upper Falls, it gains momentum for a brief stint before its next, and even more impressive descent: the Lower Falls.

Start: Frontier Bar and Campground at the intersection of US 2 and WI 169
Elevation gain: Less than 0.1 mile
Distance: 0.4 mile
Difficulty: This is not a long hike; however, it is considered difficult due to its many stairs (204).
Hiking time: About 25 minutes
Season/schedule: Open year-round from 6 a.m. to 10 p.m.; however, it's best used Apr through Oct
Fees and permits: None
Trail contacts: Potato River Falls Rd., Gurney, WI 54528, (715) 561-2922, https://www.ironcountyforest.org/
Dog friendly: Yes, on leashes

Trail surface: Dirt and wooden stairs
Land status: County park
Nearest town: Gurney, WI
Maps: USGS Potato Falls Campground
Other trail users: None
Special considerations: Many steps that may become icy and slippery when covered with snow
Amenities available: 5 rustic campsites, a picnic shelter, vault toilets, and ATV access
Maximum grade: –83 percent for less than 0.1 mile
Cell service: Limited
Waterway: Potato River
Waterfall beauty: 5
Accessibility: No

Finding the trailhead: To find the trailhead start from Frontier Bar and Campground at the intersection of US 2 and WI 169. Head south on WI 169 for 2.8 miles. Turn right (west) on Falls Road for 1.5 miles, which will bring you to the Potato Falls County Park. As you enter the park, you'll see a parking lot on your right side (west). Here you'll see signs for the trailhead for both the Upper Falls and Lower Falls. **Trailhead GPS:** N46° 27.772' W90° 31.777'

Trail conditions: This is a well-maintained trail of dirt and wooden stairs. The county park is open year-round, and these waterfalls in winter are particularly beautiful. During the rainy or winter months, the trail may be slippery.

The Hike

This hike brings you to the stunning Lower Falls situated just below Hike 25's Upper Falls. Here the Potato River provides yet another jaw-dropping cascade just as majestic as its adjacent partner upstream. The Lower Falls hiking trail leads you down to a viewing platform where you'll find an exceptional view of the falls. For more enthusiastic and athletic hikers, this trail also offers the opportunity to hike past the observation deck and down to the water's edge. A short rock-hopping hike upriver will allow you to view the falls up close near the base.

*View of the falls from the
hiking trail's first viewpoint*

The Potato Falls Lower, arguably more impressive than its older brother upstream

From the parking area in Potato Falls County Park, you'll see a trailhead sign to the northeast labeled "Lower Falls." Walk northeast from the parking area to arrive at the trailhead. From the trailhead walk northeast for less than 0.1 mile and you'll come to a set of stairs. Here you will descend a series of four separate wooden staircases divided slightly by dirt trails in between. At the top of the fourth staircase, you'll find your first viewpoint with a bench from which to take a rest and admire a view of the Upper Falls. After you descend the fourth set of stairs, the trail takes a sharp left (southeast), placing you on the last section of the hike. The final stretch of the trail includes a boardwalk and a fifth set of stairs leading you down to an observation deck with a sitting bench and a stunning view of the falls. From the trailhead to the final observation deck are a total of 204 stairs you'll climb down and then must climb back up. To arrive back at the trailhead, return the way you came.

The two designated viewpoints included in this hike are well placed and give you a beautiful, but distant view of the falls. For explorers who like to get as close as possible, these observation decks may not satisfy your curiosity or your desire for better photography. From the first trail junction, instead of turning left, follow the trail downhill (south) to the water's edge. From here you have the option of rock hopping your way upstream (southeast) toward the base of the falls. This will involve taking your shoes off (or keeping them on) and crossing the cool shallow river to arrive near the base of the falls for a fantastic view.

View of the Lower Falls from downriver at the trail's end and the water's edge

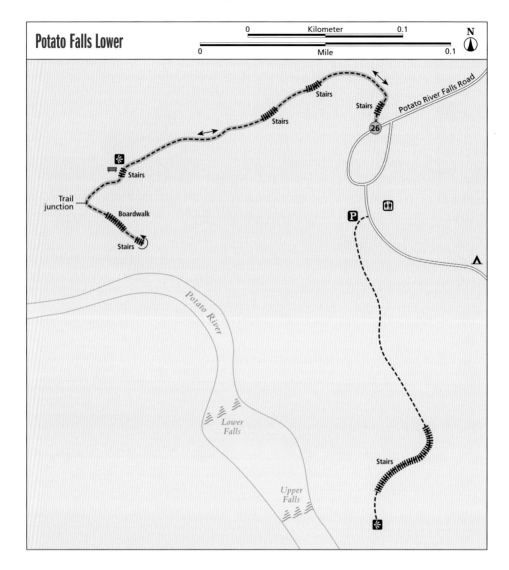

Potato Falls Lower

Miles and Directions

0.0 From the trailhead walk northwest.

0.1 Arrive at a set of stairs that descend to your left (southwest): walk down 130 stairs, which are divided briefly by short dirt paths.

0.12 Arrive at a scenic viewpoint with a bench. Here you have a beautiful view of the upper falls. Descend an additional 68 steps.

0.14 Arrive at the bottom of the stairs where you come to a boardwalk on your left (southeast). Walk southeast on the boardwalk.

0.18 Arrive at the last set of stairs. Descend six stairs.

0.2 Arrive at the trail's end with a view of the lower falls. Walk back the way you came.

0.4 Arrive back at the trailhead.

27 Wren Falls

This very hidden waterfall is worth the effort to find. Located along the legendary North Country Scenic Trail, the Tyler Forks River bursts through two dramatic rock outcropping and drops 15 feet into a scenic rocky gorge.

Start: Intersection of US 51 and WI 77 in downtown Hurley, WI

Elevation gain: Less than 0.1 mile

Distance: 0.3 mile

Difficulty: Easy

Hiking time: About 14 minutes

Season/schedule: Open year-round, but best time to hike is Apr through Oct

Fees and permits: None

Trail contacts: Iron County Development Zone, 100 Carly Rd., Hurley, WI 54534, (715) 561-2922, https://ironcountywi.com/waterfalls/

Dog friendly: Yes, on leashes

Trail surface: Dirt trail

Land status: County-owned land open to the public for recreation

Nearest town: Hurley, WI

Maps: Saxon, WI

Other trail users: Hikers of the North Country Scenic Trail

Special considerations: The roads that bring you to the parking area and trailhead are pretty rustic, and it can be easy to get lost. Keep an eye out for road signs directing you to Wren Falls.

Amenities available: None.

Maximum grade: –23.9 percent sustained for less than 0.1 mile. The steepest part of the hike is at the very end when reaching the base of the falls.

Cell service: Limited

Waterway: Tyler Forks River

Waterfall beauty: 5

Accessibility: No

Finding the trailhead: There are multiple ways to find Wren Falls if you're coming from the town of Hurley; however, I've found that coming from the north is easiest. Due to the number of unmarked gravel roads you need to take to get there, I strongly encourage you to use a GPS device or a mapping application on your smartphone. From the intersection of US 51 and WI 77 in downtown Hurley, head north on US 51 for 1.5 miles. At the traffic circle take the second exit (heading northwest) on to US 2 and drive for 15.7 miles. Turn left onto WI 169 and drive for 5.6 miles. Turn left onto Vogues Road, which becomes gravel. Here begins the more adventurous part of the drive. From here on out the roads are all dirt and gravel, and although you'll come across many signs (some handwritten) directing you to Wren Falls, the streets aren't well marked. Drive for 3.4 miles on Vogues Road until you come to a three-way intersection where Vogues Road intersects with Casey Sag Road and Wren Falls Road at a hairpin turn. Turn left (south) onto Wren Falls Road and go for 1.4 miles until you see a parking lot on your right (southwest). The trailhead is connected to the parking lot and easy to locate. **Trailhead GPS:** 46°21.141' W90°55.337'

Trail conditions: This is primarily a forested trail made of dirt and gravel that presents few uneven surfaces, obstacles, or potential hazards. The path is well worn from four-wheel-drive vehicles, waterfall enthusiasts, and hikers of the North Country Scenic Trail. The last portion of the trail has many jagged rocks that may be challenging on the ankles of even the most athletic hiker. At the trail's end there is the option to walk down to the base of the falls; however, this necessitates walking down a very steep hill of uneven loose rock, which could be potentially dangerous.

The Hike

Wren Falls is an incredibly picturesque waterfall standing approximately 15 feet high. Here the Tyler Forks River is channeled through two scenic rock outcroppings just before plunging into a rocky gorge surrounded by the lush Iron County forest. This postcard-worthy waterfall is by no means the biggest in the state, but it is arguably one of the most beautiful. The trailhead can be reached by car through a series of gravel backcountry roads or by a long and adventurous hike that connects various natural attractions throughout the Iron County wilderness.

This hike is part of the North Country National Scenic Trail (NCT), a 4,600-mile hiking and backpacking trail that travels through the northern states. Approximately 220 miles of the trail cuts through the northernmost counties of Wisconsin between Minnesota and Michigan's Upper Peninsula. On a yearly basis volunteer crews go out and work on maintaining the trails and making them easy to find and navigate.

One exciting feature of the NCT is that an 8-mile point-to-point hike exists between Wren Falls and Foster Falls, a smaller fall not featured in this book. This hike offers scenery and adventure at every turn. The trail is well maintained and runs alongside two wild rivers, past two thundering waterfalls, five established primitive campsites, and an abandoned gold mine. The hike brings you from the marshy bottoms of the Iron County Forest to vast overlooks 300 feet above. This is a great trail for anyone looking to connect with nature and do some deep woods backpacking and camping.

From the parking lot you'll see the trailhead, with a sign, on the southwest corner. Large boulders have been placed at the entrance of the trail to discourage vehicle traffic. Walk southwest on the forested trail for 0.07 mile until you come to a clearing. Continue past the clearing for 0.07 mile and you'll arrive at a primitive campsite situated just northwest of the falls. Be careful, the section of the trail just before you arrive at the campsite is a slow descent full of jagged uneven rocks. From the primitive campsite turn left (south) and the trail will lead you directly to the edge of a bluff where you'll discover a perfect view of the falls from above. Directly to your right (southwest), you have the opportunity to walk down to the riverbank and view the falls from the base. This is an incredible view of the falls, but be careful: It is a steep descent of loose jagged rock that you'll have to climb back up. To return to the trailhead and parking lot, walk back the way you came. If you plan on hiking on to Foster Falls, head east on the NCT and follow the blue vinyl decals or "blazes" on the trees. More information including maps for the NCT can be found at https:// northcountrytrail.org/trail/wisconsin/htg/.

Wren Falls falling 12 feet over ancient stone and into the rocky gorge ▶

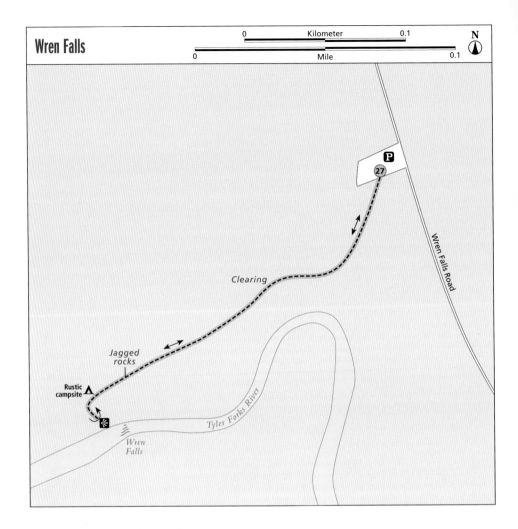

Wren Falls

Miles and Directions

0.0 From the parking lot and trailhead walk southwest.

0.1 Arrive at a rustic campsite: turn left (south).

0.16 Arrive at the trail's end with a view of the falls. Walk back the way you came.

0.32 Arrive back at the trailhead and parking lot.

Top: The Tyler Forks River dropping 12 feet over impressive rock formations
Bottom: A bluff's-eye view of the falls from the trail's end

28 Upson Falls

Located in a tucked-away campground in the charming town of Upson, WI. Here you'll discover a jagged 18-foot waterfall cascading into yet another colorful and stunning region of the Potato River.

Start: Intersection of WI 77 and US 51 in downtown Hurley
Elevation gain: 0.04 mile
Distance: 0.1 mile
Difficulty: Easy
Hiking time: About 10 minutes
Season/schedule: This community park is open year-round 6 a.m. to 11 p.m., but it's best used May through Oct (toilets are closed at the end of Oct).
Fees and permits: None
Trail contacts: 9564 Upson Park Rd., Upson, WI 54565
Dog friendly: Yes
Trail surface: Dirt and rocks
Land status: Town park

Nearest town: Hurley, WI
Maps: USGS Upson, WI
Other trail users: None
Special considerations: There is no specific path to get to the falls. Walk less than 0.1 mile along the banks of the Potato River and you'll come to multiple viewpoints of the falls. During heavy rains, the banks of the river may be slippery.
Amenities available: Campsites, vault toilets, picnic shelter
Maximum grade: Less than 0.1 mile
Cell service: Yes
Waterway: Potato River
Waterfall beauty: 3
Accessibility: No

Finding the trailhead: From the intersection of WI 77 and US 51 in the town of Hurley, head west on CR 77/WI 77 for 12.5 miles. Turn right onto Hoyt Road (WI 122) and drive 0.3 mile. Turn left onto Upson Park Road and go 0.2 mile, which will bring you to the entrance of Upson Falls Campground on your left. The parking area is a gravel patch adjacent to Campsite 7 that you will see on your left side near a white pavilion. From the parking lot walk east down a dirt path, less than 0.1 mile, to arrive at the river's edge and trailhead. **Trailhead GPS:** N46° 22.244' W90° 24.753'

Trail conditions: Rough, rocky, and unkept. This trail brings you along the banks of the river with multiple opportunities to view the falls, but no clearly defined trail. The more you hike upriver to get closer to the falls, the more climbing is involved. A sturdy pair of hiking footwear is recommended.

A view of the falls from the highest point in the hike ▶

The Hike

For waterfall hunters and nature lovers, discovering a seldom-visited hidden gem in Wisconsin's Northwoods is a treat. This waterfall, and the adventure to arrive at it, unfolds layer by layer like a Russian matryoshka doll. The hike begins on the banks of the Potato River at a rustic and out-of-the-way campground near the quaint and idyllic town of Upson. The rugged and rocky banks of the Potato River beckon you to explore upriver. Anyone willing to make the short, but somewhat treacherous, hike to the falls is rewarded with a view of an elegant and scenic cascade of multiple levels. The rust-colored Potato River gently pours over outcroppings of ancient lava rock. The exposed surfaces of the sawtooth conglomerates are covered in carpets of green moss and grizzled with faded lichens. A very scenic spot to enjoy the tranquility of a truly wild river and its unique geology.

From the designated parking area, walk less than 0.1 mile east to the trailhead on the shore of the Potato River. Here you'll see a view of the smaller rapids just downstream from the main falls. Follow the trail southeast as it hugs the shore of the river. The trail is a combination of dirt, mud, and rocks and not clearly defined. It involves some careful stepping up and over rocks. At 0.02 mile into the hike you'll arrive at a small dirt and rock hill that you must climb over to arrive at an outcropping that juts out into the river. This outcropping provides your first opportunity to view the falls. From here the trail involves a short ascent bringing you to a second view of the falls from higher up. The path continues uphill and veers southwest away from the river briefly before curving back (southeast) toward the river. At the trail's end you are situated high up on a lookout peering between the pines at a beautiful side-angle view of Upson Falls: The complex Potato River splinters over and around an array of colorful and jagged rocks. To arrive back at the trailhead, walk back the way you came.

Bonus Hike: Corrigan's Lookout. Located off WI 122 in Upson, Corrigan's Lookout is a 0.25-mile hike to a rock outcrop overlooking Upson Lake to the west, the Gogebic Range to the south, and Lake Superior to the north. More information and maps can be found at https://ironcountyoutdoors.org/corrigans-lookout.

Above: The enchanting falls drop 18 feet into the Potato River just north of Upson, WI.
Below: Many of the striking features of the falls illuminated by the morning sun

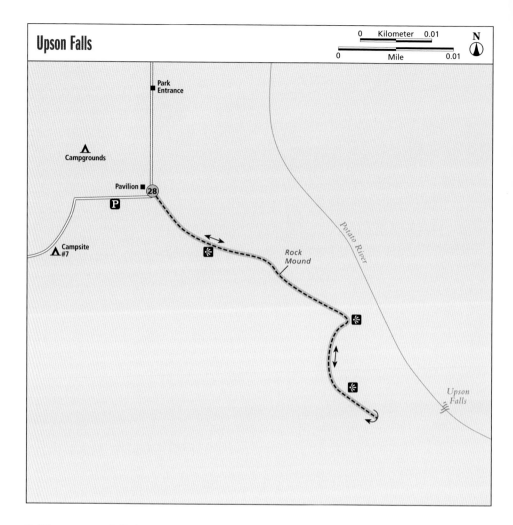

Miles and Directions

0.0 From the trailhead walk southeast.

0.01 Arrive at the first view of the falls.

0.02 Pass the large rock mound.

0.04 Arrive at the second view of the falls.

0.05 Arrive at the third view of the falls and the trail's end. Walk back the way you came.

0.1 Arrive back at the trailhead.

29 Superior Falls—Option #1

This impressive waterfall is one of the tallest in Wisconsin and drops a total of 110 feet across several levels. Two different hike options bring you to multiple vantage points, allowing you to appreciate the tremendous size of the falls and surrounding gorge.

Start: Intersection of US 51/2nd Avenue North and WI 77 in downtown Hurley, WI
Elevation gain: Less than 0.1 mile from the main trail to the edge of the bluff and trail's end
Distance: 0.3 mile (Option 1)
Difficulty: Easy due to short distance and minimal uneven terrain
Hiking time: About 18 minutes
Season/schedule: Open year-round; however, best time to hike is May through Oct
Fees and permits: None
Trail contacts: Iron County Development Zone, 100 Carly Rd., Hurley, WI 54534, (715) 561-2922, https://ironcountywi.com
Dog friendly: Yes
Trail surface: Dirt

Land status: County park
Nearest town: Hurley, WI
Maps: Superior Falls, MI
Other trail users: None
Special considerations: At the upper view of the falls, there is no guardrail keeping you from falling off the edge of the bluff. Be extremely cautious when hiking down to this viewpoint and back.
Amenities available: Porta-potty
Maximum grade: -29.7 percent sustained for less than 0.1 mile from the main trail down to the edge of the bluff
Cell service: Yes
Waterway: Montreal River
Waterfall beauty: 5
Accessibility: No

Finding the trailhead: From the intersection of US 51/2nd Avenue North and WI 77, head north on US 51 for 1.5 miles. At the traffic circle take the second exit onto WI 2/US 2 and head northwest on US 2 for 11.1 miles. Turn right (north) onto WI 122/Hoyt Road and drive for 4.2 miles, which will bring you into Michigan. Once you cross over into Michigan, the road becomes Lake Road/Lake Superior Road. Drive for 0.5 mile farther on Lake Road/Lake Superior Road and you'll arrive at an unnamed gravel road to your left. Turn left and drive for 0.1 mile and you'll arrive at the parking lot connected to the trailhead. Superior Falls is technically in Saxon, Wisconsin (Saxon, WI 54559); however, the parking lot and viewpoint is in Ironwood, Michigan (Ironwood, MI 49938). The trailhead for Option #1 is 0.01 mile southeast of the parking lot and is indicated by two wooden posts on either side and a connecting cable with an orange flag hanging from it. **Trailhead GPS:** N46° 33.841' W90° 24.897' (Option #1), N46° 33.898' W90° 24.927' (Option #2)

Trail conditions: It is a steep descent from the main trail to the bluff's edge where you'll find the best view of the falls from above. After it rains or when there are leaves on the ground, the trail may be quite slippery. The best view (and photo) of the upper falls requires getting very close to the muddy edge of the bluff.

View of the sitting area and viewpoint on the shores of Lake Superior

The Hike

Superior Falls is one of the tallest waterfalls in Wisconsin with an astounding height of 110 feet. It received its name due to its close proximity to Lake Superior and is on the awe-inspiring Montreal River, which creates a border between Michigan and Wisconsin. Superior Falls may be one of the most impressive waterfalls in Iron County. What is beautiful about this hiking trail is that it is connected to an easy-to-find parking lot and actually consists of two different trail options. Each trail leads you to separate but equally outstanding views of the falls. The first hike option leads you to the most popular viewpoint: a bluff's edge overlooking the falls from above. The second hike option leads you down a steep descent to the shores of Lake Superior and requires backtracking upriver. Both perspectives allow you to appreciate the gorgeous Montreal River and the tremendous size of the waterfall and surrounding gorge.

The trailhead for Option #2 is 0.04 mile northwest of the trailhead. The trailhead for Option #2 is indicated by two large concrete pillars and a very industrial-looking gate. The gate is usually closed and is large enough for an automobile to pass through. To the left of the gate is a trailhead: an entrance for hikers/anglers. From the trailhead walk southeast on the wide gravel path. The trail here is wide enough for an automobile or for two hikers to walk side by side. You'll notice a chain link fence on your right. In 0.1 mile you'll arrive at an Xcel Energy sign warning of the risk of rising water: turn right (west). You will begin to hear the sound of the falls. Follow the short trail down a hill for 0.02 mile to the bluff's edge. Your view will be obstructed by trees and you will not be able to see the falls clearly. Turn right (north) and walk for 0.02 mile and you'll arrive at a more appealing and less-obstructed view of the falls. To arrive back at the trailhead, walk back the way you came.

View of the falls from the base

Miles and Directions

0.0 From the trailhead walk southeast.

0.1 Arrive at the trail junction: turn right (west).

0.13 Arrive at the bluff's edge: turn right (north).

0.16 Arrive at the trail's end and view of the falls from above. Walk back the way you came.

0.32 Arrive back at the trailhead.

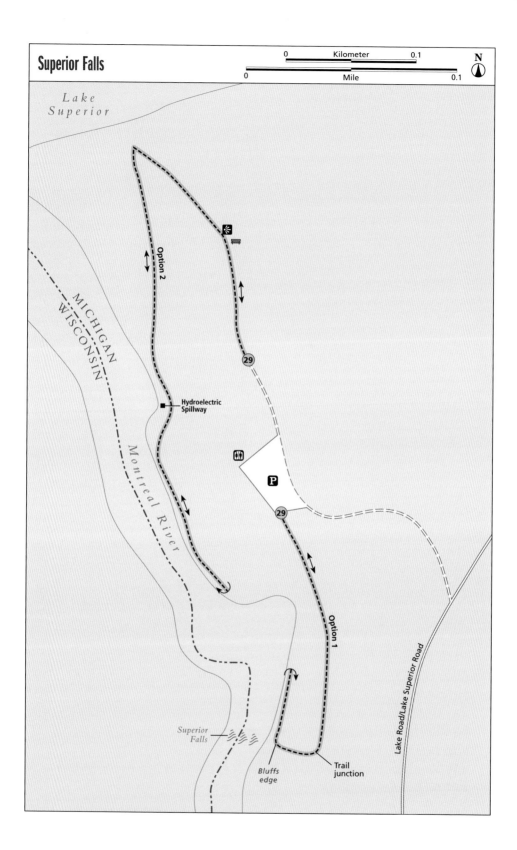

Superior Falls

0   Kilometer   0.1

0   Mile   0.1

N

Lake Superior

Option 2

MICHIGAN
WISCONSIN

Montreal River

Hydroelectric
Spillway

29

P

29

Option 1

Lake Road/Lake Superior Road

Superior Falls

Bluffs edge

Trail
junction

29 Superior Falls—Option #2

This impressive waterfall is one of the tallest in Wisconsin and drops a total of 110 feet across several levels. Two different hike options bring you to multiple vantage points, allowing you to appreciate the tremendous size of the falls and surrounding gorge.

Start: Intersection of US 51/2nd Avenue North and WI 77 in downtown Hurley, WI
Elevation gain: Less than 0.1 mile from the main trail to the edge of the bluff and trail's end
Distance: 0.6 miles
Difficulty: Difficult due to steep descent, jagged rocks, and uneven surfaces
Hiking time: About 1 hour 10 minutes
Season/schedule: Open year-round; however, best time to hike is May through Oct
Fees and permits: None
Trail contacts: Iron County Development Zone, 100 Carly Rd., Hurley, WI 54534, (715) 561-2922, https://ironcountywi.com
Dog friendly: Yes
Trail surface: Paved, dirt, and loose rock

Land status: County park
Nearest town: Hurley, WI
Maps: Superior Falls, MI
Other trail users: Anglers
Special considerations: The first 0.1 mile of the hike is a very steep descent. This may be slippery when it is wet or in the fall when it is covered in leaves.
Amenities available: Porta-potty
Maximum grade: -27.4% sustained for less than 0.1 mile from the first viewpoint down to the beach and river's edge where you take a sharp left
Cell service: Yes
Waterway: Montreal River
Waterfall beauty: 5
Accessibility: No

Finding the trailhead: From the intersection of US 51/2nd Avenue North and WI 77, head north on US 51 for 1.5 miles. At the traffic circle take the second exit onto WI 2/US 2 and head northwest on US 2 for 11.1 miles. Turn right (north) onto WI 122/Hoyt Road and drive for 4.2 miles, which will bring you into Michigan. Once you cross over into Michigan, the road becomes Lake Road/Lake Superior Road. Drive for 0.5 mile farther on Lake Road/Lake Superior Road and you'll arrive at an unnamed gravel road to your left. Turn left and drive for 0.1 mile and you'll arrive at the parking lot connected to the trailhead. Superior Falls is technically in Saxon, Wisconsin (Saxon, WI 54559); however, the parking lot and viewpoint is in Ironwood, Michigan (Ironwood, MI 49938). The trailhead for Option #2 is indicated by two large concrete pillars and a very industrial-looking gate. The gate is usually closed and is large enough for an automobile to pass through. **Trailhead GPS:** N46° 33.898' W90° 24.927' (Option #2)

View of the falls from the bluff's edge

The Hike

Superior Falls is one of the tallest waterfalls in Wisconsin with an astounding height of 110 feet. It received its name due to its close proximity to Lake Superior and is on the awe-inspiring Montreal River, which creates a border between Michigan and Wisconsin. Superior Falls may be one of the most impressive waterfalls in Iron County. What is beautiful about this hiking trail is that it is connected to an easy-to-find parking lot and actually consists of two different trail options. Each trail leads you to separate but equally outstanding views of the falls. The first hike option leads you to the most popular viewpoint: a bluff's edge overlooking the falls from above. The second hike option leads you down a steep descent to the shores of Lake Superior and requires backtracking upriver. Both perspectives allow you to appreciate the gorgeous Montreal River and the tremendous size of the waterfall and surrounding gorge.

From the parking area walk 0.04 mile northwest to arrive at the trailhead. The trailhead is indicated by two large concrete pillars and a very industrial-looking gate. The gate is usually closed and is large enough for an automobile to pass through. To the left of the gate is the trailhead: an entrance for hikers/anglers. From this trailhead walk north. In 0.05 mile you'll come to a fork in the trail equipped with a sitting bench. Follow the trail to the left as it descends steeply toward Lake Superior. The path is a combination of dirt, gravel, and concrete. There is a wire cable on your right side, which you can hold on to for support as you descend the steep path. In 0.05 mile you'll come to the bottom of the hill where you'll find a beautiful view of Lake Superior and a sitting bench. The trail makes a sharp hairpin turn left and heads south. Walk south along the river for 0.1 mile until you arrive at the hydroelectric spillway: turn right (southeast). The trail turns to concrete briefly before changing back to gravel and then dirt. Follow the path along the river until you arrive at the trail's end with a view of the falls in the distance. To arrive back at the trailhead, walk back the way you came. **Note:** It is possible to get closer to the falls for a better view; however, it involves climbing up, over, and around a section of loose jagged rocks that could be potentially dangerous. There are Xcel Energy signs informing you that changes in water level can happen rapidly. The close-up photos of the falls for this chapter were obtained by carefully climbing up, over, and around, uneven, crumbling, and jagged rock; however, this is not recommended or encouraged.

Miles and Directions (Option #2)

0.0 From the trailhead walk north.

0.05 Arrive at view of Lake Superior with a bench: turn left (northwest).

0.1 Arrive at a sharp turn in the trail: turn left (southeast).

0.2 Arrive at the hydroelectric spillway: turn right (southwest).

0.3 Arrive at the trail end. Walk back the way you came.

0.6 Arrive back at the trailhead.

30 Saxon Falls

Saxon Falls features a 90-foot drop on the gorgeous Montreal River creating another scenic waterfall on the Wisconsin/Michigan border. The scenic rocky gorge below the falls is believed to be one of the deepest in the Midwest.

Start: Intersection of US 51/2nd Avenue North and WI 77 in downtown Hurley, WI
Elevation gain: Less than 0.1 mile
Distance: 0.04 mile
Difficulty: Easy due to short distance and minimal uneven surfaces and no elevation change
Hiking time: About 2 minutes
Season/schedule: Open year-round, but best time to visit is May through Oct
Fees and permits: None
Trail contacts: Iron County Development Zone, 100 Cary Rd., Hurley, WI 54534, (715) 561-2922, www.ironcountywi.com
Dog friendly: Yes, no restrictions
Trail surface: Gravel and dirt
Land status: Xcel Energy property
Nearest town: Hurley, WI

Maps: USGS Saxon Falls Road, Saxon, WI 54559
Other trail users: Xcel Energy workers
Special considerations: This trail ends at a fenced-in overlook location on the edge of a steep cliff. For safety reasons, stay inside the fence.
Amenities available: Porta-potty
Maximum grade: 15.6 percent for less than 0.1 mile
Cell service: Yes
Waterway: Montreal River
Waterfall beauty: 4
Accessibility: Limited. The parking lot and the short trail consist of firmly packed dirt and gravel. There are no stairs or obstacles. With assistance, a wheelchair, stroller, or mobility device could navigate this trail.

Finding the trailhead: From the intersection of US 51/2nd Avenue North and WI 77, head north on US 51 for 1.5 miles. At the traffic circle take the second exit onto US 2 and head northwest on US 2 for 9.5 miles. Turn right (north) onto West CR B and drive for 2.4 miles. Turn left onto Saxon Falls Road (unpaved) and continue straight for 0.5 mile and you'll arrive at an unpaved parking area. Walk 0.01 mile northeast and you'll find the trailhead, which has a large sign that says "Saxon Falls Viewing Area." **Trailhead GPS:** N46° 32.151' W90 22.795'

Trail conditions: This is a short, easy-to-follow trail that leads you to an aerial view of the falls. This trail may become muddy and slippery when it rains, which makes it important to stay inside the fenced-in area when going near the cliff's edge.

Top: Aerial view of Saxon Falls at the trail's end
Bottom: Trying to capture the multiple tiers of the 90-foot falls

The Hike

The Montreal River is a stunning waterway that winds its way northeast and consists of wild rocky outcroppings, steep-sided canyons, and multiple waterfalls that range from pretty rapids to thunderous cascades. In some areas the canyon walls of the Montreal River reach heights of up to 300 feet, making its rugged scenery among the best in Wisconsin. Pine, spruce, and hemlock cover the steep canyon slopes, while birch and aspen cling to stone pedestals high up and the tops of cliffs. Visitors to the Montreal River are usually treated to stunning views that exist both inside its canyon walls as well as from viewpoints high above it. Saxon Falls features a 90-foot drop on the grand untamed river, creating another scenic waterfall on the Wisconsin/Michigan border.

From the trailhead follow the short, forested hike along the chain link fence to the designated overlook. Saxon Falls isn't just one waterfall; it is actually a series of about three fast-moving falls that progressively drop over approximately 90 feet. The visual spectacle presents as something of a natural waterpark. From the designated viewpoint at the end of the trail, you get an aerial view of the falls, a unique perspective you don't usually get of gorges and waterfalls. With this bird's-eye view from the trail's end, you are able to see the Montreal River Canyon at the base of the falls and better understand its beauty and complexity. According to the Iron County Development Zone, this beautiful rocky gorge is one of the deepest in the Midwest. To arrive back at the trailhead, return the way you came. The Montreal River Canyon is a popular spot for advanced whitewater paddlers and is considered by many to be one of the premier whitewater paddling spots in the Upper Midwest. Some of the canyon runs are up to 3 miles in length and include paddling over potentially dangerous rapids, falls, and edges. The features that make this gorge and waterfall scene so spectacular are also what creates its draw for adventure sports enthusiasts.

This hike connects private land, nature, and the community. Similar to Superior Falls (Hike 29), Xcel Energy owns the land in and around the Saxon Falls Project boundaries. A huge utility company such as Xcel could have easily blocked this view off with high fences and large No Trespassing signs. Instead of partitioning off this woodland path and tremendous view, they have created a hiking trail and safe overlook for the general public to enjoy. In a way Xcel Energy is expressing their appreciation for nature in a display that shows they understand how important the wild outdoors and waterfall views are to the physical and mental health of a community.

A close-up of Saxon Falls's heavy whitewater hidden behind trees ▶

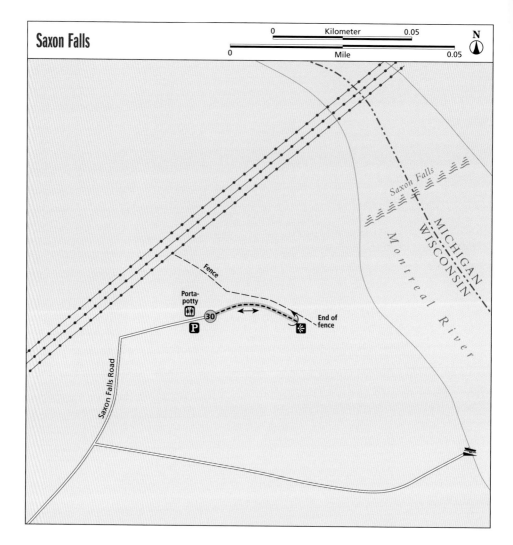

Miles and Directions

0.0 From the trailhead walk northeast along the fence.

0.02 Arrive at the trail's end. Return the way you came.

0.04 Arrive back at the trailhead.

31 Kimball Falls

This short hike brings you to a bridge view of the fast and rocky Montreal River and the quaint but attractive Kimball Falls. This trail offers hikers multiple options to explore a woodsy park offering bird-watching, fishing, and a variety of scenic views.

Start: Intersection of US 51/2nd Avenue North and WI 77 in downtown Hurley, WI

Elevation gain: Negligible

Distance: 0.02 mile

Difficulty: Easy due to short distance and no uneven or rugged terrain

Hiking time: About 1 minute

Season/schedule: The park is open year-round from 6 a.m. to 10 p.m.; however, the best time to hike is May through Oct.

Fees and permits: None

Trail contacts: Northwoods Land Trust, northwoodslandtrust.org, Town of Kimball, Iron County, (715) 561-4200

Dog friendly: Yes, on leashes

Trail surface: Gravel and bridge

Land status: Land trust

Nearest town: Hurley, WI

Maps: USGS Kimball, WI

Other trail users: None

Special considerations: None

Amenities available: Pit toilet, picnic area, playground

Maximum grade: 0.0 percent

Cell service: Yes

Waterway: Montreal River

Waterfall beauty: 1

Accessibility: Yes

Finding the trailhead: From the intersection of US 51/2nd Avenue North and WI 77 in downtown Hurley, WI, head north on WI 51/2nd Avenue for 1.5 miles. At the traffic circle take the second exit onto US 2 (northwest) and drive for 3.4 miles. Turn left (south) onto Park Road and drive for 0.2 mile. Turn right (west) onto West Town Park Drive and go for 0.2 mile and you'll arrive at a parking area connected to the trailhead, which is directly across the street from Kimball Park. Note that on some maps US 51 is also labeled Korean War Veterans Memorial Highway. **Trailhead GPS:** N46° 29.157' W90° 15.810'

Trail conditions: This is a well-maintained trail that is part of a town park. Once you cross the bridge, which goes over the waterfall, there is a gravel loop trail that brings you through a quaint park where you'll find multiple scenic views of Kimball Falls and the Montreal River.

The Hike

Kimball Falls is on the banks of the Montreal River in a tree-shaded public park. This short out-and-back hike brings you to a bridge over the river placing you directly above the falls. The trail then continues onto an optional lollipop loop through Kimball Town Park featuring amenities such as vault toilets, a picnic area, playground, basketball court, and multiple viewing areas with sitting benches.

What make this park and its well-preserved scenery unique is that it is part of the Northwoods Land Trust (NWLT), a nonprofit that promotes conservation by private

Top: Kimball Falls and the scenic footbridge from downstream northwest of the falls
Bottom: The highlight of this hike: Kimball Falls, just below the bridge

One of the many scenic viewpoints in Kimball Park where hikers can pause to admire the Montreal River

landowners of natural shorelands, woodlands, wetlands, and other natural resources. As a result, natural areas such as Kimball Falls are kept safe from development and the public benefits from having access to these protected wild spaces.

The slithery Montreal River has fast rapids, curvaceous rocky banks, slow muddy pools, and ornamental waterfalls. In and near the river is an abundance of fauna, making its preserved shores and wetlands excellent places for hiking and wildlife sightings. Aged maple and birch provide nest sites for woodpeckers, owls, nuthatches, and flying squirrels. Some trees in the park supply birds with fruits and seeds for feeding on, while others offer perching places for insect-eating birds who skim the surrounding area. Salamanders, frogs, and small mammals can be found hiding under decaying forest matter, while snakes and turtles may be perched on large rocks basking in the sun. Kimball Town Park is a destination worth a visit, offering up a local waterfall and multiple options for enjoyable nature hikes.

From the trailhead walk southwest. In less than 0.1 mile you'll arrive at a bridge with a view of the upper falls and a view of Kimball Town Park. Continue walking southwest and you'll discover a lollipop loop trail that brings you through the park and back to the bridge. On both the east and west sides of the river, you have the option of walking downstream (northwest) and observing the falls as they come out underneath the bridge. The main attraction here is a series of modest falls that begin above the bridge and end below it. During the autumn months these falls are framed by vibrant fall colors, making the Montreal River and Kimball Town Park particularly beautiful.

Top: The Montreal River just below Kimball Falls as it meanders its way toward Lake Superior
Bottom: The colorful Montreal River as it approaches Kimball Falls

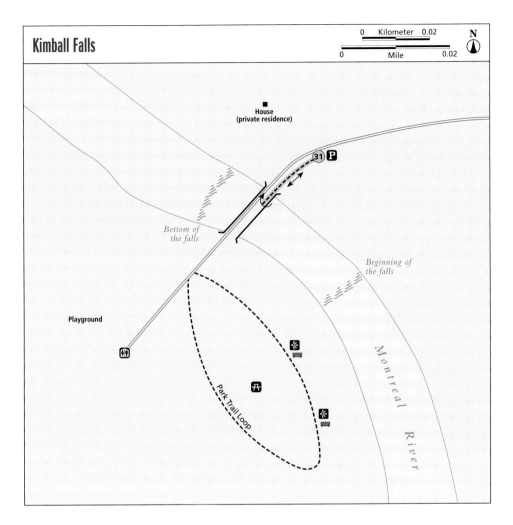

Miles and Directions

0.0 From the trailhead walk southwest.

0.01 Arrive at the bridge and view of the falls. Walk back the way you came.

0.02 Arrive back at the trailhead.

32 Interstate Falls

The east branch of the Montreal River spills over a cluster of rocks. A short but secluded nature trail leads you to a viewing deck, sitting benches, and a close-up view of the falls.

Start: Intersection of US 51/2nd Avenue North and WI 77 in downtown Hurley, WI

Elevation gain: The last 1.5 miles of the hike is an elevation change of 0.05 mile as you descend to the viewing deck in front of the falls.

Distance: 0.8 mile

Difficulty: Moderate due to length and somewhat hilly terrain

Hiking time: About 40 minutes

Season/schedule: Open year-round. This is a popular winter hike, but snowshoes are recommended due to deep snow and icy conditions.

Fees and permits: None

Trail contacts: Northwoods Land Trust, northwoodslandtrust.org, Town of Kimball, Iron County, (715) 561-4200

Dog friendly: Yes, no restrictions

Trail surface: Dirt and gravel

Land status: Land trust

Nearest town: Hurley, WI

Maps: USGS Kimball, WI

Other trail users: This trail is also open to hunters, foragers, anglers, and cross-country skiers.

Special considerations: Parts of this trail may be slippery when it rains or during the cold-weather months.

Amenities available: Porta-potty and picnic area

Maximum grade: −16.2 percent during the last 0.1 mile of the hike as you descend to the viewing platform in front of the falls

Cell service: Yes

Waterway: Montreal River

Waterfall beauty: 4

Accessibility: No

Finding the trailhead: From the intersection of US 51/2nd Avenue North and WI 77 in downtown Hurley, WI, head north on US 51/2nd Avenue North and drive for 1.5 miles. At the traffic circle, take the second exit onto US 2 West and drive for 0.6 mile until you come to Center Drive. Turn right (northeast) onto Center Drive and in 0.2 mile you'll arrive at an unpaved parking area. Turn left (north) into the parking area and you'll see a sign for the Interstate Falls Trailhead. **Trailhead GPS**: N46° 28.376' / W90° 11.958'

Trail conditions: Well maintained but muddy when it rains and icy in the wintertime. This trail is also used for anglers, cross-country skiers, hunters, and foragers.

Top: The Montreal River creating a display of beauty and enchantment
Bottom: Interstate Falls from downstream

The Hike

Interstate Falls is an 18-foot waterfall on the Montreal River, which creates a border between Michigan and Wisconsin. This is one of four popular falls on the Montreal River, which include Peterson, Saxon (Hike 30), and Superior (Hike 29). What's interesting about the rocky and rugged nature of a river adorned with so many beautiful falls is that the Ojibwe used to call it *Kawasiji-wangsepi*, which translates to White Falls River. The river was far too wild to paddle as a result of epic rock structures and waterfalls such as Interstate Falls. Allegedly Native Americans and French fur traders would portage the 42-mile Flambeau Trail to get from the mouth of the Montreal River to Long Lake in Iron County.

The rock you see as a part of these falls is from billion-year-old lava that was able to reach the surface of the earth as a result of a continental rift. This 1,200-mile arch-shaped rift extends from Detroit up through Michigan's Lower Peninsula, across Lake Superior, and then down the Wisconsin-Minnesota border. More information about the Montreal River and its geology can be found on the bulletin board at the trailhead for Interstate Falls.

Similar to Kimball Falls (Hike 31), this waterfall exists as part of the Northwoods Land Trust (NWLT), a nonprofit that promotes conservation by private landowners of natural shorelands, woodlands, wetlands, and other natural resources. As a result, natural areas such as Interstate Falls are kept safe from development and the public benefits from having access to these wild spaces and beautiful views.

From the trailhead walk east on the trail. You'll cross a bridge and in 0.07 mile you'll arrive at a trail junction with a sign directing you to your left (northwest) for Interstate Falls. Turn left (northwest) and continue on the forested trail for 0.2 mile. The trail is made of dirt rocks and tree roots and goes through a shaded pine forest. You'll pass multiple sitting benches on this trail before you arrive at a viewpoint with a picnic table. Turn left (west) and follow the trail along a wooden fence as it descends downhill and then back up again where it arrives at a set of stairs. Walk down the stairs (thirty in total) and you'll arrive at a wooden viewing platform with a sitting bench just northwest of the falls. An additional seven stairs will bring you down to the river's edge. For the best view of the falls, take your socks and shoes off and wade out to the island in the middle of the river. This will place you directly in front of the falls for some perfect photos.

Bonus Hike/Waterfall: A short distance upstream from Interstate Falls is a small, but pretty waterfall called Peterson Falls. In many online and written accounts, this modest waterfall is mistaken for Interstate Falls and is documented incorrectly. It is a separate waterfall and is part of the same hike for anyone interested in exploring further. Peterson Falls is open to the public, but located on private land.

Top: *A view of Interstate Falls from an island in the center of the Montreal River*
Bottom: *View of the falls from above*

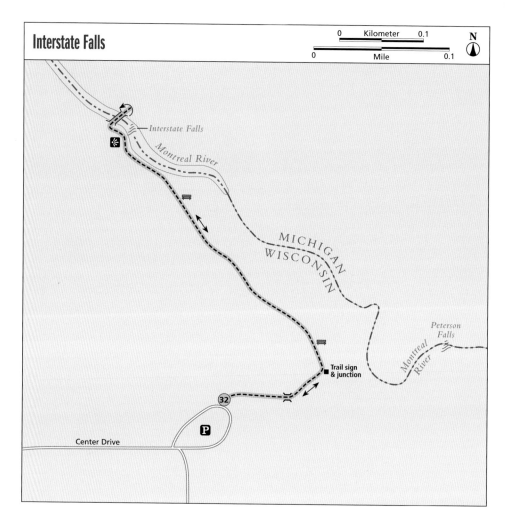

Interstate Falls

0 Kilometer 0.1
0 Mile 0.1

N

Interstate Falls

Montreal River

MICHIGAN
WISCONSIN

Peterson Falls

Montreal River

Trail sign & junction

32

Center Drive

P

Miles and Directions

0.0 From the trailhead walk east.

0.07 Arrive at a trail junction with sign: turn left (northwest).

0.3 Arrive at viewpoint and picnic spot. Turn left (west).

0.35 Arrive at the stairs to the falls. Descend thirty stairs.

0.4 Arrive at the trail end with scenic viewing platform. Walk back the way you came.

0.8 Arrive back at the trailhead.

Northeastern Wisconsin

This quadrant of the state introduces hundreds of acres of dense forest, incredible rivers, and unique geological structures. Combine these elements with a diversity of gradients and you get an abundance of scenic and fun-to-hike-to waterfalls. So many, in fact, that one county in this part of the state refers to itself as the "waterfall capital" of Wisconsin while another county proclaims itself "nature's waterpark." Wisconsin stands back to back with Michigan's Upper Peninsula. Wild rivers with even more wild nature corridors populate this quadrant. The rugged nature hikes are just as exciting as the stunning water features they lead you to. Many of the waterfall hikes in this section require maneuvering on backcountry gravel roads through dense and shady forests. To discover many of these secluded gems requires an adventurous and exploratory spirit. The result is fewer tourists and more opportunities to steal away to solitude.

Northeastern Wisconsin offers up some of the state's most popular escapes and vacation spots for nature lovers. More than 400 miles of Great Lakes shoreline make up the eastern edge as the state collides with one of the world's largest and deepest freshwater lakes: Lake Michigan. Rare birch and pine forests intersect with bogs, swamps, flowages, creeks, and streams creating a spongy water-saturated environment. Cliffs of volcanic rock outcroppings embedded with ancient fossils create scenic views and the backdrop for curtains of cascading water. The shared ecozones of Wisconsin and Michigan's Upper Peninsula combined with the landscape of abundant flowing H_2O results in some serious beauty. A sighting of an elk, black bear, timber wolf, or moose and you may just feel like you are deep in the Canadian wilderness. This scenic part of the state offers loads of opportunities to get lost in nature and stay there for as long as you wish.

33 Dells of the Eau Claire Falls

This picturesque stretch of the Eau Claire River features multiple waterfalls cascading over unusual formations of protruding bedrock. The opportunities to climb rocks and find stunning views seem endless in this lesser-known county park.

Start: Intersection of 6th and Jefferson in downtown Wausau

Elevation gain: Negligible

Distance: 0.08 mile

Difficulty: Easy due to short distance and easy-to-descend concrete stairs

Hiking time: About 2 minutes

Season/schedule: The county park is open year-round; however, the falls are best enjoyed Apr through Oct. This park is particularly beautiful during the fall when the leaves are changing colors.

Fees and permits: None

Trail contacts: P2150 CR Y, Aniwa, WI 54408, (715) 261-1550, https://www.co.marathon.wi.us/Departments/ParksRecreationForestry.aspx

Dog friendly: Yes, on leashes

Trail surface: Paved

Land status: County park

Nearest town: Wausau, WI

Maps: USGS Dells of the Eau Claire River, WI

Other trail users: During the warm-weather months, this trail is primarily used by hikers and visitors of the Dells and waterfalls. During the fall months the county park is open to hunters.

Special considerations: A sturdy pair of athletic footwear is encouraged for anyone looking to climb the rocks. When it rains the rocks are sometimes muddy and slippery.

Amenities available: Vault toilets, picnic shelter, camping, hand pump water, and swimming beach

Maximum grade: From the top of the stairs to the designated outlook, there is a maximum grade of -16.7 percent. This is sustained for less than 0.05 mile.

Cell service: Limited

Waterway: Eau Claire River

Waterfall beauty: 5

Accessibility: Yes. A large paved path connects the parking lot to the designated lookout and main viewing area of the falls.

Finding the trailhead: From the intersection of 6th and Jefferson Streets in downtown Wausau, drive north on 6th Street for 0.2 mile. Turn right onto CR Z/Franklin Street and drive for 14.4 miles. Turn left onto CR Y and in 1.5 miles you'll arrive at the entrance to the county park. The entrance road will guide you right to the parking lot connected to the trailhead. The address to the county park is P2150 CR Y, Aniwa, WI 54408. The trailhead is in the southwest corner of the paved parking lot. You'll see a large bulletin board, trail map, and a paved trail heading southwest toward the river. **Trailhead GPS:** N45° 00.326' W89' 20.267'

Trail conditions: A paved walkway and wide concrete stairs bring you right down to the main viewing area. No special footwear is required. In the cold-weather months, the stairs may be snow covered and icy.

Above: A view of three different falls as the Eau Claire flows around the various scenic conglomerates
Below: Jagged rocks and shallow swimming holes perfect for climbing and then cooling off

The Hike

Dells of the Eau Claire Falls isn't one singular waterfall as much as it is a plethora of miniature falls and rapids as this flamboyant waterway flows through a rocky gorge and passes over weathered boulders and outcroppings. The beautiful rock formations or "Dells" are the magnet for hikers and waterfall enthusiasts during the warm-weather months. What you're looking at is a type of very hard ancient volcanic rock called Precambrian rhyolite schist, which was formed billions of years ago. The protruding conglomerate formations have been shaped by the grinding actions of sand and gravel as the river flows through and around them. The result is a topography of ridges, towers, fissures, and potholes: a skyline of colorful, tilted jagged stone formations. One great thing about this natural attraction is that you are allowed to climb among the ancient volcanic rocks and wade or swim in the various channels and swimming holes.

The rocky gorge and forested area of this county park is wooded with a northern mesic forest of hemlock, sugar maple, yellow birch, and mountain maple: an excellent place for sightseeing, wildlife viewing, and bird-watching. The park contains 5 miles of hiking trails, many of which run parallel to each other on both sides of the river. Three miles of these trails are part of the Ice Age National Scenic Trail. Dells of the Eau Claire Falls County Park contains many old-growth trees, mainly Canadian hardwood species, which can be very large in diameter.

To arrive at the most scenic view of the falls, walk southwest from the parking area. In 0.01 mile you'll arrive at a set of stairs. Walk down the thirty-four stairs and you come to a designated lookout. This observation point gives you the most comprehensive view of the dells and its various cascades and rapids. To return to the trailhead, walk back the way you came. You also have the option of walking in either direction (east or west) to find beautiful views of the landscape, riverside hiking trails, and many opportunities for wildlife sightings.

Turn right (west) from the designated lookout and you'll find a trail that leads you along the high bluffs that frame the north banks of the Eau Claire River. This places you on the Ice Age Trail and brings you to multiple high elevation viewpoints with sitting benches to overlook the rock palisades from downriver (west). This section of the Ice Age Trail is also connected to hiking paths of different lengths, which loop back to the parking lot and trailhead.

If you turn left from the designated lookout, you head east on the Ice Age Trail (labeled North River Trail within the park). This leads you down to the river's edge where you can climb out on the rock formations and explore the various waterfalls from different angles. This trail continues upriver (east) and brings you to the park's campsites, a walking bridge, and a bonus waterfall. A dam that runs the entire width of the river creates a small industrial spillway. It's not as picturesque as the dells downriver, but still an elegant scene of falling water surrounded by nature. Just east of the dam is a beautiful beach and swimming area. The hiking trails in Dells of the Eau Claire County Park are well maintained and easy to follow. Trail maps are posted throughout the park and can also be found online.

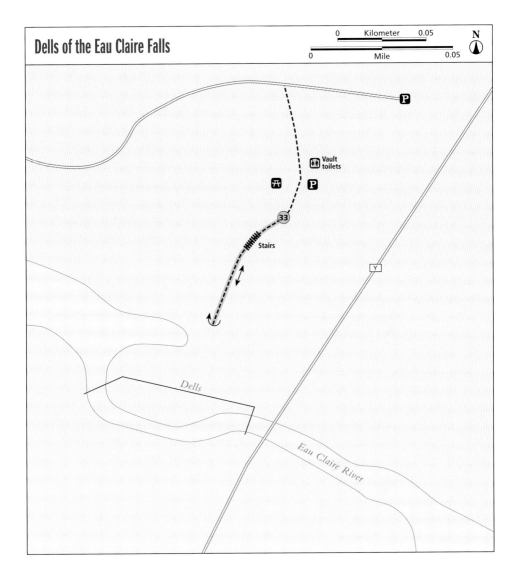

Dells of the Eau Claire Falls

0   Kilometer   0.05

0   Mile   0.05

N

Vault toilets

33

Stairs

Y

Dells

Eau Claire River

Miles and Directions

0.0 From the trailhead walk southwest.

0.04 Arrive at the designated lookout with a view of the dells. Walk back the way you came.

0.08 Arrive back at the trailhead.

*Top: A view from downstream as the river flows through ridges and towers of rock
Bottom: The rocky dells from a scenic viewpoint high up on a bluff*

34 Big Bull Falls

The Popple River splits around a wild and barbarous island creating a series of different-sized cascades. Large moss-covered boulders decorate the banks and floodplains of the river, creating scenic views in all directions.

Start: Intersection of WI 2 (Central Avenue) and CR N (Quinnesec Street) in Florence, WI

Elevation gain: Less than 0.1 mile

Distance: 0.4 mile

Difficulty: Moderate due to length and rugged terrain

Hiking time: About 16 minutes

Season/schedule: Open year-round. Hiking is best May through Oct, though winter waterfalls make excellent photographs.

Fees and permits: None

Trail contacts: Florence County Forestry and Parks, 5617 Forestry Dr., Florence, WI 54121, (715) 528-3207, exploreflorencecounty.com

Dog friendly: Yes, on leashes

Trail surface: Grass, dirt, and gravel

Land status: County forest

Nearest town: Florence, WI

Maps: USGS Popple River

Other trail users: Anglers

Special considerations: Once you turn west off of WI 101, you are on backcountry gravel roads that have little to no signage. In this case, there is not ample signage directing you to Big Bull Falls like you'll find for LaSalle Falls (Hike 37) and Breakwater Falls (Hike 38), and the majority of the forks, trails, intersections, and turnoffs are unmarked. Many of these intersecting roads are ATV trails, logging roads, or private drives. Maps can be found at the Wild Rivers Interpretive Center and their use is encouraged. The Wild Rivers Interpretive Center is at 5638 Forestry Dr., Florence, WI 54121. Big Bull Falls can be found on Google Maps and many other popular smartphone mapping applications. The roads that lead to Big Bull Falls are primarily dirt and gravel and sporadically contain large rocks and potholes. During the spring thaw and during wet periods, the roads may be difficult to drive on. The trailhead can be reached carefully with a small automobile; however, a high-clearance (preferably four-wheel-drive) vehicle is best. The lands surrounding these falls are open to the public, but are part of a private forest management program. Driving on these back roads may be difficult during logging operations.

Amenities available: None

Maximum grade: –6.4 percent. This hike has two short descents where the maximum grade is –6.4 percent, which lasts for less than 0.1 mile.

Cell service: No

Waterway: Popple River

Waterfall beauty: 2

Accessibility: No

Finding the trailhead: From the intersection of WI 2 (Central Avenue) and CR N (Quinnesec Street) in Florence, head west on US 2 for 0.3 mile. Turn left (southwest) onto WI 70 and drive for 2.4 miles. Turn left (south) onto WI 101 and drive for 10.6 miles. Just north of the Popple River off of WI 101, you will see a sign for Big Bull Falls: turn left (west). This is West River Road. Drive for 0.6 mile on West River Road and you will see a sign for Big Bull Falls trailhead on your left (south) and a parking lot to your right (north). Park in the unpaved parking area and walk less than 0.1 mile south to the trailhead. **Trailhead GPS:** N54° 47.996' W88° 24.514'

Trail conditions: The trail is a well-maintained and easy-to-follow path of dirt and grass through a heavily wooded area. There are no major elevation changes; however, the path does consist of occasional rocks and tree roots. The trail may become muddy and slippery when it rains or covered in snow or ice during the cold-weather months. A sturdy pair of athletic shoes or hiking footwear is encouraged.

The Hike

Waterfall hiking/hunting is an excellent activity to bring you into nature and enjoy the health-promoting and longevity benefits of the great outdoors. Research is continuing to show that being in nature can boost your mood and improve mental health. It reduces stress, calms anxiety, and can lead to lower risk of depression. Consider the hike to Big Bull Falls a wonderful tool to support your mental health and overall well-being. This hike is one of those beautiful outdoor experiences that make you think, "Florence County, *another* pleasant nature hike that ends at a stunning waterfall? Well done!"

This 0.4-mile out-and-back hike brings you on a hiking path with natural scenery typical of the Popple River Corridor. One-hundred-year-old white and red pine tower overhead, while Canada mayflower, big leaf aster, and north-bush honeysuckle frame the narrow trail on both sides. As you near the falls, you begin to see large boulders along the banks and floodplains, the major contributing factors to what make the waterfalls and river views so appealing. The Popple River Corridor is a complex region of wetlands and uplands that create dense and beautiful forests perfect for a nature stroll.

Big Bull Falls are formed by the presence of an island in the middle of the Popple River. The north channel creates the 7-foot main attraction here, while the south channel forms a cascade of smaller, but equally pretty falls. From the trailhead walk southeast. The path is a well-defined and easy-to-follow trail of trampled dirt, leaves, pine needles, and tree roots. The trail meanders through the forest until you arrive at the trail's end with a view of the falls. Along the path the main trail intersects with multiple offshoot trails to your left (east), which lead you down the river's edge for some epic views. Continue past all the trail junctions and offshoots until you arrive at the falls. The trail ends at a viewpoint just above the falls where you have unbelievable scenery in all directions, including overlooking the falls from above where the tannin-colored water spills over the mammoth rocks. To get a view of the falls from the front, take one of the unofficial rustic trails downstream (northeast), and you'll find multiple views from the river's edge looking upstream at the falls. On the west bank of the river are massive rocks sitting decoratively on the shores creating small flat-top bluffs. These colossal tabletop perches create perfect places to sit and relax, listen to the falls, enjoy a picnic, or read a book. To arrive back at the trailhead, return the way you came.

Above: View of the falls and the rocky bluff from downstream
Below: The turbulent falls, foamy river, and scenic rock formations of Big Bull Falls

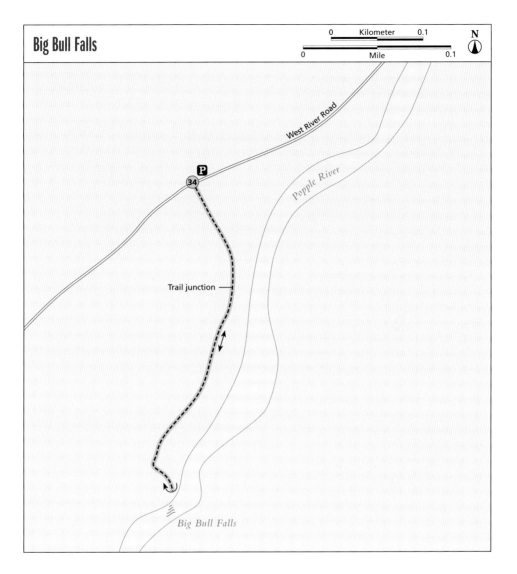

Miles and Directions

0.0 From the trailhead walk southeast.

0.2 Arrive at the end with a view of the falls. Walk back the way you came.

0.4 Arrive back at the trailhead.

Above: Looking north on the Popple River from above the falls
Below: A view of the tranquil river far north of the falls

35 Meyers Falls

This quaint yet intricate waterfall offers scenic views from multiple different vantage points. A short out-and-back hike brings you to a small canyon-like environment with modest-size bluffs on the vigorous Pine River.

Start: Intersection of WI 2 (Central Avenue) and CR N (Quinnesec Street) in Florence, WI

Elevation gain: Less than 0.1 mile

Distance: 0.4 mile

Difficulty: Easy due to short distance and flat even terrain

Hiking time: About 30 minutes

Season/schedule: Open year-round. Hiking is best May through Oct; however, trails are open year-round and winter waterfalls make excellent photographs.

Fees and permits: None

Trail contacts: Florence County Forestry and Parks, 5617 Forestry Dr., Florence, WI 54121, (715) 528-3207, exploreflorencecounty.com

Dog friendly: Yes, on leashes

Trail surface: Grass, dirt, and gravel

Land status: County forest

Nearest town: Florence, WI

Maps: USGS Pine River Flowage, WI

Other trail users: Anglers

Special considerations: Once you turn west off of WI 101, you are on backcountry gravel roads that have little to no signage. In this case, there is not ample signage directing you to Meyers Falls like you'll find for LaSalle Falls (Hike 37) and Breakwater Falls (Hike 38), and the majority of the forks, trails, intersections,

and turnoffs are unmarked. Many of these intersecting roads are ATV trails, logging roads, or private drives. Maps can be found at the Wild Rivers Interpretive Center and their use is encouraged. The Wild Rivers Interpretive Center is at 5638 Forestry Dr., Florence, WI 54121. Meyers Falls can be found on Google Maps and many other popular smartphone mapping applications. The roads that lead to Meyers Falls are primarily dirt and gravel and sporadically contain large rocks and potholes. During the spring thaw and during wet periods, the roads may be difficult to drive on. The trailhead can be reached carefully with a small automobile; however, a high-clearance (preferably four-wheel-drive) vehicle is ideal. The lands surrounding these falls are open to the public, but are part of a private forest management program. Driving on these back roads may be difficult during logging operations.

Amenities available: None

Maximum grade: –215 percent for less than 0.1 mile

Cell service: Limited

Waterway: Pine River

Waterfall beauty: 2

Accessibility: No

Finding the trailhead: From the intersection of US 2 (Central Avenue) and CR N, head west on US 2 for 0.3 mile. Turn left (southwest) on WI 70. Go for 2.4 miles and you'll come to an intersection with WI 101: turn left on WI 101 (south). Drive for 6.7 miles and just as WI 101 begins to curve south you'll see a gravel road straight ahead (west) labeled Norway Price Lake Road (on Google Maps it is just labeled Price Lake Road): continue straight. Here is where you begin the next 5.8 miles on backcountry dirt and gravel roads. Drive straight on Norway Price Lake Road for 0.2 mile until you come to a sharp right turn (northeast): turn right. This is also considered Pine Lake Road Drive, but there is no signage. After you turn right (northeast) the road zigzags a bit and it becomes one lane, which can be problematic if someone is driving in the opposite direction. Take precautions! Drive 1.4 miles and you'll come to a fork in the road: stay right (to the left is a private driveway). At this fork you will also see a sign cautioning you, "end town road and snowmobile route." Continue driving past the sign for 1.1 miles and you'll arrive at a second fork in the road: stay left. In 0.9 mile you'll pass a sign welcoming you to the Pine-Popple area. Continue past the sign for 1.1 miles and you'll come to an intersecting road with a sign stating "Lake Access" if you turn right: do not turn right, continue straight. In 0.6 mile you'll arrive at an intersection with signs stating "Pine River Access" to your right and "Meyers Falls" straight ahead. Continue straight for 0.6 mile and you'll arrive at the parking area and trailhead for Meyers Falls. **Trailhead GPS:** N45° 53.933' W88° 26.013'

Trail conditions: Good. Flat and well maintained, but quite possibly muddy and slippery when it rains. The trail may also be covered in snow or ice during the cold-weather months.

The Hike

This is a short hike that brings you to a pretty 7-foot cascade where the lively Pine River narrows, and the brandy-colored water is forced through rocky bluffs and over a scenic outcropping. Here nature has created a dynamic and turbulent waterslide that is both soothing to listen to and visually appealing to gaze at.

Meyers Falls is one of the select waterfalls that are part of the federally safeguarded Pine-Popple Wild Area. What makes this area so special for hiking enthusiasts and nature lovers is that 33 miles of the Pine River is protected by the Department of Natural Resources and is being kept in a natural free-flowing condition. The area is rugged and undeveloped, creating a truly wild experience for adventure seekers. The Pine River is one of Wisconsin's more remote rivers as is this waterfall and the hike to arrive at it. Finding the trailhead may seem challenging, but the payoff is getting to visit this preserved natural area that delivers you to the doorstep of an attractive and out-of-the-way waterfall.

From the trailhead begin walking northwest. You'll notice the trail is maintained but not packed down from frequent foot travel. At the beginning of the hike, the trail is grass and both sides of the trail are framed by wild dandelion, burdock, buffalo grass, and young maple. The forest canopy is less dense at the start, which allows sunlight into the forest floor creating a vibrant green understory. After a short distance (less than 0.1 mile), the trail enters a thick-wooded forest with a more substantial canopy and you begin to hear the roaring sounds of the falls. The path continues to be wide, well maintained, and easy to follow. The trail leads you right to the falls, where you'll see two very attractive outcroppings. Huge boulders emerge from the forest floor and frame the river on all sides constructing gorge-like walls. The river shoots between the bluffs before foaming and crashing into the lower portion of the Pine River. These falls and the surrounding area become jaw-dropping river scenes you might expect in the mountains of Wyoming or Montana, but not in northern Wisconsin. Approaching the waterfall, the Pine River is peaceful and framed by forest on all sides. The waterfall is the end of the designated hiking trail; however, there is potential to hike up and down the river from this point. The trails that head upriver and downriver offer plenty of opportunities to climb the bluffs or enjoy the falls from different vantage points. Take precautions since the bluffs can be quite steep and slippery and have no railings. To return to the trailhead, hike back the way you came.

The peaceful Pine River rapids just before Meyers Falls

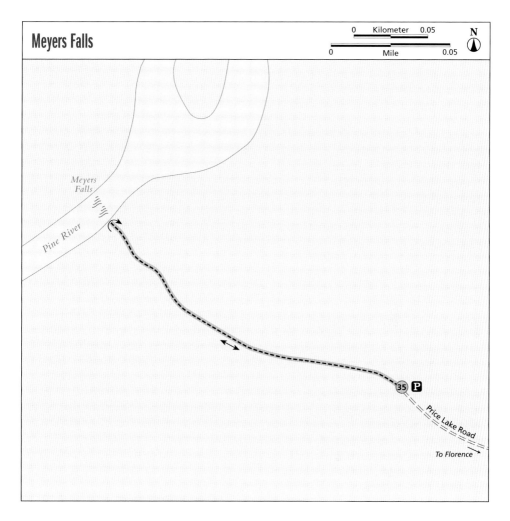

Meyers Falls

Meyers
Falls

Pine River

35 🅿

Price Lake Road

To Florence →

Miles and Directions

0.0 From the trailhead walk northwest.

0.2 Arrive at the trail end. Return the way you came.

0.4 Arrive back at the trailhead.

◀ *Top: Taking in the entire breadth of Meyers Falls from a vantage point downstream*
Bottom: A view of the falls from a rock outcropping

36 Washburn Falls

Washburn Falls is one of the most scenic and peaceful views in Florence County. A secluded forest trail leads you to a truly tranquil viewpoint and sitting area directly next to the falls.

Start: Intersection of WI 2 (Central Avenue) and CR N (Quinnesec Street) in Florence, WI

Elevation gain: Less than 0.1 mile

Distance: 0.16 mile

Difficulty: Easy due to short distance and flat easy terrain

Hiking time: About 10 minutes

Season/schedule: Open year-round. Hiking is best May through Oct, though winter waterfalls make excellent photographs.

Fees and permits: None

Trail contacts: Florence County Forestry and Parks, 5617 Forestry Dr., Florence, WI 54121, (715) 528-3207, exploreflorencecounty.com

Dog friendly: Yes, on leashes

Trail surface: Grass, dirt, and gravel

Land status: County forest

Nearest town: Florence, WI

Maps: USGS Popple River Flowage, WI

Other trail users: Anglers

Special considerations: Once you turn west off of CR 101, you are on backcountry gravel roads that have little to no signage. And to complicate things further, on all sides of the road are ATV trails, logging roads, and private drives that intersect with the main, but unmarked, roads. You will encounter many signs directing you toward Washburn Falls; however, the parking lot for Washburn Falls is unmarked. Maps can be found at the Wild Rivers Interpretive Center and their use is encouraged. The Wild Rivers Interpretive Center is at 5638 Forestry Dr., Florence, WI 54121. Washburn Falls can be found on Google Maps and many other popular smartphone mapping applications. If you use a GPS unit or mapping app/device and follow the signs to Washburn Falls, you shouldn't get lost. The roads that lead to Washburn Falls are primarily dirt and gravel and sporadically contain large rocks and potholes. During the spring thaw and during wet periods, the roads may be difficult to drive on. The trailhead can be reached with a small car; however, a high-clearance (preferably four-wheel-drive) vehicle is ideal. The lands surrounding these falls are open to the public, but are part of a private forest management program. Driving on these back roads may be difficult during logging operations.

Amenities available: None

Maximum grade: –215 percent for less than 0.1 mile

Cell service: Limited

Waterway: Popple River

Waterfall beauty: 2

Accessibility: No

Finding the trailhead: From the intersection of WI 2 (Central Avenue) and CR N (Quinnesec Street) in downtown Florence, head south on CR N (Quinnesec Street) for 9.5 miles. Turn right (west) on CR C and drive for 6.9 miles. Just after passing a large sign for Florence County Forest ("Managed in cooperation with Florence County Forest and WDNR"), you will arrive at Sunrise Drive with a sign for Washburn Falls and Popple River access: turn right (north) onto Sunrise Drive. This is a winding gravel road with sporadic potholes that intersects with multiple other gravel backcountry roads: continue straight. In 2.7 miles you will cross Lamon Creek Road, which is your indicator that the parking lot for Washburn Falls is coming up on your left (northwest). In 1.1 miles you'll arrive at a circular parking area on your left (northwest). It is 3.8 miles from the turnoff onto Sunrise Drive to the parking area for Washburn Falls. On Sunrise Drive you'll see multiple signs for Washburn Falls that guide you toward the parking area and trailhead; however, the parking lot itself is unmarked. Once you turn into the parking area, you'll see a bulletin board with hiking information connected to the easy-to-identify trailhead. **Trailhead GPS:** N45° 48.623' W88° 21.843'

Trail conditions: This hike brings you on a short, easy-to-follow dirt trail through a heavily wooded area. The trail may become muddy and slippery when it rains or covered in snow or ice during the cold-weather months. A sturdy pair of athletic shoes or hiking footwear is encouraged.

The Hike

Another hidden beauty among an already opulent region of the Northwoods, from beginning to end this hike delivers the visual and auditory experience that high-priced health spas try to re-create. This hiking trail is challenging to get to and is far enough removed from the more touristy ones in the area that you are almost guaranteed solitude. This short hike ends at a sitting bench with a serene and tranquil view of the falls and the surrounding wilderness. The wild Popple River comes around a frothy curve and then tumbles 6 feet over a series of rock ledges and ends with a flurry of mist and white foam.

The speedy Popple River tumbling over multiple tiers of flat rock

View of Washburn Falls from the scenic park bench located at the trail's end

From the trailhead walk northwest. You will enter a type of forest common along the Popple River corridor. Pine, maple, and northern white cedar tower overhead while the trail is flanked on both sides by an understory foliage of wild raspberry, bracken fern, and beaked hazelnut. You will begin to hear the falls immediately as you embark on this short hike on the shaded and well-defined trail of gravel and dirt. From beginning to end this hike offers a serene visual and auditory experience. In 0.08 mile you'll arrive at the trail's end, which places you just southeast of the falls where you'll find a wooden bench and a beautiful side-angle view of the two-tiered cascade and the picturesque rapids just above the falls. Another excellent view is from a peninsula that juts out in front of the falls just northeast of the trail's end. To arrive at this viewpoint, walk northeast less than 0.05 mile, which will lead you down a short but steep hill and across a narrow stream. Here you'll find a perfect place for a picnic or to just relax and enjoy the view. The peninsula viewpoint is also a popular location for anglers trying their luck in this popular Class II trout stream. To arrive back at the trailhead, walk back the way you came.

Top: A torrent of foamy amber water, as the Popple River progressively rushes downward ▶
Bottom: View of Washburn Falls while standing on one of the
many large mossy boulders that sit on the shore

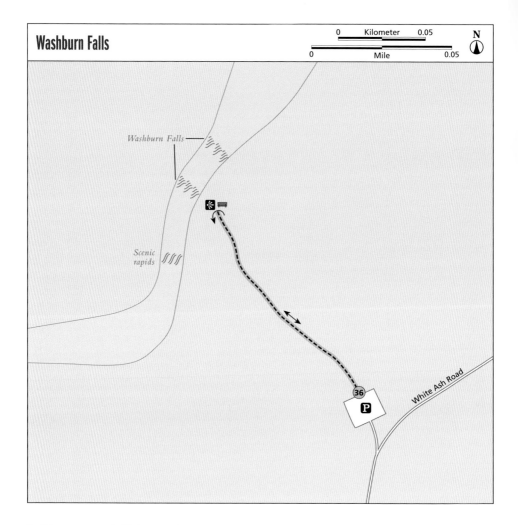

Washburn Falls

Washburn Falls

Scenic rapids

White Ash Road

Miles and Directions

0.0 From the trailhead walk northwest.

0.08 Arrive at the trail's end with a view of the falls. Walk back the way you came.

0.16 Arrive back at the trailhead.

37 LaSalle Falls

On this hike you'll discover one of the most impressive water features in Florence County. This dramatic and roaring waterfall bursts over a scenic rock outcropping and into a steep-walled 0.5-mile-long gorge.

Start: Intersection of US 2 (Central Avenue) and CR N (Quinnesec Street) in Florence, WI

Elevation gain: This hike requires gradual climbing up and down a series of hills; however, the elevation gain is less than 0.1 mile and the ascents and descents are never sustained for very long.

Distance: 2.0 miles

Difficulty: Difficult due to length, elevation change, and rugged uneven surfaces

Hiking time: About 1 hour

Season/schedule: Open year-round. Hiking is best May through Oct, though winter waterfalls make excellent photographs.

Fees and permits: None

Trail contacts: Florence County Forestry and Parks, 5617 Forestry Dr., Florence, WI 54121, (715) 528-3207, exploreflorencecounty.com

Dog friendly: Yes, on leashes

Trail surface: Grass, dirt, and gravel

Land status: County forest

Nearest town: Florence, WI

Maps: USGS Pine River Flowage, WI

Other trail users: Anglers

Special considerations: The driving directions may seem complicated because once you turn west off of either of the major highways (CR N and CR C) you are on backcountry gravel roads that have little to no signage. And to complicate things further, on all sides of the road are numerous ATV trails, logging roads, and private drives that intersect with the main, but unmarked, roads. Fortunately, Florence County has ample signage directing you to LaSalle Falls so that you don't get lost. LaSalle Falls is also on Google Maps and many other popular mapping apps. Using mapping apps or a GPS device is encouraged. The roads that lead to LaSalle Falls are primarily dirt and gravel and sporadically contain large rocks and potholes. After it rains, the roads can be difficult to drive on. The trailhead can be reached with a small car; however, a high-clearance (preferably four-wheel-drive) vehicle is ideal.

Amenities available: None

Maximum grade: This hike is quite hilly; however, the ascents and descents are gradual and spread out for the most part. In the last 0.25 mile there is a sharp ascent and a sharp descent before arriving at the trail's end. The maximum grade on the ascent is 40.7 percent, which lasts for 0.05 mile. The maximum grade for the final descent is -61 percent and lasts less than 0.1 mile. This also happens to be the most rugged portion of the hike, which involves many exposed tree roots, large rocks, and uneven surfaces.

Cell service: No

Waterway: Pine River

Waterfall beauty: 4

Accessibility: No

Finding the trailhead: From the intersection of US 2 (Central Avenue) and CR N (Quinnesec Street) in Florence, head south on CR N (Quinnesec Street) for 7.8 miles. Take a sharp right (west) on Power Dam Road and drive 1.3 miles until you come to a fork in the road. Stay to your left (west) and follow the signs for LaSalle Falls. The road you're on becomes River Road and in 0.9 mile you will come to another three-way intersection. Follow the road as it veers to your left (southwest) and the road becomes River Flowage Road. Go 0.4 mile and you'll come to an intersection. Turn right (northwest) onto Pine Flowage Road and go for 0.9 mile. You'll come to an intersection where if you go left (southeast) you stay on Pine Flowage Road and if you turn right (northwest) you are on LaSalle Falls Road. Turn right (northwest) onto LaSalle Falls Road, cross the bridge over Halls Creek, and in 0.4 mile you'll see signs telling you to turn right (north) to arrive at the trailhead for LaSalle Falls. **Finding the trailhead from Washburn Falls parking area:** To arrive at LaSalle Falls from Washburn Falls, turn left (north) out of the parking area and follow the gravel road as it curves right and heads east. Sunrise Drive will become Washburn Road. Follow Washburn Road for 4.1 miles and you'll see signs for LaSalle Falls to your left (north). **Trailhead GPS:** N45° 49.281' W88° 17.241'

Trail conditions: This is a 2-mile out-and-back hike. The trail is a well-maintained and easy-to-follow path of dirt and grass through a heavily wooded area. There are minor elevation changes as well as rugged terrain consisting of rocks and tree roots. The trail may become muddy and slippery when it rains or covered in snow or ice during the cold-weather months. A sturdy pair of athletic shoes or hiking footwear is encouraged.

The Hike

This fun out-and-back hike brings you through an enchanting forest on a well-maintained and easy-to-follow trail. Your adventure ends at a 35-foot-high, two-billion-year-old bedrock outcropping. The unique geology of the Pine River is what makes this particular waterfall so visit-worthy. The Niagara Fault runs across the Pine River watershed causing pretty and unusual rock formations made of ancient basalt, slate, and granite. The emerging boulders and bluffs contain no fossils since they pre-date life on Earth. According to Florence County historical records, the outcroppings you see here at LaSalle Falls are from the Precambrian period: older than the bedrock at the bottom of Grand Canyon. Glacial meltwater buffed, scoured, and sculpted the layers of bedrock; what is left behind are the bluffs and waterfalls you see here and in other areas of Florence County.

At the trailhead you'll discover a large bulletin board with a trail map and information regarding the Pine-Popple Wild Rivers Project. Due to the popularity of this hike, the trail is packed down from frequent foot travel, making it difficult to get lost. From the trailhead walk north on the dirt and gravel path as the trail enters the forest. The path curves clockwise to the east and slowly climbs up and over a hill. The hill is not steep and the elevation gain is less than 0.1 mile. As you arrive at the bottom, you'll come to a bench adjacent to a babbling stream: an excellent resting

LaSalle Falls is one of the few waterfalls in Florence County where you can paddle up to its base in a canoe or kayak. The trip is approximately 4.1 miles and begins downstream. A local adventure travel company offers canoe and kayak rentals as well as guided tours. For more information, check out www.natureswaterpark.com or www.exploreflorencecounty.com.

Above: View of the falls from above as it plummets over a rock outcropping
Below: View of the falls as the mighty Pine River approaches the 22-foot drop

The rapids upstream from the falls as you head northwest up the Pine River

spot and a place to enjoy the mood-elevating properties of nature. Cross the bridge over the stream and the path ascends quite quickly. Just beyond the bridge you'll pass a sign warning "rugged terrain." The terrain the sign refers to is dirt, exposed tree roots, large rocks, and a steep incline ahead. As you ascend into this more rugged terrain, the surrounding forest opens up. The trees and understory foliage become less dense, increasing the likelihood of wildlife sightings. Crested blue jays and red-headed woodpeckers can be found flittering throughout the high branches of the deciduous environment while northern chipmunks and red squirrels scurry around the forest floor, attempting to be elusive. You'll arrive at a trail junction with a bench and a trail sign informing you to stay to your left for LaSalle Falls. Just past this trail junction you'll arrive at a steep descent that involves a set of four stairs made from dirt, logs, and exposed tree roots. Here you'll also discover an offshoot trail to your right (northeast), which leads you to the first view of the falls: slightly downriver and from the top of a bluff. Continue down the stairs (Careful! They may be muddy and slippery!) and you'll arrive at a trail junction: turn right (southeast) and in less than 0.05 mile you'll arrive at the trail's end. Here you will discover a beautiful rock outcropping that places you directly above the falls. After enduring the long hike, you are in a perfect place to enjoy a picnic or just relax and take in the falls and surrounding nature. To return to the trailhead, hike back the way you came.

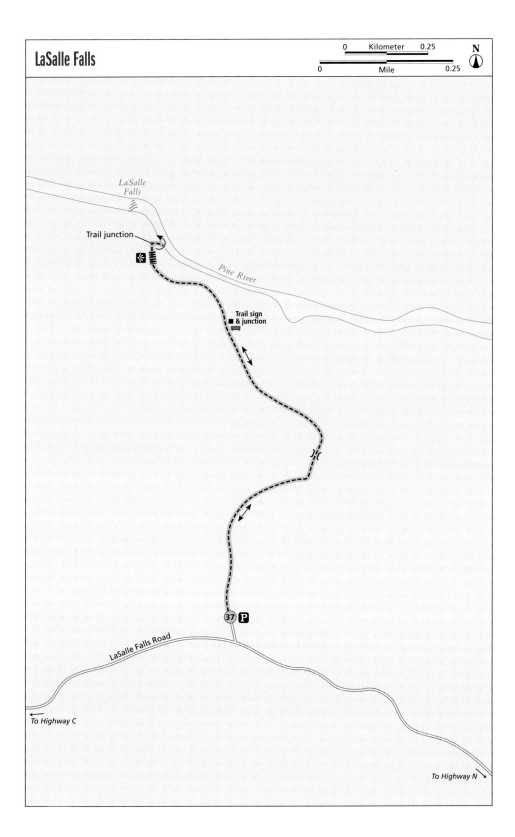

LaSalle Falls

LaSalle Falls

Trail junction

Pine River

Trail sign & junction

37 P

LaSalle Falls Road

To Highway C

To Highway N

0   Kilometer   0.25

0   Mile   0.25

N

A scene of the falls from the top and the gorge below

Miles and Directions

0.0 From the trailhead walk north.

0.4 Cross a bridge and continue to follow the trail northeast.

0.7 Pass a trail sign with a bench directing you to stay left.

0.9 Arrive at the first viewpoint just above a set of stairs of natural construction.

0.95 Arrive at a second trail junction. Turn right (southeast).

1.0 Arrive at the waterfall. Return the way you came.

2.0 Arrive back at the trailhead.

38 Breakwater Falls

This thunderous three-tiered waterfall cascades down 60 feet of the Pine River just below a marvel of human engineering: the Pine River Power Plant Dam. Here you'll discover a secluded and rugged hiking trail traversing a pine and moss forest that will lead you to multiple photo-worthy viewpoints.

Start: Intersection of US 2 and CR N in Florence, WI
Elevation gain: Less than 0.1 mile
Distance: 0.8 mile
Difficulty: Difficult due to rock climbing and potentially slippery uneven surfaces
Hiking time: About 1 hour
Season/schedule: Open year-round. Hiking is best May through Oct, though winter waterfalls make excellent photographs.
Fees and permits: None
Trail contacts: Florence County Forestry and Parks, 5617 Forestry Dr., Florence, WI 54121, (715) 528-3207, exploreflorencecounty.com
Dog friendly: Yes, on leashes

Trail surface: Gravel, grass, and dirt
Land status: County forest
Nearest town: Florence, WI
Maps: USGS Pine River Flowage, WI
Other trail users: Anglers
Special considerations: Some of the rocks near the river's edge may be slippery.
Amenities available: Vault toilet
Maximum grade: 46 percent near the beginning of the hike; duration less than 0.1 mile
Cell service: Limited
Waterway: Pine River
Waterfall beauty: 5
Accessibility: No

Finding the trailhead: From the intersection of CR N (Quinnesec Street) and WI 2, head south on CR N for 7.8 miles. Turn right (west) onto Power Dam Road and go 1.3 miles. On Power Dam Road the road turns from pavement to gravel. In 1.25 miles you will come to a fork in the road with a sign telling you to stay to the right for Breakwater Falls. Follow the fork to the right for 0.3 mile and you will arrive at a dead end and parking roundabout, or cul-de-sac, connected to the hydroelectric plant. Park here and you'll see a gate on the northwest end of the parking area with signs stating "Foot Travel is Welcome" and that Breakwater Falls is just ahead. Walk around the gate and continue heading northwest. In less than 0.1 mile you'll arrive at the trailhead. **Trailhead GPS**: N45° 49.617' W88° 14.905'

Trail conditions: The first portion of the trail is well maintained and easy to follow; however, once you enter the forest it becomes more rugged and precarious. The trail may become muddy and slippery, and there are large rocks that you must climb over. A sturdy pair of hiking footwear is recommended.

Top: *Shore view of the middle tier of Breakwater Falls*
Bottom: *A side view of the falls from one of the many viewpoints along the trail*

The Hike

This hike begins on a well-marked and exposed gravel trail along a service road. You may be initially confused as to what makes this hike so interesting, until you find yourself thrust into a misty pine forest along the descending banks of the river. Here you'll discover Hollywood scenery reminiscent of a *Lord of the Rings* movie. The biodiversity appears damp, shaggy, and unkept like you've just stepped foot into a rainforest. Vibrant greens of the forest canopy contrast against the rusty iron color of the pine needle floor. Large moss-covered boulders are interspersed among the trees providing scenic beauty as well as opportunities for relaxation or a spontaneous picnic. The primitive and rugged trail brings you to the water's edge, where you'll discover a breathtaking 60-foot multitiered waterfall. There are roughly three separate falls to take in here; although there are so many smaller waterfalls, it is difficult to separate them into individual falls. The entirety of this portion of the river consists of water spilling over multiple levels of billion-year-old protruding bedrock. There is far too much beauty than one can take in from any one viewpoint, so you must continue hiking downriver to observe it all from the various lookouts. Until recently these falls went unnamed and were not found on any popular waterfall maps (you still can't find them on Google Maps): something of a local best-kept secret.

From the parking lot you'll see a large brick building to the north and a gate to the left (east). There signs let you know that "Foot Travel is Welcome" and that walking around the gate is the way to Breakwater Falls. You will find the trailhead less than 0.1 mile just beyond the gate. From the trailhead walk northwest on the wide gravel road. The trail is well maintained and wide enough for a vehicle to drive on. As you walk you'll pass two separate trail signs along the path letting you know that Breakwater Falls is straight ahead. In approximately 0.26 mile you'll arrive at a fork in the trail where you'll see a third trail sign directing you to the right (west). Follow the trail as it veers right, off the gravel road and onto a grass path. In less than 0.1 mile you'll see another sign for Breakwater Falls telling you to turn right (northwest) and into the woods. Follow this path into the pine forest and you'll find an easy-to-follow, but potentially muddy, dirt path guiding you to the first waterfall and viewpoint. Here you see a juxtaposition of industry and nature. The first-tier waterfall presents as a masterpiece of nature in the foreground with a large man-made spillway

> The Pine River is an aesthetically pleasing and challenging place to fish. According to the US Department of Agriculture and Forest Service, the Pine River is considered a "Blue Ribbon" cold water trout stream. Fishing is one of the most popular activities on the river, and anglers come from all over to enjoy its scenic shoreline while attempting to pull in brook, brown, and rainbow trout.

Long-range view of the falls from downriver

in the background. This may seem a little off-putting to some, but as you walk north-east along the banks of the Pine River, you venture farther from the hydroelectric plant and into the surrounding beauty that makes this hike so worthwhile. There is no singular clearly defined path that brings you downriver; however, there are multiple paths carved through the forest by boots of hikers and anglers. One option is to stay close to the shoreline, which involves climbing over multiple large moss-covered rocks. This route brings you to multiple viewpoints to see the different falls. A second option is to take a slightly higher ground that meanders through the forest and then redirects you back toward the river so you can stop and view the falls from a middle and lower viewpoint.

There is a fifty-one-stair canoe portage on the east end of the parking lot that will bring you down to the river's edge well below the falls. At the base of the stairs there is no direct route or easy-to-follow path to bring you upstream to arrive at the falls, since you would have to walk in the water and hike around the power plant building. These stairs are a viable option to arrive at the lower portion of the river, but they are not a viable option to get to the base of the falls.

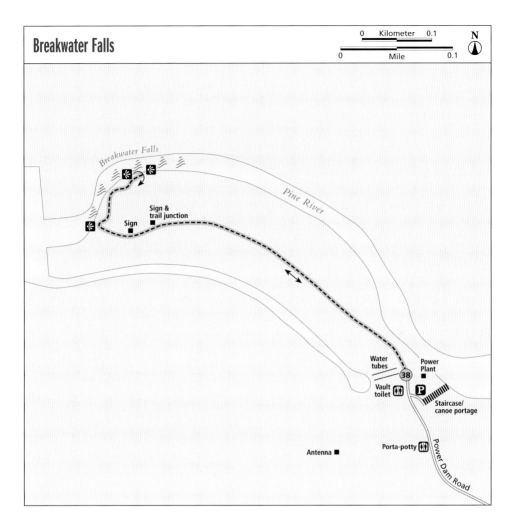

0   Kilometer   0.1

0   Mile   0.1

N

Miles and Directions

0.0   From the trailhead follow the gravel path toward Breakwater Falls.

0.26 Arrive at a trail junction with trail sign. Stay right.

0.29 Follow the trail sign indicating you turn right (northwest) into the forest.

0.3   Arrive at first viewpoint: upper falls.

0.37 Arrive at second viewpoint: middle falls.

0.4   Arrive at third viewpoint: lower falls. Retrace your steps and return the way you came.

0.8   Arrive back at the trailhead.

39 Strong Falls

This small, but powerful waterfall is aptly named. The mighty Peshtigo River splits in two and divides itself around a large boulder-strewn island, creating multiple powerful and stunning falls.

Start: Intersection of Coleman Avenue and WI 141/US 141, just south of the Driftwood Fuel and Sport in downtown Amberg, WI
Elevation gain: Less than 0.1 mile
Distance: 0.34 mile
Difficulty: Easy, due to flat even terrain and minimal elevation change
Hiking time: About 30 minutes
Season/schedule: Open year-round; however, best enjoyed May through Oct
Fees and permits: Yes
Trail contacts: Marinette County Parks, 1926 Hall Ave., Marinette, WI 54143, (715) 732-7530, www.marinettecounty.com
Dog friendly: Yes, on leashes
Trail surface: Gravel, dirt, and boardwalk
Land status: County park
Nearest town: Amberg, WI
Maps: USGS Goodman Park, WI; https://www.marinettecounty.com/parks/

Other trail users: This is a popular county park.
Special considerations: None
Amenities available: Vault toilets, water, camping, cabins for rent, picnic area, and drinking water
Maximum grade: −27.2 percent sustained for less than 0.1 mile
Cell service: No
Waterway: Peshtigo River
Waterfall beauty: 2
Accessibility: Limited. The first portion of the trail is firmly compacted gravel and dirt that, with assistance, could be navigated by a wheelchair, stroller, or mobility device. The boardwalk/bridge that crosses the river and brings you to the final view of the falls is also navigable with assistance.

Finding the trailhead: Start at the intersection of Coleman Avenue and WI 141/US 141, just south of the Driftwood Fuel and Sport in downtown Amberg, WI. Head southwest on Coleman Avenue for 0.4 mile until you come to Grant Street: turn right (northeast). In 0.2 mile the road curves left (west) and becomes Dow Dam Road. Continue straight (west) on Dow Dam Road for 3.2 miles until you come to a three-way intersection with Mathis Road and Benson Lake Road. Stay to your right and continue on Benson Lake Road for 14.8 miles. The road makes some twists and turns and becomes gravel. Once you pass the intersection of Benson Lake Road and Parkway Road, the entrance to Goodman County Park will be 1 mile ahead on your left (southeast). Turn left (southeast) onto Goodman Park Road and drive for 0.3 mile and you'll arrive at a parking lot connected to the trailhead. The address to Goodman Park is N15201 Goodman Park Rd., Athelstane, WI 54104. **Trailhead GPS:** N45° 31.128' W88° 20.377'

Trail conditions: This hike brings you through a park on a wide, well-maintained path of gravel and firmly packed dirt. The trail meets up with a bridge and a boardwalk that bring you up and over a bridge. The trail, bridge, and boardwalk may become icy and slippery during winter months. No specific footwear is required.

Above: The coppery Peshtigo River as it plunges over Strong Falls
Below: A beautiful view of the aptly named falls from downstream

The Hike

Strong Falls is an aptly named waterfall for its forceful appearance and visual appeal. Located on the pristine Peshtigo River, Strong Falls is a popular destination with locals as well as out-of-town campers and hikers due to its beautiful views, large campgrounds, and wide-open spaces. An easy-to-follow gravel trail leads you down to the water's edge where you stand face-to-face with the energetic falls. The hiking trail then continues over a walking bridge leading you to a secluded wooded island and a second, more hidden, set of smaller falls. The beautiful thing about this hike is that it offers the opportunity to be a short out-and-back hike, or a longer more physical adventure, depending on what you're looking for. In fact, you could easily turn your day excursion into an overnight adventure by renting one of the charming cabins onsite or camping at one of the spacious sites in the designated campgrounds.

Many of the rustic, log cabin–style buildings and landscaping you see around Goodman Park were constructed between 1936 and 1938 by the Civilian Conservation Corps (CCC). In the depths of the Great Depression, the CCC was one of the first relief programs created by President Franklin Roosevelt. It put young men to work on environmental projects and development of state parks. A number of these CCC camps were in Wisconsin and have had a lasting impact on our state parks. The park area you walk through to get to Strong Falls was built by CCC Company 1696 based out of Dunbar, Wisconsin.

From the parking lot walk west until you arrive at a trail junction with a sign for Strong Falls. On your right you'll see some of the featured buildings built by the CCC including small cabins, a garage, vault toilets, and a caretaker's abode. From this trail junction turn left (southwest) and follow the trail to the river's edge. The trail changes from gravel to grass and then dirt as you pass informational signs, a large pavilion on your right, and a picnic area on your left. At the river's edge you'll arrive at your first view of the falls. To your right (west) you'll see the rust-colored Strong Falls where the Peshtigo River swiftly crashes in between decorative rocks covered in shaggy mosses and lichens. From here turn right (southwest) and follow the trail along the river until you come to a pedestrian bridge with a sign that says, "Walking Bridge." Follow the trail over the walking bridge (southwest), which will lead you to an island in the center of the river. To your right (northwest) you'll see decorative rapids as the nature-shrouded river flows through narrow reddish-brown rock formations. The smell of the surging river combined with fresh pine and cedar will awaken your senses as you pause to enjoy the turbulent mini falls. Continue over the bridge to the trail's end where you'll arrive at a sitting bench and a view of the falls from the other side (southwest). To return to the trailhead, walk back the way you came.

The second, and more hidden falls, as you cross the walking bridge to the other side of the river

When you reach the trail's end on the other side of the Peshtigo River, you'll find an optional hiking trail that leads northeast along the river. This walking path connects to McClintock Park 4 miles away—also situated on the Peshtigo River—located southeast of Goodman Park. This trail offers multiple different "loops," which all vary in length for different ability levels and will easily bring you back to where you started. If you make the 4-mile trek along the scenic trail to McClintock Park, you'll be rewarded with a series of picturesque footbridges that bring you to a variety of small falls and rapids. This hike is particularly beautiful when the leaves are changing in the autumn months.

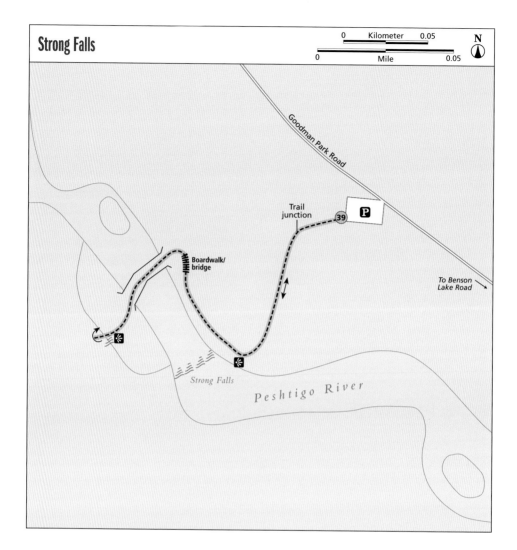

Miles and Directions

0.0 From the parking lot that is connected to the trailhead, walk west.

0.01 Arrive at a trail junction with a trail sign directing you toward the falls: turn left (southwest).

0.07 Arrive at the view of the falls: turn right and follow the path along the river.

0.12 Cross the bridge and boardwalk.

0.16 Arrive at a view of the second falls.

0.17 Arrive at the trail's end. Walk back the way you came.

0.34 Arrive back at the trailhead.

40 Dave's Falls

This hike has everything nature lovers and waterfall enthusiasts are looking for. A pleasant forested trail brings you to multiple different water features including a pretty waterfall, humble rapids, and a 10-foot jaw-dropping gusher.

Start: Intersection of Amberg Street and US 141 in downtown Amberg

Elevation gain: Less than 0.1 mile

Distance: 0.48 mile

Difficulty: Moderate due to a portion of the trail involving rugged terrain and rock climbing

Hiking time: About 20 minutes

Season/schedule: Open year-round 5 a.m. to 10 p.m, but best enjoyed May through Oct

Fees and permits: Yes

Trail contacts: Marinette County Parks, 1926 Hall Ave., Marinette, WI 54143, (715) 732-7530, www.marinettecounty.com

Dog friendly: Yes, on leashes

Trail surface: Paved, dirt, forest, and boardwalk

Land status: County park

Nearest town: Amberg, WI

Maps: USGS Dave's Falls County Park, WI

Other trail users: None

Special considerations: This park does not have any trail maps posted, and the hiking trails have minimal signage. Once you cross over the footbridge to the other side, the terrain becomes a bit more rugged and there are no clearly defined trails or loops. What you'll discover is a string/collection of unofficial trails that allows you to explore however you wish. Don't expect a lot of signage or posted trail maps in Dave's Falls County Park, but the park is small and it is difficult to get lost.

Amenities available: Vault toilets, camping, picnic area

Maximum grade: −43.2 percent sustained for less than 0.1 mile. For this short descent you are walking down a portion of the trail that is a well-constructed staircase.

Cell service: Limited

Waterway: Pike River

Waterfall beauty: 4

Accessibility: No

Finding the trailhead: Dave's Falls County Park is along US 141 near Amberg, WI, along the Pike River. You'll be able to easily spot signs along the highway, and the entrance to the parking lot is clearly marked with a big wooden sign. From the intersection of Amberg Street and US 141 in downtown Amberg (just north of the Driftwood Fuel and Sport gas station), head south on US 141. Drive for 0.9 mile until you see signs for Dave's Falls County Park to your right. Turn right onto County Park Road and in 0.2 mile you'll arrive at two parking lots: one on both the east and west side of the trailhead. The trailhead is just northeast of the playground and picnic area and it's marked by a large bulletin board. The address for Dave's Falls County Park to put into map apps or navigation devices is Old 141 Road, Amberg, WI 54102. **Trailhead GPS:** N45° 29.689' W87° 59.306'

Trail conditions: This is a well-maintained trail. The first portion is paved as it slowly ascends toward a forested trail. The second portion is packed down due to frequent travel.

The exciting and historic waterfall named after a river crew boss who lost his life while trying to free a log jam

The Hike

Dave's Falls County Park is one of the gems in Marinette County's waterfall circuit, and it will not disappoint. It is a place of scenic falls and outstanding rock formations. A short congenial nature hike leads to a string of unofficial trails, spectacular views, and two noteworthy waterfalls. The falls featured in this park are not thunderous cascades crashing from towering rock tables overhead. Here you'll find an ornate collection of scenic rapids, tumblers, and forceful chutes, decorated on all sides by the bounty of geology and nature. One of the most exciting features of this park is that there are no fences or guardrails. You are free to hike up and down the shores, clamber among the rocks, or wade in the water to view and enjoy the falls from different vantage points.

On both sides of the river, there are colossal and beautifully placed rock formations. Dave's Falls is caused by a great volume of water flowing between two high-quality granite outcroppings. Amberg, and the surrounding region, is one of the most extensive geological areas of its kind due to something called the Wisconsin magmatic terrane, a belt of plutonic volcanic rock formed by a tectonic plate collision millions of years ago. The result of the collision is a sought-after type of

The Pike River as it splits and creates eye-catching cascades around a wild and unkept river island

granite known for its strength and attractiveness. Within the park property lies an abandoned granite quarry that at one time produced some of the region's most beautiful igneous rock.

At the trailhead you'll see a sign with arrows indicating right (east) for the lower trail and right (west) for the main trail. If you follow the lower trail, a short hike will bring you to the base of the lower falls. For the sake of a more enjoyable and diverse hike with stellar views, we will be following the main trail.

From the trailhead walk northwest as the trail curves clockwise, enters a lush green forest, and comes to a small set of stairs. Descend the stairs and the trail comes to a T where you'll see a sign directing you to the left (west) for "waterfalls" and "foot bridge." To your right (east) there are more waterfalls (you will later retrace your steps and follow this trail east to visit the lower falls). Follow the trail to your left and you'll follow a forested trail of dirt and rock with large exposed tree roots. Large boulders sit decoratively on both sides of the river as you come to a footbridge that straddles some small rocky rapids. Continue past the footbridge and you'll arrive at a view of the upper falls. The Pike River splits and divides itself around collections of cumbersome rocks causing multiple small, but fun to look at, falls. What these

THE HISTORY OF DAVE

These falls were originally called Pern-a-wan Falls but were later named Dave's Falls to honor a local lumberjack and river crew boss. Dave Frechette lost his life here while trying to free a log jam in 1881. More details are available at the Amberg Historical Society in town.

Dave's Falls downstream. This is an exciting hike that includes some amazing viewpoints.

The humble rapids and footbridge of Dave's Falls

miniature waterfalls lack in size they make up for in serene beauty and a pleasant hypnotic sound. Return the way you came and head east at the T trail junction that you previously visited at the base of the stairs. This rugged trail leads you to the lower falls. There is no clearly defined trail and it requires a lot of athletic rock stepping to arrive at the falls. Here you will find a breathtaking view of a large bluff overlooking the Pike River as it narrows and is forced through decorative moss-painted boulders, creating a forceful waterslide of frothy reddish-brown water. These falls are medium sized, but powerful, audible, and scenic. The topography and surrounding

Enjoy rock climbing? Adjacent to Dave's Falls County Park is an abandoned granite quarry on public land. The quarry is popular with park visitors and rock climbers since it hosts some of the best bouldering. The quarry was once known as the "Aberdeen Quarry" and was owned by the Amberg Granite Company in the late 1800s. It produced the iconic "Amberg Red" granite, which was used in Chicago for curbing blocks and street paving. It was also used for buildings such as the Minnesota State Capitol and buildings in Chicago and Cincinnati. The Amberg Museum has a unique exhibit that features a pictorial history of quarrying in Amberg along with a collection of quarrying tools and other memorabilia.

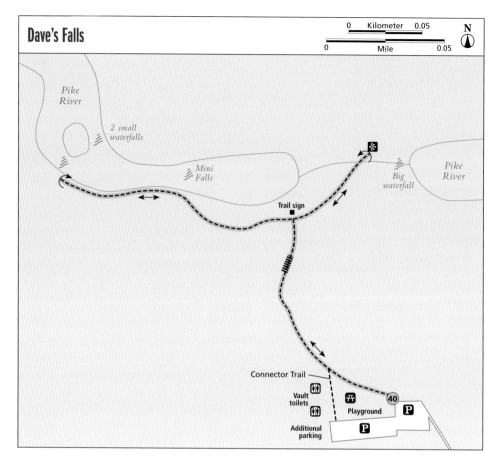

Dave's Falls

Pike River

2 small waterfalls

Mini Falls

Big waterfall

Pike River

Trail sign

Connector Trail

Vault toilets

Playground

40

Additional parking

beauty make you want to sit and stay a while. The large smooth rocks offer plenty of opportunities to sit and relax, read a book, or have a picnic. It will quickly become evident to you why this location is so popular with the locals. To return to the trailhead, walk back the way you came.

Miles and Directions

0.0 From the trailhead walk northwest.

0.07 Arrive at a set of stairs: walk down the stairs.

0.09 Arrive at a T in the trail: turn left (northwest). Walk along the forested trail toward the footbridge.

0.16 Arrive at a footbridge; continue straight (east).

0.21 Arrive at a view of the upper falls. Walk back the way you came.

0.31 Arrive back at the T in the trail. Continue straight (west).

0.35 Arrive at a view of the lower falls: retrace your steps.

0.48 Arrive back at the trailhead.

41 Twelve Foot Falls

Discover a sparkly and luminescent waterfall where the height matches the name. A gratifying hike through the forest brings you right up close to the falls where you can interact with it. This county park and campground includes a bonus hike that leads to a second waterfall almost as exciting as this one.

Start: Intersection of US 8 and US 141 in Pembine, WI

Elevation gain: Less than 0.1 mile

Distance: 0.28 mile

Difficulty: Moderate due to rugged terrain

Hiking time: About 30 minutes

Season/schedule: Open year-round 5 a.m. to 10 p.m., but best enjoyed May through Oct

Fees and permits: Yes

Trail contacts: Marinette County Parks, 1926 Hall Ave., Marinette, WI 54143, (715) 732-7530, www.marinettecounty.com

Dog friendly: Yes, on leashes

Trail surface: Dirt, gravel, and forested

Land status: County park

Nearest town: Pembine, WI

Maps: USGS Dunbar, WI; https://www.marinettecounty.com/parks/

Other trail users: Anglers

Special considerations: Between the second and third viewpoint, the trail has very uneven terrain due to exposed tree roots. Hikers are encouraged to be extra careful.

Amenities available: Picnic area, camping, and vault toilets

Maximum grade: 5.8 percent sustained for less than 0.1 mile

Cell service: No

Waterway: Pike River

Waterfall beauty: 2

Accessibility: Yes

Finding the trailhead: Getting to the trailhead involves navigating some winding backcountry gravel roads. Using a mapping device and/or a GPS unit is encouraged. Begin at the intersection of US 8 and US 141 in Pembine, WI. Head west on US 8 for 5.7 miles. Turn left (south) onto Lily Lake Road and drive for 1.5 miles. When you come to an intersection with Twin Lakes Road, stay to your right (south) to continue on Lily Lake Road: drive for another 3.1 miles. When you arrive at an intersection with Trout Haven Road, turn right (west) and drive for 1.7 miles (past the intersection for Trout Haven Lane). Beware, the names of the streets can get confusing. Turn right (north) on 12 Foot Falls Road and drive for 0.8 mile. You'll see signs for Twelve Foot Falls County Park on your right (east). Turn right (east) into the park and stay to your right as you follow the road for 0.26 mile to arrive at the parking lot connected to the trailhead. This parking lot is connected to the trailhead for both Twelve Foot Falls and Eight Foot Falls. The address for Twelve Foot Falls County Park, which can be used in a mapping application such as Google Maps, is Twelve Foot Falls Road, Dunbar, WI 54119. **Trailhead GPS:** N45° 34.850' W88° 08.153'

Trail conditions: The trail is well worn and easy to follow due to frequent travel. The majority of the trail is sand and dirt. Just past the bridge the path has many exposed tree roots that make the surface uneven.

The Hike

Arriving at this waterfall hike involves a lot of backcountry dirt road driving. As you pull into the parking lot, you are immediately treated to a beautiful view of the shiny falls. Just off the trailhead, front and center, you discover a captivating viewpoint equipped with sitting benches. What you see is the elegant falls pouring into a lagoon-like feature where the Pike River grows slow and wide. A 0.2-mile S-shaped nature trail leads you through a forest of red pine, pin oak, aspen, and birch. The path is well worn and easy to follow. A trail with a soft surface of pine needles and sand is adorned on both sides by herbaceous vegetation including forest grasses, sedges, and forbs. The trail ends just northwest of the falls where you have a stunning view overlooking the lagoon and the surrounding photogenic nature. Here you have the ability to climb on the rocks, interact with the falls, or just take a well-deserved rest: a place for mental and physical rejuvenation.

From the trailhead follow the path east until you arrive at a trail junction with a view of the falls and two sitting benches (directly south you'll find the path to Eight Foot Falls). Turn left (north) and walk less than 0.1 mile, which will bring you to another viewpoint offering an opportunity to pause and enjoy the falls from a different perspective. From here continue northwest on the trail and follow it over a small bridge that crosses a creek. Just beyond the bridge the terrain becomes quite rugged with many exposed tree roots, making the hike a bit rougher on one's ankles. The trail curves clockwise to your right (heading east) and then begins to gradually head uphill (rising less than 0.1 mile in elevation). The trail pauses next to the falls before ending at a view just behind them. At the trail's end you are rewarded with a stellar view overlooking the lagoon in the direction of the trailhead. To arrive back at the trailhead, return the way you came.

Bonus Hike: Just northeast of the trailhead, you'll see signs for Eight Foot Falls, yet another blandly named waterfall where the height matches its name. The trailhead can be found directly south of the first trail junction. To arrive at Eight Foot Falls, walk northwest on the trail. Continue to follow this exciting trail as it crosses boardwalks over a soft damp marsh. This trail zigzags through the forest and traverses uneven terrain, exposed tree roots, and large rocks. Here in this forest the smell of mature pine, fresh moss, and the moist forest floor will invigorate your senses. This trail is 0.2 mile one way and will lead you to a small postcard-worthy waterfall where the Pike River plunges between large rock outcroppings: short, quick, and pretty. The trail's end and surrounding forest invite you to unwind and enjoy the landscape of Wisconsin. To arrive back at the trailhead, return the way you came.

Top: Twelve Foot Falls observed from the first viewpoint ▶
Bottom: Twelve Foot Falls from the second viewpoint

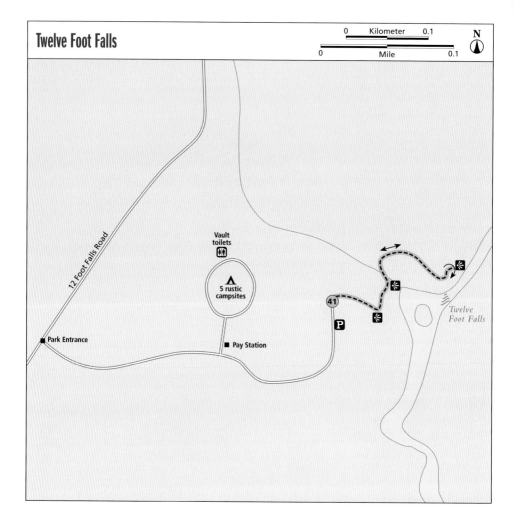

Twelve Foot Falls

Vault toilets

5 rustic campsites

12 Foot Falls Road

41

P

Park Entrance

Pay Station

Twelve Foot Falls

0   Kilometer   0.1

0   Mile   0.1

N

Miles and Directions

0.0 From the trailhead walk east.

0.04 Arrive at a trail junction and viewpoint with sitting benches: turn left (north).

0.05 Arrive at a second view of the falls. Continue straight (northwest). Follow the path over a small bridge and through rugged terrain as it curves right (east).

0.13 Arrive at a third view of the falls.

0.14 Arrive at the trail's end. Return the way you came.

0.28 Arrive back at the trailhead.

Top: Twelve Foot Falls as seen from the trail as you stand directly above it ▶
Bottom: The Pike River cloaked in nature as it meanders toward the falls

42 Eighteen Foot Falls

Simplicity in its title, but complexity in its beauty. A narrow woodsy trail leads you to an 18-foot slide-like waterfall surrounded by an impenetrable dark green forest.

Start: Intersection of US 8 and US 141 in Pembine, WI
Elevation gain: Less than 0.1 mile
Distance: 0.4 mile
Difficulty: Difficult due to uneven rocky terrain and steep drops. There is a point on this hike where the trail splits and gives you the option of "Extreme" if you go to the right and "Moderate" if you go to the left. The path converges again before the trail's end.
Hiking time: About 26 minutes
Season/schedule: The park is open year-round from 5 a.m. to 10 p.m. Hiking is best May through Oct.
Fees and permits: Yes
Trail contacts: Marinette County Parks, 1926 Hall Ave., Marinette, WI 54143, (715) 732-7530, www.marinettecounty.com

Dog friendly: Yes, on leashes
Trail surface: Dirt, rock, and forest
Land status: County park
Nearest town: Pembine, WI
Maps: USGS 18 Foot Falls, Dunbar, WI 54119
Other trail users: Anglers seeking trout
Special considerations: This is a strenuous hike with a narrow path, steep drops, and uneven terrain. Keep a close eye on small children.
Amenities available: Vault toilets
Maximum grade: -25 percent near the trail's end, sustained for less than 0.1 mile
Cell service: Limited
Waterway: Pike River
Waterfall beauty: 3
Accessibility: No

Finding the trailhead: Starting from the intersection of US 141 and US 8, head west on US 8 for 5.7 miles. Turn right onto Lily Lake Road and go for 1.5 miles until you come to the intersection of Twin Lake Road. Stay to your right (south) on Lily Lake Road for less than 0.1 mile and then take a right (west) on Twin Lake Road. Go for 0.5 mile on Twin Lake Road and turn left (south) on Twelve Foot Falls Road. Drive for 2 miles on Twelve Foot Falls Road and you'll come to the entrance of Eighteen Foot Falls County Park. Turn left and drive for 0.2 mile and you'll arrive at a parking lot connected to the trailhead. **Trailhead GPS:** N45° 35.239' W88° 07.997'

Trail conditions: This trail is a narrow and hilly dirt path through the woods that requires stepping onto and over large rocks. When it rains, the path may become muddy and slippery. A sturdy pair of walking shoes or hiking footwear is encouraged.

The Hike

This trail has rocky and hilly terrain that demands a sturdy pair of walking shoes. It is a strenuous hike, with a narrow path and steep drops. But the promise of an 18-foot waterfall will keep you moving forward. This is perhaps one of the most enjoyable nature hikes in the area: a rewarding trail for both nature lovers and waterfall enthusiasts. As I hiked this trail, I was greeted by toads and tree frogs that leaped out of the

Above: The Pike River as it drops, you guessed it, 18 feet over a scenic rock outcropping
Below: Here you see the beautiful cascade from a viewpoint directly above the falls.

A view of the falls from a distance as the surrounding forest complements the amber-colored river

way of my slow methodical footsteps. An unfazed garter snake slithered over my foot as I was chirped at by an energetic red squirrel. Then a hummingbird suddenly flew directly into the side of my head. I thought to myself, "This ecosystem is alive and well. The forest is teeming with life!"

From the trailhead walk southeast. You'll pass a sign for Eighteen Foot Falls indicating that you're on the right path and that the waterfall lies ahead. After this trail sign you are thrust onto a narrow rocky path teeming with wildlife. To your left (north) is an impenetrable forest of pine, birch, and trembling aspen. To your right (south) is a steep descent leading down to the river's edge. At 0.05 mile past the trail sign, you'll arrive at a fork in the trail. To your left the sign reports the hike as "Moderate." To your right the sign reports the hike as "Extreme." The "Extreme" trail involves a slight elevation change (less than 0.05 mile) and large rocks protruding from the earth that you will need to step over. The "Moderate" trail involves a less hilly path of dirt, gravel, and pine needles. For the sake of a more interesting and dynamic hike, I mapped this one out using the "Extreme"

The attractive Pike River just before it reaches the falls

route, which involves a short scenic nature hike, interesting geology, and some fun and athletic rock stepping. The trails only diverge for 0.03 mile before converging again, and both are manageable by anyone with a moderate level of physical fitness and a sturdy pair of walking shoes. In 0.07 mile past the trail convergence you'll arrive at the trail's end. You will find yourself placed just northeast of the falls with a beautiful view of the descending Pike River as it creates an 18-foot torrent of descending white wash. What makes the scenic end of this already enjoyable hike special is how close you can get to the falls. This is another example of a Marinette County waterfall that allows you to get up close and interact with it. As you stand on the rocky shores of the falls and look to your right (north), you are treated to a serene view of the Pike River and surrounding majestic forest. Pine, spruce, and emerald green fern cling to the shores as the river makes a lazy voyage south. Turn your gaze right (south) and you witness the river becoming turbulent as it is channeled between two narrow rocky shorelines emptying into a shallow pool. To arrive back at the trailhead, return the way you came.

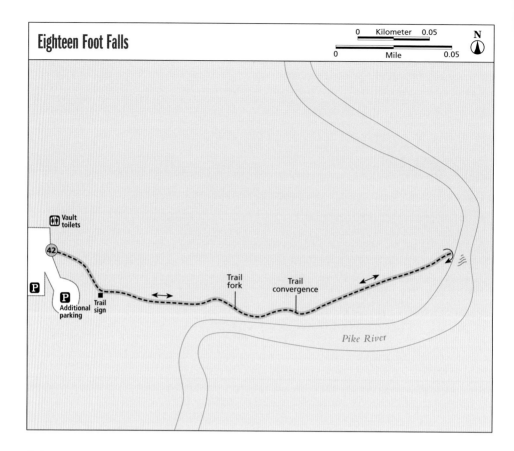

Miles and Directions

0.0 From the trailhead walk southeast.

0.03 Arrive at a trail sign for Eighteen Foot Falls: continue straight (east).

0.1 Arrive at a fork in the trail with a trail sign. To your left the hike is labeled "Moderate." To your right the hike is labeled "Extreme." In 0.03 mile the trail will converge again.

0.2 Arrive at the trail's end. Walk back the way you came.

0.4 Arrive back at the trailhead.

43 Long Slide Falls

In this tucked away county park, the Pemebonwon River narrows and forcefully threads itself through immense moss-covered boulders. The copper-colored river then plunges one last time into a steamy cauldron before peacefully carrying on like nothing ever happened.

Start: Intersection of WI 8/US 8 and WI 141/US 141 in Pembine, WI

Elevation gain: Less than 0.1 mile

Distance: 0.35 mile

Difficulty: Moderate difficulty due to the steep hill that brings you down to the falls, which you must climb back up to return to the trailhead

Hiking time: About 40 minutes

Season/schedule: The park is open year-round from 5 a.m. to 10 p.m. Hiking is best May through Oct. Winter waterfalls make excellent photographs; however, take precautions because the trail may be slippery.

Fees and permits: Yes

Trail contacts: Marinette County Parks, 1926 Hall Ave., Marinette, WI 54143, (715) 732-7530, www.marinettecounty.com

Dog friendly: Yes, on leashes

Trail surface: Gravel, dirt, and forested trail

Land status: County park

Nearest town: Pembine, WI

Maps: USGS Long Slide Falls County Park

Other trail users: None

Special considerations: To arrive at the base of the falls requires walking down a hill and then returning the way you came. The climb back up may be challenging for less athletic hikers.

Amenities available: Vault toilets and picnic area

Maximum grade: The first viewpoint of the upper falls requires descending down from the main trail. At this point there is a maximum grade of 307 percent sustained for a very short period: less than 0.1 mile. Then you return to the main trail and descend down to the base of the lower falls on a path with a maximum grade of -71 percent; however, the majority of the trail is -18.8 percent, sustained for 0.1 mile from the top of the hill to the bottom.

Cell service: Limited

Waterway: North branch of the Pemebonwon River

Waterfall beauty: 5

Accessibility: No

Finding the trailhead: From the intersection of US 8 and US 141 in Pembine, WI, head north on US 141 for 6.3 miles until you come to Morgan Road: turn right (southeast). Drive for 1.6 miles until you come to Long Slide Road at the entrance for Long Slide County Park: turn right (south) onto Long Slide Road. Go 0.2 mile and you'll arrive at a parking lot connected to the trailhead. The trailhead is in the south end of the parking area. **Trailhead GPS:** N45° 41.019 W87° 55.946'

Trail conditions: The majority of the trail is gravel; however, viewing the upper and lower falls requires walking on dirt trails that may become muddy when it rains.

The Hike

Long Slide Falls is yet another one of the many dazzling cascades on Marinette County's waterfall tour. Behold one of the largest slide falls in the Northeast Wisconsin region and one of the most impressive waterfalls of the Lake Michigan watershed. Tucked away in a dark green forest, the Pemebonwon River drops approximately 50 feet in a violent display of foamy chutes and then plunges over multiple tiers of mammoth rocks. These falls are so immense and elongated that it is impossible to view them all from any one place, which makes them difficult to photograph. The benefit is that you get multiple exciting trails that bring you to different incredible views of the flowing root beer–colored water. These falls are easy to find, easy to park near, and always big and robust, maintaining a consistent flow, regardless of the season. Smalley Falls, Twelve Foot Falls, Eighteen Foot Falls, and Dave's Falls are all very close by and could be combined in a day or weekend excursion.

From the trailhead walk south on the gravel path. In 0.01 mile you'll arrive at a trail sign and a roundabout offering paths to your right (west) and left (east). If you turn right (west), the trail leads you to the middle and upper falls. Here you'll find multiple offshoot trails that allow you to get right up to the rocky banks of the falls. Here you're able to observe how the falls got their name. The tannin-colored water swiftly and violently maneuvers a collection of mossy boulders in a waterslide-like fashion. Towering pines on both sides of the falls bow to each other over the slide-like falls creating a shaded place of solitude. This area offers many large rocks to sit and enjoy the falls and linger a while. Retrace your steps (east) and you'll arrive back at the gravel trail and roundabout. Head east on the path and follow it downhill as it curves southeast. In 0.07 mile you'll come to a sharp hairpin turn: turn right (west). Continue on the trail for 0.05 mile, over a wooden boardwalk, until you arrive at the trail's end. Here you'll find yourself at the bottom of the falls where the river explodes in a fury of activity. You are gifted with the final and best view of the falls as you feel its sheer force and cold spray on your face. To arrive back at the trailhead, walk back the way you came.

◀ *The Pemebonwon River as it tumbles down one of nature's most artful waterslides*

*View of the intricate and highly structured
rock formations of the upper falls*

The brandy-colored Pemebonbon River as it makes its way downstream from the falls and through the county park forest

Bonus Hike: Smalley Falls is a waterfall located 0.5 mile northwest of Long Slide Falls and is absolutely worth a visit. This smaller waterfall is also located on Pemebonwon River and provides an energetic show as the rust-colored river squeezes through a miniature ravine of large moss-stained rocks. I read reports online that you can hike there, but I was never able to find a suitable hiking trail other than walking out to the main road and strolling along the shoulder. To get to the trailhead from Long Slide Falls, drive back out to Morgan Park Road and head northwest for 1.4 miles. Turn left (southwest) when you see the sign for Smalley Falls. Address: 20545 Morgan Park Rd., Niagara, WI 54151.

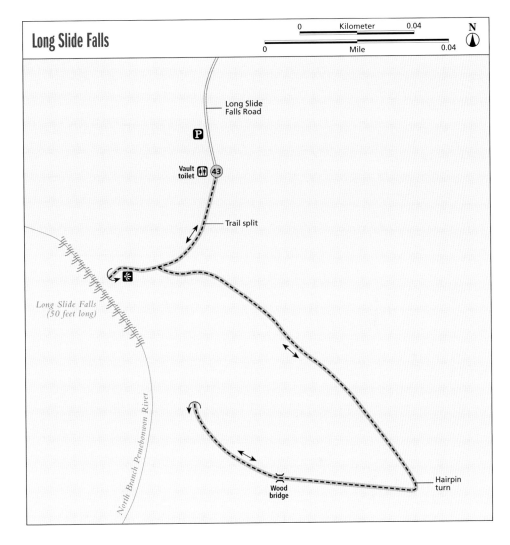

Miles and Directions

0.0 From the trailhead walk southwest.

0.01 Arrive at a fork in the trail: stay right.

0.03 Arrive at a scenic viewpoint of the upper falls. Retrace your steps and walk down the gravel path.

0.12 Arrive at a sharp hairpin turn in the trail: take a hard right (west).

0.2 Arrive at the trail end. Return the way you came.

0.35 Arrive back at the trailhead.

◀ *The turbulent water of the upper rapids just before cascading over the lower falls*

44 Veterans Falls

This short out-and-back hike brings you to an observation platform where you can view two falls on the Thunder River. Here you'll discover a scenic pedestrian bridge extending over the pretty upper falls.

Start: Intersection of CR W and CR A in downtown Crivitz
Elevation gain: Less than 0.1 mile
Distance: 0.14 mile
Difficulty: Easy due to a short well-maintained gravel path with minimal elevation change
Hiking time: About 6 minutes
Season/schedule: Open year-round 5 a.m. to 10 p.m., but best enjoyed May through Oct
Fees and permits: Yes
Trail contacts: Marinette County Parks, 1926 Hall Ave., Marinette, WI 54143, (715) 732-7530, www.marinettecounty.com
Dog friendly: Yes, on leashes
Trail surface: Gravel
Land status: County park
Nearest town: Crivitz, WI
Maps: USGS Veterans Memorial Park, WI
Other trail users: Anglers
Special considerations: None
Amenities available: Picnic area and vault toilets
Maximum grade: -88 percent sustained for less than 0.1 mile
Cell service: Limited
Waterway: Thunder River
Waterfall beauty: 4
Accessibility: Yes

Finding the trailhead: From the intersection of CR W and CR A in downtown Crivitz, head west on CR W/Main Avenue for 10.6 miles. Turn right onto Parkway Road and drive for 3.1 miles until you come to the entrance of Veterans Memorial Park: turn left. Drive past the road for the campgrounds and follow the main road for 0.3 mile and you'll arrive at a parking lot connected to the trailhead. Here you'll see a sign for Veterans Falls. The road into the park that ends at the waterfall is well marked and easy to find. To find this location using a mapping application, the address is W12171 Parkway Rd., Crivitz, WI 54114. **Trailhead GPS:** N45° 16.096' W88° 12.758'

Trail conditions: This is a large easy-to-follow gravel trail that is accessible. A second trail exists just southwest of the parking lot that will bring you to the falls by way of a short vertical descent down a set of stairs.

The Hike

This hike is in Veterans Memorial Park on the Thunder River, one of the many wild serpentine waterways of Marinette County. The Thunder River originates in northern Oconto County near Thunder Mountain and then travels downhill into Marinette. It is one of the county's wild and untamed main attractions with an equally wild and intriguing name. It's a cold-water river alive with biodiversity: fish, crustaceans, insects, plants, and an assortment of amphibians and reptiles. In and near the Thunder River is an abundance of food sources for wildlife, making it a great

*View of the falls looking
down from the bridge*

Located approximately 5 miles away and just upstream from Veterans Falls on the Thunder River is the legendary Thunder River Hatchery. It began as a tourist destination for the adventurer in the early 1900s because of its waterfall and scenic beauty. It became a showcase fish hatchery as part of President Roosevelt's New Deal Program in 1936 and has been producing trout for 76 years. Most of the year there will be up to 140,000 brown trout onsite, and you can visit it several times a year and watch the trout grow.

place for fishing as well as wildlife viewing. Bald eagles and turkey vultures patrol the waterway from the forest canopy while black bear, porcupine, river otter, and other wildlife may be seen close by in the surrounding woodlands.

Here in Veterans Park the Thunder River is channeled through a narrow gorge of solid granite under a scenic footbridge, creating a highly photogenic waterfall. A short accessible trail leads to a wooden observation deck with a view of the upper and lower falls and a tranquil pool at their base. This is not one of the giant thunderous cascades that you'll find in other areas of Marinette County and the state. This is a small, but scenic series of falls with interconnected walking trails, serene viewpoints, and sitting benches. This hike brings you to a quiet slice of unspoiled wilderness where you may want to linger and spend some time soaking up the high vibrations of the river and forest. For those interested in spending a full day, or even longer in the area, Veterans Memorial Park also offers vault toilets, a picnic area, a playground, and fifteen rustic (no electricity) campsites.

From the trailhead walk southeast. A large well-groomed gravel path will lead you to an observation deck overlooking the upper and lower falls. Just south of the observation deck is a trail that brings you down to the water's edge. Be careful. This is a steep unofficial trail consisting of gravel and loose rock, and requires a degree of athletic ability. At the bottom you're able to wade into the Thunder River and view the falls from different angles and get some excellent photos. North of the observation deck is a walking path that leads you to the bridge that goes over the upper falls. On the other side of the bridge, you'll find two walking paths, one west and one south, which go for less than 0.1 mile before they end. To return to the trailhead, walk back the way you came.

Top: A view of the upper falls with the scenic footbridge over the top ▶
Bottom: View of the lower falls from downriver

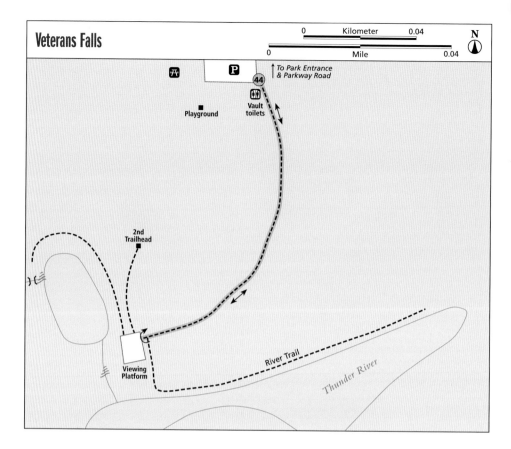

Veterans Falls

0   Kilometer   0.04

0   Mile   0.04

N

To Park Entrance & Parkway Road

Playground

Vault toilets

2nd Trailhead

Viewing Platform

River Trail

Thunder River

Miles and Directions

0.0 From the trailhead walk southeast.

0.07 Arrive at the end and a view of the falls. Walk back the way you came.

0.14 Arrive back at the trailhead.

View of the upper falls from a distance ▶

45 Keller Lake Falls

This waterfall is tucked away at the far end of a sleepy and beautiful lake. This scenic tumbler drops 30 feet into one of Wisconsin's most treasured rivers.

Start: Intersection of CR S/W Ramsdell Street and WI 110/South Main Street in downtown Marion

Elevation gain: Less than 0.05 mile

Distance: 0.26 mile

Difficulty: Easy due to short distance, flat trail, and minimal elevation change

Hiking time: About 13 minutes

Season/schedule: The county park is open year-round; however, the waterfall is best enjoyed May through Oct.

Fees and permits: None

Trail contacts: Waupaca County Parks and Recreation, 811 Harding St., Waupaca, WI 54981, (715) 258-6243, https://www .waupacacounty-wi.gov

Dog friendly: Yes, on leashes

Trail surface: Paved, dirt, and rocks

Land status: County park

Nearest town: Marion, WI

Maps: USGS Keller Lake, WI

Other trail users: Anglers

Special considerations: None

Amenities available: Five rustic campsites, picnic pavilion, vault toilets, children's play area, and basketball court

Maximum grade: -7.3 percent sustained for less than 0.05 mile near the trail's end and view of the falls

Cell service: Limited

Waterway: Keller Lake pouring into the South Branch of the Pigeon River

Waterfall beauty: 4

Accessibility: No

Finding the trailhead: From the intersection of CR S/W Ramsdell Street and WI 110 /South Main Street, drive south on WI 110 for 1.7 miles. Turn right onto CR G and drive for 4.1 miles. Turn left into the county park and drive for 0.4 mile and you'll arrive at a paved parking area that is adjacent to a picnic area, playground, basketball court, and vault toilets. The trailhead is in the northwest corner of the parking lot. The address for Keller Lake County Park is N11250 County Highway G, Marion, WI 54950. **Trailhead GPS:** N44° 58.585' W88° 58.635'

Trail conditions: The first portion of the trail is paved. Once you turn off the main road, you enter a short, forested trail that leads you down to the base of the falls. The trail is dirt and rock, and has a relatively flat surface with a slow steady decline. It may be muddy and slippery when it rains.

The Hike

This 80-acre site is heavily wooded with a mixture of native hardwood and coniferous species including jack, white, and Norway pines. What makes this waterfall unique is its history. The long sudsy cascade was created in 1937 when Waupaca County intentionally dammed up the Pigeon River. The dam was constructed to create a recreation park for northern Waupaca County as well as an optimal location

The dammed-up Pigeon River making a steamy and scenic falls

A view of the falls looking down from the top

for propagating game fish. The result is a beautiful lake and woodsy campground that still offer multiple possibilities for Wisconsin nature lovers. The waterfall appears to have been created as a byproduct of building the dam, and, however serendipitously, it is now one of the most scenic in this region.

From the trailhead walk south on the paved trail that connects the parking lot to the main road. Walk 0.06 mile following the contour of the road until you arrive at a trail junction just northeast of the falls. To your right (northwest) you'll see a bulletin board with historical information regarding the dam and the history of Keller Lake. Just beyond the informational bulletin board is a stellar view of Keller Lake. To your left is a descending trail leading into the forest. Turn left (southeast) and follow the path down toward the river. On your right you pass two different side trails, short in length, which lead you to different views of the falls. Once you arrive at the river's edge turn right (northwest), and in less than 0.05 mile you will arrive at the base of the falls with a stunning view. To arrive back at the trailhead, walk back the way you came.

◀◀ *Top: A view of the misty falls at dawn*
Bottom: A view of Keller Lake at sunrise, standing above the falls

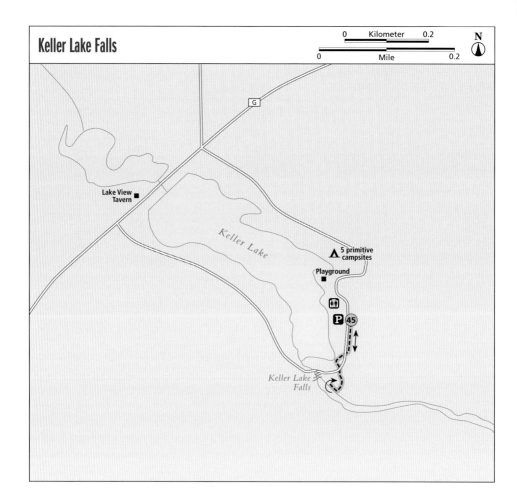

Miles and Directions

0.0 From the trailhead walk south on the paved service road. Continue on the trail past the picnic area and the information board.

0.06 Arrive at the trail junction: turn left (southeast) and follow the trail into the woods. Continue southeast on the forested dirt trail.

0.12 Arrive at the banks of the Pigeon River: turn right (northwest). Continue walking straight.

0.13 Arrive at the trail's end with a view of the falls. Walk back the way you came.

0.26 Arrive back at the trailhead.

46 Fonferek's Glen Falls

This historic and beautiful waterfall is truly nestled in the heart of America's Dairy-land. The short but rewarding out-and-back trek is connected to a lovely nature preserve offering plenty of options for bird-watching, hiking, and nature exploration.

Start: Intersection of WI 57 and US 141/Main Street in downtown Green Bay
Elevation gain: Less than 0.1 mile
Distance: 0.16 mile
Difficulty: Easy due to a well-maintained trail with minimal elevation gain
Hiking time: About 6 minutes
Season/schedule: This waterfall is best enjoyed Apr through Oct; however, the nature preserve that this waterfall is connected to is open year-round. The park is open 8 a.m. until sunset.
Fees and permits: None
Trail contacts: Brown County Parks, PO Box 23600, Green Bay, WI 54305, (920) 448-6242, www.browncountyparks.com
Dog friendly: Yes, on leashes
Trail surface: Dirt, gravel, and grass
Land status: County park
Nearest town: Green Bay
Maps: USGS Green Bay, WI
Other trail users: Hunters

Special considerations: This county park is adjacent to a privately owned farm with a clearly defined border and *many* No Trespassing signs. Make sure to stay on the county park property. The outside gate closes at 8 p.m., so make sure you don't get locked in after sunset. If you arrive and the parking lot is full, you are encouraged to visit on another day. *Do not* park on the surrounding streets. Sheriffs have been known to give out tickets. This park has dangerous conditions including steep cliffs and rugged terrain. Take caution outside of the designated use areas where no marked trail exists.
Amenities available: Porta-potties and picnic area
Maximum grade: From the trailhead to the end the maximum grade is -7.3 percent. The duration of the decline lasts for less than 0.1 mile.
Cell service: Yes
Waterway: Bower's Creek
Waterfall beauty: 2
Accessibility: Yes

Finding the trailhead: From the intersection of US 141/Main Street and WI 57, head southeast on US 141 and drive for 6.5 miles. Turn right (south) on Glenmore Road and go for 1.7 miles. Turn right (west) onto Dutchman Road and drive for 0.6 mile: on your right you'll see a sign for the entrance for Fonferek Glen County Park. Technically the entrance is considered Memory Lane, but this is only visible on map applications such as Google Maps. Turn right (north) onto Memory Lane, which will bring you into the park, and drive for 0.1 mile: You'll arrive at a parking lot adjacent to the trailhead. The address for Fonferek Glen County Park is 2825 Dutchman Rd., Green Bay, WI 54311. **Trailhead GPS:** N44° 25.464' W87° 56.436'

Trail conditions: A short gravel, dirt, and grass path that meanders through a well-maintained county park and ends at a scenic viewpoint. No special footwear is required. In the cold-weather months, the path may be snow covered and icy.

The beautiful glen and its waterfall cloaked in the bounty of nature

The Hike

This 30-foot waterfall is the centerpiece of the Fonferek's Glen Conservancy Area. Similar to Wequiock Falls in Hike 47, the rocky precipice that creates the falls is an extension of the larger Niagara Escarpment. A short and sweet hike brings you through a meadow of native grasses and wildflowers and ends at a designated overlook platform. Here you'll find a stunning view of the glen and the veil-like falls where Bower's Creek gently pours over a colorful cliff of textured dolomite and trickles into a shallow pool.

Fonferek's Glen is popular with nature lovers and waterfall hunters. It is in a 74-acre protected wild area that contains a variety of hiking trails as well as a gravel quarry, limestone cliffs, agricultural fields, and 15 acres of former farmland that have been restored to natural prairie. One of the geological features of the conservancy is a natural stone archway that was created when erosion opened up a skylight in the precipice walls. Like the falls and the rocky glen, this archway is an extension of the Niagara Escarpment, and here you have a close-up inspection of this regional geological gem. This ecologically diverse county park has proven to offer visitors a lot more to explore beyond just the decorative falls.

Remnants of ancient organisms can be found here. Fossils of tabulate coral have been spotted in the dolostone layers of the glen behind and around the falls. Tabulate coral is an extinct form of coral from the early Ordovician Period over 450 million years ago. It consists of hexagonal cells called coralites, which form a honeycomb shape and act as a skeleton for calcite. Sightings of this type of coral make this hike particularly exciting for fossil hunters and geology buffs.

The trailhead is in the northeast end of the parking lot. From the trailhead walk north and follow the trail as it curves clockwise around a large barn. You'll notice a farmhouse to your right (east) with plenty of signage stating "private property" and "no trespassing." Continue past the porta-potty on the north side of the barn and head east on the trail, which will pass through a wide-open meadow. In 0.08 mile you'll arrive at the trail's end, which includes an observation deck with guardrails and a sitting bench.

From the observation deck there are multiple options to view the glen and falls from different vantage points. If you turn right (south), you can walk around the upper rim of the glen and end up at Bower's Creek just before it plunges over the falls. Bower's Creek above the falls is shallow and descends toward the glen in multiple stair-like tiers. You can continue walking along the banks of the creek upstream for less than 0.1 mile before you begin seeing many large No Trespassing signs.

If you turn left (north) from the observation deck, the trail descends into the 75-acre county park, which seems to have endless magnificent views. Multiple unofficial trails wind their way through the conservancy allowing any curious hiker the opportunity for more free-spirited exploring. There are also a variety of designated trail loops that begin and end at the scenic falls and vary in length to suit different ability levels. One of the more popular loops found in the conservancy is a 1.4-mile trek that leads you through the various landscapes of the glen, offering multiple opportunities for bird-watching and lots of potential for wildlife sightings.

During the spring snowmelt the falls become full-bodied and fast moving. The springtime also brings a botanical bloom where the prairies onsite come alive with wildflowers, blanketing the surrounding area with bright and exquisite colors. The flower-strewn prairies combined with a strong and voluminous waterfall make Fonferek's Glen a destination worth a visit.

Fonferek's Glen Falls

Miles and Directions

0.0 From the trailhead walk north.

0.02 Arrive at the barn and porta-potty: follow the trail to your right (east).

0.08 Arrive at the view of the falls. Return the way you came.

0.16 Arrive back at the trailhead.

◀ *Top: The Fonferek's Glen waterfall sitting at the precipice of a 75-acre nature preserve*
Bottom: View the descending glen from above the falls

47 Wequiock Falls

Just east of Lake Michigan, this frequently visited park contains a Zen-like walking path and a punchbowl-style ravine with fascinating geological and historical significance. At the end you'll discover beautiful ribbons of water falling over ancient Cambrian rock into a shallow pool.

Start: Downtown Green Bay or Sturgeon Bay
Elevation gain: Less than 0.1 mile
Distance: 0.28 mile
Difficulty: Difficult due to stairs and uneven rocky surfaces
Hiking time: About 40 minutes
Season/schedule: The park is open year-round 8 a.m. to 8 p.m. This waterfall is best enjoyed in the spring: Apr through June. The flow of the waterfall tends to slow down during the dry summer months.
Fees and permits: None
Trail contacts: Brown County Parks Department, 2024 Lakeview Dr., Suamico, WI 54173, (908) 448-6242, https://www.browncountywi.gov
Dog friendly: Yes, on leashes

Trail surface: Pavement, gravel, wooden stairs, and dirt
Land status: County park
Nearest town: Green Bay, WI
Maps: USGS Wequiock, WI
Other trail users: None
Special considerations: Stairs and uneven ground as the trail follows the creek
Amenities available: Water, flush toilets, and picnic shelter
Maximum grade: –57 percent sustained for less than 0.1 mile while walking down stairs and into the ravine
Cell service: Yes
Waterway: Wequiock Creek
Waterfall beauty: 3
Accessibility: No

Finding the trailhead: From the intersection of US 141/Main Street and WI 57/Monroe Avenue in downtown Green Bay, head northeast on WI 57. You'll cross over the East River and WI 57 will turn clockwise and start heading southeast. Stay on WI 57 for 9.4 miles until you arrive at Van Laanen Road. Turn left (west) on Van Laanen Road and go for 0.1 mile: make a sharp right into Wequiock Falls County Park. Drive less than 0.1 mile and you'll arrive at a parking lot. The address for the park is 3426 Bay Settlement Rd., Green Bay, WI 54311. **Trailhead GPS:** N44° 34.081' W87° 52.756'

Trail conditions: Good. The first portion of the trail is a combination of pavement, gravel, and wooden stairs. Once you walk down the stairs and enter the ravine, the path along the creek is an uneven surface of stone and dirt. There's a sign letting you know that the park does not maintain that area.

The Wequiock Creek creates an elegant curtain of falling water into the scenic rocky glen. ▶

Ribbons of water trickle into the small glen of million-year-old rock from the Niagara Escarpment.

The Hike

Wequiock Falls is in a roadside park along a historic stretch of northeastern Wisconsin known as the "Wis 57 Transportation Corridor." Along this historic corridor are multiple archaeological sites with artifacts dating back 11,000 years or more. Throughout this region there are ancient relics ranging from as far back as the first Paleoindian inhabitants and all the way up to its first European settlers. One of the fun attractions of Wequiock Falls Park is its display of informative signs explaining in great detail the history of the surrounding area and the evidence of previous civilizations.

The hike to the falls leads you through a wide-open green space and descends into a rocky ravine where hikers can see a close-up inspection of a regional geological wonder called the Niagara Escarpment, a long cliff-like ridge of land and rock that extends westward from New York and runs through Ontario, Michigan, Wisconsin, and Illinois. Here you get to see a portion of the escarpment where layers of ancient rock formed over millions of years are shaped by the erosion of weather and streams. The centrally located waterfall you'll see is a result of Wequiock Creek plunging over a composite of dolostone and shale rocks. In the spring or after a good rain, the falls are more robust and thunderous. In the drier months they are minimized to a modest yet elegant veil of falling water: not as energetic, but still visually appealing and worth the hike.

From the trailhead walk northeast on the paved path, which will bring you over a bridge that crosses Wequiock Creek. Walk 0.01 mile past the bridge and you'll arrive at a trail junction: turn left (northwest). Here you'll find yourself on a gravel path that hugs the upper edge of the ravine with a wooden fence to your left. Walk along the fence for 0.04 mile until, just before arriving at Bay Settlement Road, you come to a trail junction connected to a set of stairs that brings you down into the ravine. The first set of twenty-nine steps brings you to an observation deck where you have a perfect long-distance view of the waterfall and the entire ravine. The entire area is incredibly photogenic, and this observation deck is one of the best locations for photography. An additional seventeen steps bring you from the observation deck down to the dirt and rock path along the shore of the creek. From here to the trail's end, the path is quite rugged and uneven. Head 0.02 mile along the edge of the creek (south) until you come to the trail's end near the base of the falls. You'll find yourself on the east side of the creek, just northeast of the falls. A path of flat stones crosses the creek creating an opportunity to visit the other side and admire the falls from multiple vantage points. To arrive back at the trailhead, return the way you came.

One beautiful feature of these falls is the nature of their juxtaposition. Standing in the center of the peaceful ravine, you can look south and lose yourself in a masterpiece of nature. Turn your gaze 180 degrees and you'll observe the meandering creek disappear under an industrial bridge decorated with a colorful graffiti mural. Wequiock Falls offers a small piece of serenity, with historical geological significance, just a short drive from the busy city center of Green Bay.

A view from downstream as the sunshine illuminates the falls and the shallow pool below

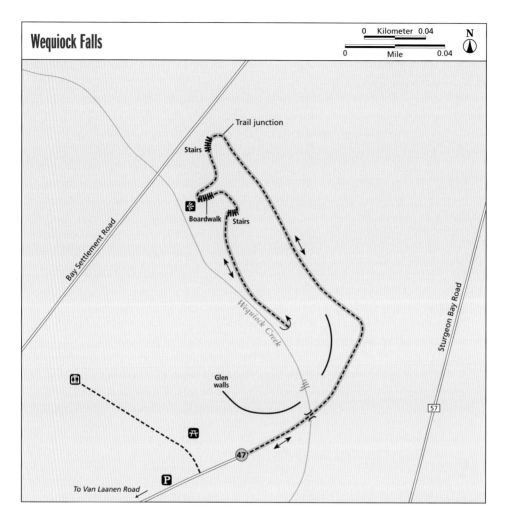

Miles and Directions

0.0 From the trailhead walk northeast.

0.04 Arrive at the first trail junction: turn left (northwest) and follow the trail along a fence.

0.08 Arrive at a second trail junction and staircase: walk down the stairs.

0.14 From the bottom of the stairs walk south until you arrive at the trail's end. Return the way you came.

0.28 Arrive back at the trailhead.

Hike Index

THE TEN ESSENTIALS OF HIKING

American Hiking Society

American Hiking Society recommends you pack the "Ten Essentials" every time you head out for a hike. Whether you plan to be gone for a couple of hours or several months, make sure to pack these items. Become familiar with these items and know how to use them. Learn more at **AmericanHiking.org/hiking-resources.**

1. Appropriate Footwear

6. Safety Items (light, fire, and a whistle)

2. Navigation

7. First Aid Kit

3. Water (and a way to purify it)

8. Knife or Multi-Tool

4. Food

9. Sun Protection

5. Rain Gear & Dry-Fast Layers

10. Shelter